Successful Research Careers

SRHE and Open University Press Imprint
General Editor: Heather Eggins

Successful Research Careers

Sara Delamont and
Paul Atkinson

Society for Research into Higher Education
& Open University Press

Open University Press
McGraw-Hill Education
McGraw-Hill House
Shoppenhangers Road
Maidenhead
Berkshire
England⁻
SL6 2QL

email: enquiries@openup.co.uk
world wide web: www.openup.co.uk

and Two Penn Plaza, New York, NY 10121-2289, USA

First published 2004

A catalogue record of this book is available from the British Library

ISBN 0 335 21201 8 (pb)   0 335 21202 6 (hb)

Library of Congress Cataloging-in-Publication Data
CIP data applied for

Typeset by YHT Ltd, London
Printed in the UK by MPG Books Ltd, Bodmin, Cornwall

Contents

Preface and acknowledgements

We have written this book in hope: hope that those who read it can feel empowered to survive in the current higher education system. It is based on what we learnt from our mentors, from careers we watched go badly wrong, from the research, from the campus novels, and from our experience. To make the book vivid and even entertaining we have illustrated our points with fictional episodes, featuring a set of characters from vice-chancellors to doctoral students. Some of these characters recur in different chapters, having various triumphs and disasters. These characters all have names and careers, and weave their way round seven universities, six in England and one in Scotland. We have invented seven fictional universities, six in fictional English places and one in a real Scottish city that does not have a university: Arlinghurst, Beauminster, Castleton, Mallingford, Penbury, Wedmarsh and Perth.

Arlinghurst is an 'old' British university, founded in the 1880s in a large, thriving city: it has all the disciplines including medical and dental schools. Beauminster has medieval origins and is both very traditional and high status. Castleton is in an old market town near the bigger town of Penbury, and is struggling to recruit students and retain its status. Mallingford was a college of London University until the 1950s, has a wide range of disciplines including pharmacy and engineering, and is in a cathedral city. Penbury was a polytechnic until 1992, is in an industrial town, and had active researchers in only some of its subjects before 1992. Wedmarsh was founded in the 1960s on a greenfield site in a rural area, and does not have any of the big expensive science and vocational departments such as medicine, architecture or engineering: its strengths are in humanities and social sciences. We also pretend that there is an old Scottish university in Perth, and has been since 1583. The pseudonyms for the six English universities are taken from Josephine Tey.

We have also invented five publishing houses, none of which bears any relation to any publishing house we have ever worked with or for. These are Snipcock and Tweed, Polegate and Pettifer, Arlinghurst University Press,

Beauminster University Press and Castleton University Press. Snipcock and Tweed is a high-status, long-established publisher with a bias to history, classics and literature. Polegate and Pettifer is a more modern firm with lots of science journals, strong in social science. Arlinghurst University Press is 60 years old, and produces a strong list in the disciplines long established at Arlinghurst, such as archaeology, geography and architecture. Beauminster University Press is medieval in origin, and very high status. Castleton University Press is small, and rumoured to be struggling.

Various academics, men and women, old and young, successful and aspiring, appear as staff of the seven universities. Some staff from the five publishing houses also appear. Our characters move between our seven universities, and judge themselves against their peers at the other places. By the end of the book, the seven institutions will have become as familiar to you as your *alma mater*. None of our fictional characters is intended to portray any living person.

Many of the books written for, or about, life in universities are dull, pessimistic, report atrocity stories and generally encourage the idea that young staff are victims. We have tried to be interesting, optimistic, report success stories and promote the idea that young staff can have glittering careers.

In preparing this book we have tried to write in as direct a fashion as we can. After all, we want the book to be read and acted upon. In order to illustrate our themes we have included a number of fictional episodes and vignettes. They are intended to capture in a vivid fashion some of the good and bad outcomes that commonly occur. Like most fiction, they are loosely based on real events and real experiences. But they have been transformed. The characters, their names and details have been changed. No character constructed here therefore has any direct relationship with any of our own colleagues, past or present.

The chapter titles are all modified phrases from J.I.M. Stewart's (1976) novel *A Memorial Service*, the third volume in his quintet of novels, *A Staircase in Surrey*. In these novels a Scot, Duncan Pattullo, experiences life in Oxford as a young student and as a middle-aged fellow after 25 years away from the University. Surrey is his fictional college. In *A Memorial Service* Duncan is a novice facing a new academic career. The novels are not as well known as C.P. Snow's Cambridge sequence, but they are much more insightful.

We are grateful to the four referees of the original proposal, and to all the colleagues we have worked with over the years. Rosemary Bartle Jones typed several of the chapters from Sara's handwriting: a staunch effort.

1

Introduction: 'plain words by a truth-telling friend'

The purpose of this book is self-explanatory. It is intended to help younger academics *and* to help those who find themselves responsible for building and sustaining research and research cultures, perhaps in mid to late career, and their mentors – especially in the social sciences, business and law, arts and humanities – to build research cultures, groups and careers. It thus provides – in a very different style and format – a kind of modern parallel to Cornford's little classic *Microcosmographia Academica*. There Cornford outlined his advice for young academics on the practical politics of academic (actually Oxbridge) life. That work was a gently satirical view of universities, but contained a good deal of insight into academic culture, much of which remains valid to this day. We have each had a copy of Cornford's book for a long time: Sara was given a copy by one of her own most influential mentors, Gerry Bernbaum; Paul was given a copy by Sara. The world has changed since Cornford's day, and universities have changed out of all recognition (except perhaps Oxbridge). Cornford is still a valuable and amusing *vade mecum*, although it is really a guide to a world we have lost. The imperatives of academic politics and careers are now very different. Higher education is now a very competitive environment. Universities compete with one another for recognition and resources; departments within universities compete for recognition and support; individuals compete for jobs and promotion. The need for advice and explicit planning is even more pressing than it was for the 'young men in a hurry' whom Cornford poked fun at.

Advice on research careers will not be to everybody's taste. In many ways the things we write about go against the grain of many people's ideals and values. The academy seems all too often to betray the things for which it exists – disinterested learning, the intrinsic rewards that scholarship brings, collegiality – in favour of competitiveness, and an undue preoccupation with material rewards. It is easy to distance oneself from current realities, and to deplore the kinds of competition that prevail. Careerism is still disdained in enough quarters to make the kind of practical advice we offer here seem disreputable. The recurrent exercises of external surveillance that bedevil universities, and the sometimes desperate scramble for scarce resources, do little to enhance the intellectual value of the work that is done in higher education. An obsession with performance indicators, quality mechanisms, transparency reviews and research assessments threatens to overwhelm the academy with bureaucratic procedures that function as displacement activities, distracting us all from the real tasks of teaching and scholarship. If we are not all careful the performance indicators become ends in themselves, and 'research' a form of alienated activity that is prosecuted for the extrinsic rewards it brings rather than for its inherent value.

In writing a book of practical advice for today's academics, we do not endorse the policies and practices that lie behind these new pressures. Clearly a system of mass higher education – whatever one thinks of its intrinsic merits – will have a culture and management procedures that differ from those of a small, elite system. The political culture of the later twentieth century has ensured an almost obsessive concern with accountability and surveillance in all aspects of the public sector. There is no reason to assume that the academy could ever escape change.

Many of the changes that have overtaken higher education are concerned with teaching and financial management. They are beyond our scope here. Academic staff can no longer be assumed to be able to teach undergraduates, engage in curriculum planning, plan and conduct assessment, supervise practical work, with no training or reflection. There is a useful book on all aspects of building an academic career by Blaxter, Hughes and Tight (1998) which we recommend to British readers. In the USA Sage publish a series, *Survival Skills for Scholars*, all of which are useful. Heads of increasingly large and complex academic departments need management training. But this is not our focus here. We are concerned almost exclusively with the imperatives of research-led careers and cultures. Research is the single most important area in which individuals and groups need advice in the current academy, and where advice is most singularly lacking.

The question for readers of this book, or at least our implied readers, is whether they want to be in control of the current stress on research productivity and quality, or whether they want to be victims. There is clearly no point in railing against it, even if one wanted to. There is no going back to a gentler age in which academics could operate as autonomous liberal professionals, with little or no scrutiny of their activities. (The liberal professions have largely lost their 'professional' autonomy too.) Research is no longer a matter of private scholarship pursued with magnificent disregard for timetables, outputs and accountability. On the whole, therefore, we do not advocate throwing oneself on the guns, however much one may dislike the current climate. For the record, we are not 'managerialist' in ethos: we are not wholehearted supporters of contemporary systems of scrutiny and accountability. We do not like the way in which academics keep being pulled up at the roots to see if they are still growing. We do not think that research necessarily flourishes under conditions in which short-term performance takes precedence over long-term inquiry, or in which the likelihood of attracting research funds can outweigh curiosity-driven scholarship. Equally, however, we do not think that everything about today's universities is bad. We argue that explicit reflection on academics' lives and work is no bad thing. There is no virtue in keeping unproductive academic staff who do not fulfil their basic contractual obligation to undertake research and to disseminate it into the public domain. Counting up publications with a train-spotting mentality is dubious, but 'research' that remains unpublished is just a hobby that wastes public money and personal time.

The purpose of this book, however, is neither to defend nor to denounce the current climate of British higher education. Rather, we want to provide a book of practical advice on how to make the best of it. The question for all of us is whether we want simply to be victims of the system, or whether we want to exercise control. Moreover, if we want to achieve what we want, then we have to manoeuvre ourselves into positions where we can do so. If research is increasingly perceived as important, increasingly subject to scrutiny, and increasingly competitive, then we might as well try to work out how to compete successfully.

Our credentials for writing a book of this sort are a mixture of research and professional experience. In terms of experience, we have both occupied positions of responsibility in higher education. We have both spent the majority of our careers at Cardiff University, which has itself undergone extraordinary change in the quarter century that we have both been there. We have both been Head of Department at Cardiff. Sara has been Dean of two different Faculties; Paul has been a Pro Vice-Chancellor. In those positions we have been directly involved in institutional change, and have, in small ways, helped in the transformation of Cardiff from a rather lowly position among UK institutions to being a research-led university, a member of the high-status Russell Group of research universities, with considerable success in the national Research Assessment Exercise, and substantial growth in external research income. We make no false claims here. We have been a part of that process of change, and it has helped us to gain insight into some of the key problems and processes involved. We have, of course, also been research active ourselves. Indeed, we are proud of the extent to which we retained active research and publishing careers while occupying managerial positions. We have experience of attracting external research funding, from a variety of sources, and therefore of managing research. We have had some success in establishing and fostering a particular kind of research tradition, and research continuity amounting to a modest 'research group' at Cardiff. Our own academic research has included work directly relevant to this book. We directed two projects funded by the Economic and Social Research Council that were specifically focused on doctoral students and their supervisors in UK universities. In the process of that research we inevitably found ourselves gaining a broader insight into the management of research groups, research cultures, and individual researchers.

In constructing this book we have also drawn on our experience of conducting staff development activities at our own university and elsewhere. It is, of course, part of the modern ethos of the academy that staff development should be a routine activity. Gone are the days when academic staff could implicitly view each other as automatically qualified to research, teach, manage and provide pastoral care. Even if not formally trained to high levels, academics can now take seriously the idea of staff development, linked to periodic appraisals and self-assessment. We are now able to see that, as a minimum, academics can help themselves and help one another to realize their plans by thinking about things systematically and purposefully. Staff development can be thought of as the extension of the best qualities of academic life – the collective exploration of specific goals or problems, using one's intelligence and engaging in open discussion. We intend that this book should be thought of in much the same way. It is not meant to be an 'idiot's guide' because neither we nor our readers are idiots. Equally, we hope that it does not come over as a managerial harangue on how to shape up in a tough, competitive world. We prefer to think of a book such as this as providing the opportunity to demystify key aspects of our collective problems and to reflect upon some possible solutions.

We are responding to the fact that research is the key to personal and institutional success. This is not to denigrate teaching, or to reinforce the division between research and teaching. We are ourselves thoroughly committed to the idea that teaching benefits from research. We endorse the significance attached to the mix of teaching and research, and that is the hallmark of the major university. Teaching and research are mutually reinforcing. Moreover, the development of research and teaching come together in the development of postgraduate students through the provision of research training. Equally, of course, 'research' is not something that is undertaken in a vacuum. We do not think that you can dream up good research quite apart from wider personal, intellectual and public contexts. Research ideas cannot be conjured out of nothing, and we do not mean to create that sort of impression.

Nonetheless, the processes surrounding research have considerable significance for the individual and collective fates of academics. In the majority of institutions and departments, the improvement of research is a major institutional goal. We shall bracket for the moment what 'improvement' could and should consist of, but the fact remains that most of today's academics need to develop explicit plans and projects to improve their own research performance. Here research does not mean just conducting private scholarly work. It also involves transforming those inquiries into published papers and books. It may well involve winning external research funds to support that research. Moreover, the promotion of research is often a collective activity. It may involve the development and maintenance of a research grouping within one's department. It may increasingly involve the development of research links across disciplinary boundaries, and across institutional boundaries as well. Consequently, when we start to think about enriching research environments, we are not addressing only the development of individual academics. We need to address the collective promotion of research, by the support of research groupings and the development of collective research strengths.

This book is intended to be of value to several constituencies within the academy. We want to address younger or less experienced academics who need and want to develop their own career: contemporary higher education is especially hard for such colleagues. They are subject to increasingly stringent demands if they are to be employable, gain permanent employment, get promoted, and be rewarded. Few of them will have embarked on an academic career on the basis of 'careerist' ambition. Anybody who wants to be well paid will have looked elsewhere; anybody who wants to be famous will have tried other avenues. Most people commit themselves to an academic career because they have a fire in their belly about their subject, their own research, the excitement of publishing scholarly work, and the opportunity to teach. Having made that commitment, however, there is no reason why they should pursue that work in unworldly ignorance. We believe that younger colleagues benefit from explicit coaching and mentoring about the management of their work and their career.

It is also our intention to address more senior academic staff too. As research careers and contexts become increasingly important at the institutional level, it is apparent that they call for management. Inexperienced academics, research associates and postdoctoral fellows, research students – they all need supervision and mentoring. Their work and their professional development need guidance. Previous generations of younger academics were left to find out the mysteries of their craft for themselves. If they were lucky, they were taken under the wing of a sensible supervisor, mentor or role model; if they were not, then they could flounder. Nowadays, if we want our research groups to flourish and our departments to succeed, then more experienced academic staff need to take responsibility for their less experienced colleagues. Research groups need some degree of leadership. Departments and divisions need academic leadership. This latter term is often bandied about in universities. When senior posts are advertised it is common to find that their further particulars specify 'academic leadership' among the desiderata for the successful candidate. The precise meaning of academic leadership is almost always left implicit. It is the sort of thing that most other senior academics think they recognize when they see it, even if they cannot quite define it. We are not going to define academic leadership either, but it must mean the capacity to promote and manage research – to help research students, researchers, younger academics and others to conduct research, publish research, attract funds, develop a sense of collective purpose, and to prepare themselves for assessment.

The need to exercise 'leadership' (in those terms) is increasingly the responsibility of a large number of academics. Many, if not all, of us need to demonstrate academic leadership. That is, we need to promote and manage research, mentor research fellows and research assistants. We have to

supervise research students. We need to provide mentoring, staff development and act as role models for more junior academic staff. Even though
higher education is poorly rewarded in material terms, and even though
secure job tenure is not what it once was, there are still gifted men and
women who want to pursue higher degrees, work as postdoctoral
researchers, and pursue careers as academics in universities. Increasingly we
see these potential recruits and junior colleagues as an investment, to be
nurtured and cherished. So we become 'managers' of 'human resources'.
Those are not the terms in which the work has traditionally been couched,
but whatever we choose to call it, we all need to grapple with the reality.

All academics are therefore faced with the kinds of issues we pursue in
the course of this book. Our experience and our research covers a broad
range of academic disciplines, but the everyday realities of the laboratory
sciences are sufficiently different from the arts and social sciences as to
make it difficult to do justice to the entire spectrum of subjects. We
therefore concentrate our attention on the disciplines we know best – the
arts and humanities, business and law, social and cultural studies. We focus
on those disciplines for another reason too: the laboratory sciences have
cultures and mechanisms that treat research funding and research management as normal, unremarkable features of disciplinary culture and
organization. The supervision of postdoctoral and postgraduate researchers
has long been conducted within the organizational context of research
groups. While nothing is straightforward in any domain of the academy, the
laboratory sciences have experienced things differently from the humanities and social sciences.

In the chapters that follow, therefore, we address a number of key themes
to do with the development of research and research cultures in university
departments, and the concomitant development of research careers. Just
like 'academic leadership', 'research culture' is a pretty nebulous term.
Again, it is not our intention to define it. It does not have a precise
denotation. Its general connotations are clearly comprehensible, however.
It refers to a constellation of values, expectations, organizational arrangements and everyday practices that foster the pursuit of research as a
collective commitment. Research cultures transform the private work of
reading and writing, collecting and analysing data, translating and editing
texts, into shared 'public' activities. Departments, research centres and
groups are focused on the common purposes of shared research commitments. Research cultures reflect the work of academic leaders. Successful
departments, and hence successful institutions, are able to create these
shared commitments. Moreover, they are able to demonstrate them to the
outside world. Collective action thus enters the public domain, through
scholarly publishing and other academic activities.

Our book is partly for those who need to promote and sustain research
cultures and research groups 'from the top'. We thus address ourselves to
department heads, senior research-active academics, directors of research,
chairs of research committees and the like. We write about building research

groups. Our book is also for those who need to build their own careers within such environments. Our advice is for those more junior colleagues who have their way to make. We thus try to provide advice about how to become a successful academic in terms of research and publication. Many aspects of collective work are the same whether you are senior or junior. In fact, much of the work of building research depends on the direct collaboration of senior and junior academics. Hence advice to younger colleagues is also, indirectly, advice to their more senior mentors on how to help them.

This is not intended to be a handbook on how to succeed in the Research Assessment Exercise. We have included a chapter on the UK RAE itself, but our purpose is wider than that. As will be seen from the chapter itself, we do not think that there are any short cuts or magic formulae for the RAE. There is good advice that is often shared among heads of department and others, and there is the sort of advice that subject panel chairs make public before and after each assessment exercise. We have tried to distil such advice and pass it on. There are also rumours and myths about the RAE, some of which sound downright odd. Indeed, there is now almost a genre of urban myths and legends surrounding the RAE and the behaviour of subject panels that someone (else) should be documenting. We try to avoid such myths and rumours. Equally, individual departments and institutions like to think that they have particular successful strategies in preparing for the RAE. These are jealously guarded – although as far as one can ascertain, most institutions follow much the same sort of approach. We have tried to avoid trespassing on such local practices. Indeed, our own institution regards our specific preparations for the RAE as confidential, and we respect that confidentiality, even when it seems redundant. On the other hand, there is already a great deal of public domain knowledge and understanding about the exercise in general for us to be able to bring together some practical advice about external research assessment and how to cope with the periodic exercises.

In many ways, however, research assessment is not the primary focus here. Indeed, it should not be the primary focus of research leaders or research-active academics. Pragmatically, careful preparation for research assessment is idle unless the research itself has been done successfully and turned into publications of good quality. Research assessment is not about spin-doctoring. Presentation cannot compensate for weak research. Consequently, the real effort lies in the creation of research cultures and the promotion of sustained, high quality research. It also lies in the construction of centres of excellence, research groups or clusters (the nomenclature matters little). This means treating research as a collective effort that is subject to some degree of planning, that develops over time, that is more than the sum of its parts (the individuals concerned). Consequently, we devote a chapter of this book to the processes that go into developing a research group. Again, there may be resistance to such notions. It may sound too like the managerial imposition of constraints and targets. We make clear that this is not necessarily the case. Indeed, we make clear that success is not achieved through 'top-down' control. The development of research groups is, or should be, the extension of the kinds of activities that academics normally claim to endorse and to enjoy. It is about collaborating with others; talking to each other; planning together; sharing plans and ideas. It is about the more experienced helping the less so; the junior members learning from their more experienced mentors. There is obviously nothing spurious about these activities. They are intrinsically good, and they have more tangible rewards as well. We discuss, therefore, what goes into research groups and how to think about them.

Research and its evaluation all depend on aspects of 'peer review'. Peer review is used to evaluate bids for research funding, journal submissions, book proposals and promotions to senior lectureships, readerships or chairs. It is an imperfect system but the best we have. Academics spend a good deal of their time judging the work of others. We shall, therefore, spend some time talking about general principles of peer review. More to the point, we also discuss how one becomes a 'peer'. In other words, how one comes to be part of that generalized exchange of expert opinion; how one comes to be recognized by one's fellow academics as someone whose opinion is valued. Moreover, there are some general maxims to follow when it comes to responding to requests for peer review from others. Research group leaders and mentors need to think about how they become well-informed judges and opinion-formers – how they get to be on the 'inside track', and how they will encourage their more junior colleagues to do likewise. Less experienced academics need to understand how peer review works and what they need to do to become part of the key networks.

A key area in which peer review operates is the evaluation of research bids for external funding. Research funding is a research input, not an output or a performance indicator of research quality in itself. Nevertheless, there are few, if any, fields in which research cultures and research productivity are not enhanced by research grants and contracts. There are many kinds of research that are virtually impossible without such external support. Moreover, research income is a widely used indicator of success. The very fact that research grants are peer reviewed and are competitive means that they are *ipso facto* indicators of peer approval. We therefore devote a chapter to some of the mechanics of research grant-getting. Obviously, there are things that cannot easily be accommodated within a relatively brief hand-book like this one. We cannot tell you how to have what counts as a brilliant research idea in your field. But brilliant ideas do not always receive funding. We know: some of our best ideas were turned down for funding, while we have been successful with proposals that were certainly no better intellec-tually. But one thing is for sure. If you do not apply for research funds, you will never get any. And if you write inept research bids the chances will be heavily against you. Consequently, some practical advice on research pro-posals that work is offered here, with the proviso that these things remain competitive, and success is never guaranteed. All we can help to do is shorten the odds a bit.

Research that is not published is pointless. We therefore devote a chapter each to publication in academic journals and to the publication of academic books. The same considerations apply here. We cannot give you the inspiration to come up with an outstanding idea for a paper or a book. But – like grant-getting – we can help prevent the sort of elementary mistakes that can spoil any hope of success. It is remarkable that so many academics, who have got where they are by reading mounds of books and journal papers, struggle to publish successfully themselves. As editors and reviewers ourselves, we see many inadequate efforts, and it would seem that there are some simple precepts that, if followed, can help authors to avoid the most elementary pitfalls. Clearly, publication in any format depends on writing. It is strange how many academics seem to struggle with writing, and find it a burden. We think that writing is the very best thing about being an academic. That does not mean we think writing is just 'fun', or that it comes easily. It is not always easy. It is, however, something that can be worked at and thought about. It can be treated as a collective activity, and something that can be talked about explicitly. We need always to break down images of writing that represent it as a private effort. Writing among research groups, collaboration and co-authorship can be encouraged as part of the collective research effort. We therefore devote a chapter to the issue of writing in general, with some practical advice on how to encourage oneself and one's colleagues to treat writing as a professional craft skill and not a matter of romantic inspiration or a natural 'gift'.

In dealing with these various topics, therefore, we intend to help our professional colleagues to reflect on their own practices, and those of their colleagues. The academy is becoming an increasingly stressful and competitive domain. We are not trying to make things worse by drawing attention to these issues of research culture and career. Rather, we think that if academics are to cope with and to thrive in the contemporary academic context, then they need the resources to reflect on the pressures they face and the demands made upon them. If there is one single message we try to impart to our own doctoral students and our own colleagues it is this: you can be in control, or you can be a victim. If you want to be in control, then you need to understand the world in which you work, and understand how to stay in control of your work and your career. Equally, you need to invest some of the energy you devote to your research to making that research count for something in the public and professional domains. It is always surprising how many academics put a great deal of effort into their own research, but are not prepared to put even a fraction of that effort into thinking about all the issues surrounding that research: how to support it and promote it, how to ensure it has an impact, starts a trend, and leads to intellectual development.

In writing this book, then, we have tried to address a number of potential audiences within our profession – the 'younger' colleague who is just embarking on her or his professional career; the mid-career academic who is established personally, but who needs to build up research, possibly developing a research group and promoting collaborations with other people; and the senior academics and academic managers, who need to promote research cultures and research-led careers throughout their department, faculty or institution. The great majority of institutions in higher education aspire to being 'research-led' at least in some areas. The elite – such as the members of the Russell Group of universities – claim research-led excellence in virtually all areas. Academics in UK universities increasingly need to look to international levels of collaboration and comparison if they are to flourish. Academic staff at all levels, therefore, need to have an informed understanding of what this entails.

We realize that some of our readers may feel that there is little or no prospect of their developing successful research-led careers, or building research groups and cultures around them. In the United Kingdom, as throughout the global higher education system, the rankings of university institutions – and of research centres of excellence within them – are becoming increasingly polarized and impermeable. Successive assessment exercises in the United Kingdom have been leading inexorably towards the concentration of core government funding in a relatively small number of elite departments, which are themselves concentrated within a small number of elite institutions. Institutions in the Russell Group of the leading 19 research-led universities mop up a substantial amount of research funding, attract large numbers of research students from home and overseas, and enjoy the highest esteem. Within that grouping are institutions in the 'golden triangle', defined by Cambridge, Oxford and London (Imperial College, University College, King's College and the LSE). Core funding for highly-rated departments means superior student-staff ratios, better facilities, and more time and better support for research. Those elite universities also include those institutions that have better endowments, richer alumni and other material advantages. There are similar tendencies in the United States, where the elite research universities have resources – material and symbolic – that far outweigh the majority of other institutions. As the hierarchies become apparently ever more fixed, and the tiering of universities ever more evident, the vast majority of academics who work outside of the elite sectors may feel that research development is all but impossible. They may – with some justification – feel that the odds are so heavily stacked against them that they have no chance of fighting their way out of relative poverty and lowly ratings.

We recognize the force of such feelings, and the constraints under which individuals, groups and institutions may labour. But we are not convinced that it is impossible to improve one's performance, or to enhance the collective levels of success enjoyed by one's department and university. To some extent we base this assertion on personal experience. Between us, without moving and without changing the kind of research we do, we have been members of groups rated 2, 3, 4, 5, and 5* (all at Cardiff University) in different Research Assessment Exercises. We have, therefore, been part of a process that has seen our department receive enhanced ratings, and our university improve its overall position in the research league tables. To some degree the improvements in rating reflect 'grade inflation', and – like many such exercises – may also reflect improved game-playing techniques. But they also reflect some real differences in the research environment: changes in personnel have made a difference, but so too have redoubled efforts to attract major research grants, to place research development at the heart of the department's shared culture by promoting interdisciplinary and also inter-institutional research collaborations.

In many ways, research is getting more demanding. There are enormous pressures, especially on those in mid-career and those making their way, to compete for research funding and to publish in 'the best' journals (which are by definition normally the hardest to get into). Those competitive pressures are real. But they are not the whole story. There are increasing numbers of research opportunities in the current academic world. In the research environment we know best, that of UK social science, there is more Research Council funding than ever before (in real terms). There are huge amounts of research funding circulating within the European Union. Although endowments have taken a hit following falls in equity prices, there are still substantial opportunities from major charities. Likewise, while publishing the very best papers may seem a very competitive game to play, the fact remains that there are many, many more journals than ever before in virtually all disciplines. Commercial publishers have responded to the academic marketplace by launching ever-increasing numbers of titles, as have many learned societies and other interest groups; the possibilities of electronic publishing are creating even more opportunities for academic dissemination. We discuss these and related issues later in this book.

So one need not despair: the possibilities for developing and conducting research are still there. For an ambitious individual, the potential rewards are still there too. Promotion within one's institution, enhancing one's own research group's performance, or moving to a more successful institution – these are all possible. For the ambitious head of department, dean or vice-chancellor, research enhancement is still possible. For the institution, as for the individual, it needs *work*. It needs investment of time, effort and other resources; it needs staff development and training; it needs shared efforts, including culture change if necessary; it needs people of above-average intelligence to pit their collective wits against the kinds of problems and limitations they face.

Peer review

In many ways, the entire theme of this book, and the culture it addresses, is that of peer review. This is a pervasive feature of contemporary academic life. It operates in many formal contexts, and it is also there in less formal ways. Academics experience peer review from two complementary perspectives. They should *be* peers and do reviewing, and they should be submitting their work *for* peer scrutiny. In the early stages of a career there are three main impacts of peer review: of conference papers and posters, of journal articles and book proposals, and of grant applications. Of course, the examination of the PhD thesis is a form of peer review too: it is the last time one is examined by one's superiors *and* the first peer review, both going on simultaneously, but it is not experienced like that by most candidates. The experience of being peer reviewed often starts before the first job, but it should be more frequent in one's early posts.

Peer review can be done anonymously ('blind') or by names. The judges and the judged can be either anonymous or known: that is, there can be anonymous applicants judged by anonymous referees, anonymous applicants judged by named referees, named applicants judged by anonymous referees, and named applicants judged by named referees. Peer review is largely an Anglo-Saxon phenomenon. It is much rarer in other countries than it is in the USA, Britain, Canada, Australia and New Zealand. Hess (1991), for example, has shown that Brazil works with other systems. In Britain there have been inquiries into the system: for example, the Advisory Board of the Research Councils in the UK had a panel on the topic a decade ago. Such inquiries conclude that, while peer review is an imperfect system, other devices would be worse. It is used by reputable journals to vet articles submitted to them, by editors of books who wish the chapters to have the same status as refereed journal articles, by grant-giving bodies to decide which applications to fund, by bodies awarding prizes and honours, by government departments, and by learned societies electing fellows. In fully anonymous peer review, a journal article is sent out to referees who do not know who the author is, or which institution they are from, so the referees do not know the identity or status of the author. This means a paper from a full professor at Harvard and one from a PhD student at Penbury will be judged on the same criteria, against the aims of the journal. Equally, the authors will not know whether the referees were full professors at Yale and Columbia, or research associates at Wedmarsh and Normal, Illinois, because when they receive the feedback on their submission it is anonymized. Journals vary a good deal in whether 'blind', or 'anonymous', refereeing takes place. In some fields all journals engage in anonymous refereeing, in others there is a variety of journals with different practices.

However, much peer review is not and cannot be of this kind. If a team of British earth scientists or physical geographers who are experts in using remote sensors want to have time on the centrally funded airborne survey of the Arctic, they have to be judged by experts who can scrutinize their records as scientists. The referees have to know the names, university, grant-getting record, publications and previous Arctic experience of all applicants to reach a sound judgement about the quality of the application. Inevitably, the Natural Environment Research Council (NERC) panel will include friends, enemies, competitors and supporters of the applicants. The team from Beauminster will probably be famous, that from Penbury unknown. NERC might use referees overseas, who would not be direct competitors for the same money and aircraft space, but these experts would still 'know' the work and reputation of the applicants.

There were two cases when peer review became newsworthy in the 1990s – the Sokal hoax and the Swedish research by Wenneras and Wold (1997). The Sokal hoax publicized peer review of journal articles; the Wenneras and Wold investigation raised questions about the review of scientific grant applications. Alan Sokal is a physicist at New York University. He published a paper in a journal called *Social Text* which purported to be a postmodern analysis of some aspects of maths and physics (Sokal 1996). After it had been published, he wrote another triumphal paper exposing the *Social Text* paper as a hoax, designed to reveal the nonsensical nature of post-modernism, social studies of science, feminism, Africancentric theories, and everything else Sokal dislikes about American academia. Sokal revealed that he had taken words, phrases and sentences that sounded like a postmodern argument, added some completely meaningless mathematics and physics, and produced a piece of gibberish, which, because it had been published, proved that all of humanities and social sciences were nonsense. The resulting disputes do not concern us here, and if you missed them you can follow up the events in Labinger and Collins (2001). One aspect which does concern us here is the status of *Social Text* and its editorial policies. Opponents of Sokal argued that *Social Text* was not a refereed journal. If it had been, and the Sokal paper had been refereed, the fallacious nature of its arguments would have been exposed, the paper rejected, and the standards of social science defended. This is probably not true, but it displays the faith that academics have in the peer-reviewed journal.

Sokal's case did not prove the point he wanted to make, but it does prove something about peer review and journals. The system is not well designed to detect hoaxes, because it is based on an assumption that submissions are genuine attempts submitted in good faith to meet a standard. It is designed to *select between* submissions, so the best work gets published. Referees may well be asked to comment on papers at the edges of their expertise, and Sokal's paper, which claimed to be from physics, might have fooled referees as well as the editors. However, if it had been sent to sociologists who worked on physics, and been scrutinized by them, it *might* have been recognized as garbage. Many commentators have drawn the conclusion that *Social Text* is a poor journal because it does not use peer review, rather than abandon their own research area. Further on in the chapter we explore why peer reviewing is an important task that benefits the reviewers' careers and the careers of those subjected to it. Peer review of science grant applications is also sacrosanct, yet it too was challenged in the 1990s, although not by a hoax. Wenneras and Wold are Swedish biomedical scientists who investigated one peer-review system and published their results in the high-prestige science periodical *Nature* (Wenneras and Wold 1997). The case study involved applicants for the Swedish Medical Research Council's postdoctoral positions. They had access to 114 applications made by 52 women and 62 men, and the peer-review ratings evaluating them made by

55 senior scientists. The reviewers were asked to judge the candidates on three criteria: scientific competence, relevance of the research project, and the quality of proposed methods. Women scored lower than men, especially in the category of scientific competence. Wenneras and Wold constructed objective measures of the candidates' scientific achievements, such as total number of publications, the number on which the applicant was first author, the impact factor of the journals in which the papers were published, and the number of citations to their work in the citation index in 1994. When they compared how the referees had rated the applicants with the objective measures they had calculated, they found that male applicants consistently received higher ratings than women with equal objective competence scores. On further investigation they found that applicants got higher scores from the referees if they were male, if they were productive, and if they had a prior affiliation with the referee.

The sex difference was very striking. A woman needed to be more than twice as productive as a man to get the same competence rating from a referee: for example to have published 20 more journal articles in good journals. Subsequently, a pair of Danish studies reported similar findings, one of biomedical grant applications in the UK found women applicants had an equal success rate (Grant, Burden and Breen 1997), and one of Dutch postdoctoral awards reported a pattern like that seen in Sweden (Brouns 2001). The consequences of this research are not yet clear, but those anxious to keep more women in science careers (Glover 1999; Rees 2001) are perturbed by these findings. Researchers in the sociology of scientific knowledge (Collins and Pinch 1993, 1998) would not find these results surprising, but would want to argue that the so-called 'objective' measures are neither objective nor useful for understanding how science works. That is not a debate we intend to enter into here. In a culture, such as science, where objectivity is very highly prized, and belief in meritocracy strong, the discrepancy between the objective, bibliometric data and the subjective ratings by the senior judges was disquieting. None of the commentary on the Wenneras and Wold data from inside science has focused on a campaign to abolish peer review: rather commentators are all arguing that it needs to be made more objective or meritocratic and have sexism stripped out of it. This research study is one of the reasons why women scientists cannot afford to absent themselves from opportunities to collect patrons. Women in science are less likely to be known by senior males, and their work is cited less often. Yet they need sponsors and patrons more if they are to prosper.

A third area of peer refereeing surrounds getting conference papers accepted. The peer review of proposed conference papers and posters is rarely 'blind' or 'anonymous': the panel running the conference or strand within a conference is usually known, and submissions are usually judged with names and institutions on them. Senior staff need to explain how peer review works in their sub-speciality to younger colleagues, checking that there are the relevant sections on the CV headed '*Refereed* Journal Papers' and '*Refereed* Conference Papers and Posters' and that the refereed papers are listed in separate sections from the non-refereed ones, and explain why that matters.

In Cardiff we have tried to de-mystify the processes of peer review by exploring it in classes for postgraduate students and in staff development courses. We run a couple of staff development sessions: one is essentially didactic, we provide materials on how journals work and discuss the procedures; the other is more of a simulation, in which we provide a set of materials mimicking an imaginary journal – mission statement, advice for authors, paper, report sheets – and get the participants to role play being editor, then referee, then editor again, and finally author. In the didactic session we start by ensuring that everyone knows about different categories of publication, from book review to single-authored monograph, and the existence and coding frame of the CVCP/UUK categorization system (explained in Appendix 2). That leads on to a focus on journal and book publication. The simulation exercise follows the didactic session: students attending the exercise need to have grasped the basics covered in the didactic session. In the simulation the participants are pre-circulated with a dreadful submission, full of every kind of error. Then they come to the session, and are given material about the fictitious journal. They then role play being the editor of the journal, being the referee and again being the editor, and actually handle the decision-making stages. So each person sends out the paper to someone else in the workshop, and receives it from another to referee. Then they return their comments to 'their' editor, and receive comments from 'their' referees and have to reach a decision. The same is repeated for grant applications: one two-part session where the ESRC forms are explained and salary scales and so on issued, then, a week later, participants return with the forms completed for a brain storm. In parallel is a simulation of refereeing a grant proposal, in which participants role play refereeing a specimen application for a grant.

It is, of course, not always clear to young staff why they should engage in peer review: they do not necessarily accede to requests to do it, and when they do they are not always sure what to do. Some senior colleagues are not good role models: their rooms are piled high with submissions to journals they have not bothered to referee or even to return to the editors so other referees can be appointed. One way to introduce younger colleagues to the necessity of altruistic work, such as peer review, is to explain the selfish benefits to the reviewer and to show how it is a task done by the intellectual elite. Zuckerman (1977) found that refereeing journal submissions was the one altruistic 'service' role that Nobel laureates undertook. Their work refereeing articles and editorial board work on journals mattered to them, they called it 'keeping the literature clean' (p. 201). The benefits to the reviewer are not always clear. On a cold winter evening after a long day, the 'benefits' of refereeing three journal submissions are not obvious. There is, of course, an altruistic reason: much of academic life depends on disinterested reciprocities: if we want refereed journals to exist so we can publish our papers in them, we have to safeguard their existence, survival and standards by refereeing papers for them, or others like them. If we do not, and others follow us, the system collapses. More selfishly, an individual can put on her CV that she referees for that journal, she might get invited on its editorial board, she learns about the type of paper that gets submitted to it, and about the common errors that would-be authors make. Also, if the papers are any good, you will have to read them eventually. If you referee them you have read them six months to two years before they are published, so you stay at the front of the field. Similarly, if a scholar referees grant proposals, she learns how to write them, even though she cannot put that work on a public curriculum vitae. She could, however, list it on confidential documents for appraisal or promotion.

In many ways, therefore, building successful research careers and cultures is about becoming adept at understanding peer review, of becoming a part of that general peer review process oneself, and about deriving success and esteem from one's professional peers. The successful development of research cultures and groups within an institution or a department is partly dependent on sponsoring and mentoring more junior staff in such a way that they become socialized into the systems of review and evaluation.

A concern with peer review and esteem is not confined to the development of junior staff, however. All academics and their institutions must be concerned with the promotion of excellence, the markers of esteem, and their rewards. Probably because academic life is not well paid, markers of success and prestige are rarely monetary: indeed, producing a bestseller, doing a successful TV series, writing a column in a tabloid, or winning a car or cash on a game show, are all despised – terms like 'popularizer' and 'selling out' fly around. It is necessary to learn what the indicators of prestige and success are, and how to recognize some of the 'badges' worn.

At a more basic level, it is important for academics to become participants in the circuits of esteem, recognition and influence. This often means involvement with learned societies, with advisory bodies, with research councils and major charities, and being visible as public intellectuals. As an article in the publication *Research Fortnight* (August 2003) pointed out, being a member of an advisory board or committee is often advantageous. As with all the processes of peer review and participation, such work often requires an investment of considerable time. The time is spent reading papers, travelling to meetings, attending those meetings, writing reviews, and so on. The (intangible) rewards include the opportunity to see the peer review process in action, to get a broad understanding of the research environment in one's own and related fields, to learn a lot about best practice and mistakes to avoid, to network with other members of such committees, to influence research policy and direction.

Becoming one of the 'peers', therefore, depends on being known in one's field. This means *involvement* in various activites, as well as publicly visible research productivity. One route for visible engagement is through subject associations or defence groups. Then there are the learned societies.

These vary in their age, royal patronage, and exclusivity; some take anyone who wants to join who will pay the subscription, others require nomination and election. For example, the Royal Economic Society and the Royal Anthropological Institute have royal patronage, whereas the Women's Studies Network and the Leisure Studies Association do not. Simple membership, while necessary for any academic career, is not in itself career-enhancing; office-holding, prizes and work for the society, such as running conferences, study groups, and summer schools, are career-enhancing. To build a career it is sensible to run a regional conference, the national conference, serve on the committees, and generally get a reputation as a loyal, hardworking member. Being Treasurer of the British Tourism Studies Association is useful for career purposes, but being President is better. The UK has a very large number of learned societies and subject defence groups in the arts and social sciences. There are 129 on the database maintained by the British Academy, and at least another 40 that are not on that list. They vary a good deal in status and size. They also represent overlapping research interests, so that multiple membership is intellectually possible. It is possible for one academic to be affiliated to, or a member of, a good many of these societies at once.

A hypothetical, but not improbable, example will illustrate this. A professor of French has been chosen for this hypothetical example, but there are parallel cases in all the other modern languages, English, history and most social sciences. A professor of French with an interest in politics could be an individual member of the Association of University Professors and Heads of French (AUPHF), the Association of French Language Studies (AFLS), the Association for the Study of Modern and Contemporary France (ASMCF), the Political Studies Association (PSA), the Society for French Studies (SFS) and the University Association for Contemporary European Studies (UACES). Through her institution, she could also be affiliated to the Standing Conference of Heads of European Studies (SCHES), the University Council of Modern Languages (UCML), the Council of Deans of Arts and Humanities (CUDAH) and the Standing Conference of Arts and Social Sciences (SCASS). In addition the British Academy could be held to be a voice for her interests. All of these bodies are always looking for keen people to sit on committees, hold office and organize events.

There are ten chapters in this book. In Chapter 2 we explore how a young scholar can build a research group and a head of department can build a research culture. In Chapter 3 we address the vital issue of supervising and mentoring colleagues to help them become research active. Then, in the next chapter, Chapter 4, we focus on raising research funds. The second half of the book focuses on the outputs of research. Chapter 5 addresses academic writing in general, Chapter 6 the publication of journal articles, Chapter 7 the publication of books, and Chapter 8 the dissemination of research by other means. All these chapters are relevant throughout the anglophone world: getting published in Canada, or setting up a website in the USA, are ways to build a career that are essentially similar to the UK. In

Chapter 9 we focus on a more parochially British topic, the periodic Research Assessment Exercises. Our conclusions occupy Chapter 10.

2

Building a research culture and a research group: 'holding their place'

In *A Memorial Service*, which is set in the early 1970s, there are productive and unproductive Oxford dons. One of the productive scholars is an old friend of the hero's called Ranald McKechnie, who expounds upon the difference. McKechnie, a distinguished classicist, explains to Duncan Pattullo that in real disciplines, scholars 'have to keep thinking hard to hold their place at all' (pp. 180–1). Since the coming of the Research Assessment Exercise, all disciplines have become 'real' (in the sense that everyone in an institution has a collective interest in how their members perform and are evaluated) and everyone has to 'keep thinking hard', to keep themselves and their departments holding 'their place'. In this chapter we explore strategies for individuals and departmental heads.

The actions necessary, and appropriate, to create, develop, rescue, recreate or to sustain a research culture are different in different institutions, and at the various levels in any one institution. The role to be played by a single lecturer inside a department is very different from that of her professorial department chair, or her vice-chancellor. We have illustrated this with accounts of two of our fictional universities, building up from what Althea Sclander can do in her department of politics and sociology at Arlinghurst to build her own career, through what a new head of department, Lalage Hunstanton, can do at Wedmarsh to revitalize a declining geography department's research.

Althea Sclander is a lecturer in her late twenties or early thirties, expecting to apply for promotion to senior lecturer in the current year. At Arlinghurst all staff are expected to be research active, and to have sufficient publications to be 'returned' in every RAE. Her department makes two returns, to sociology and politics. Althea has been in the post since 1992 and has been returned in 1992, 1996 and 2001. She and her appraiser, and as far as she knows her head of department, are not concerned about her individual career. However, she now needs to show leadership and start building up a research group.

Professor Lalage Hunstanton has been appointed Head of Geography at

Wedmarsh, from the Grade 5 department at Mallingford. Wedmarsh Geography Department is in decline: from a 5 in the 1992 RAE it had slipped to a 3a in 2001. The former head has taken early retirement, and one of the other professors has left for a post at Arlinghurst, taking his £400,000 NERC grant with him. Wedmarsh expects all units of assessment to get at least 4s. Two other units that got only 3as have been closed. At her appointment committee Lalage was told Geography had been allowed a second chance because of buoyant undergraduate recruitment, including many joint degrees with other science subjects that have recruitment difficulties, such as chemistry and geology, as well as all the social sciences that Wedmarsh is strong in. Lalage has been appointed to rebuild the geographical research at Wedmarsh: to get a 4 in 2007. She can make one new professorial appointment, and one lectureship is vacant: a bright young scholar left in 2000 for a post in the USA, the post was 'frozen' for two years and is now available for Lalage to make an appointment of her choice.

One major fact: the leader has to go on publishing and getting grants him- or herself. Exhortation from seniors or line managers who have stopped being research active themselves is pointless. If Lalage and Althea are to lead teams, departments, and whole universities to higher things, the first thing they have to do is make sure they set time aside to write for publications for themselves. Althea and Lalage will have to prioritize getting grants as well. Althea has to get a grant which will provide a job for a research associate or research assistant, and then help that research associate or research assistant start or continue their career. The research assistant needs to do, or finish, a PhD, get some training and career development, get some publications, go to conferences, and get another job. And, of course, Althea has to ensure that the project is completed and the final report delivered. Sometimes in the rough and tumble of running a research project the career development of the research staff gets overlooked. This prevents the longer-term development of the research group. The British Research Councils have a concordat with the universities that staff employed on Research Council grants are given staff development, but the evidence is that this is often ignored.

If Althea gets a grant and employs someone who has not yet done a PhD, then getting that degree should have priority, and the research assistant should get all the training in research methods and related skills that a full-time PhD student would. (It is reasonable to negotiate that some of this and some of the PhD work is done in the research assistant's 'own' time: this is good preparation for an academic career, with its 60–100-hour working weeks.) If the employee has a PhD, then other staff development is necessary.

Teaching: it is a good idea for all research staff to do a little bit of teaching, and to embark upon a postgraduate diploma in teaching in higher education, and start a portfolio for membership of the Institute for Learning and Teaching (ILT). The teaching should include some lectures and some tutorials, ideally to different levels of student, such as year one/

level one and masters level. Systematic classes on publication and grant-getting are desirable. Althea should check what is available at Arlinghurst provided by staff development teams for the whole university, or more informally at faculty and at departmental level. If there is nothing she should raise the lack in her department, and, perhaps via the Association of University Teachers, with the personnel department. The research assistant or associate needs to keep a log of this staff development: because the Research Councils issue a questionnaire at the end of the grant, because it can go on the CV for job applications, and because the concordat between the funding body and the university requires it. Part of building a research group is ensuring that the research staff get access to the research culture: in science and engineering, this is easier than in social science and arts where much research is private (Deem and Brehony 2000). But research staff have to learn how to judge which conferences to go to, which sessions to attend, which journals to target, and these things are not blindingly obvious to novices. Much of the rest of this book is devoted to how such staff development could be organized, especially Chapter 3.

Changing the culture of a whole department is harder than building one's own personal research group. However the first step is to be research active oneself, but not boast about it. Do it, and let the product slide into colleagues' consciousness. There are several hard decisions to be made. First, can all tenured staff be research active, or are there some who cannot – people who never have been, people who have burned out? If a university is prepared to offer the unproductive incentives to leave, or to threaten them with dismissal, the head of department has an easier task. At present a university can have two types of academic staff, research active and teaching only, without damaging their research ratings. It is possible to designate staff teaching only. So unless Wedmarsh has decided not to have such staff, one strategy Lalage could adopt is to see if the never active and the burnt out could be officially designated as teaching only. Such people can be much happier with a different job description. If Wedmarsh does not have such an official policy, Lalage can start discussions with her new colleagues about how they want to structure their work in future. They could decide to pool their efforts, perhaps by alternating heavy and light teaching semesters, and rotating the administration, so that everyone gets blocks of research and writing time.

The department has to decide if it is going to become a dual labour market, or the research active are going to carry the inactive on projects and publications. Either has consequences, but these are rather different. If a staff group agree to a dual labour market, or to a strong carry the weak model, then the group is highly bonded. More commonly, though, the research active are unwilling to carry the 'unproductive', and want a dual labour market of a more purposive kind, where higher teaching and administrative loads are given to those without publications, who also get denied funding for conferences, for travel, sabbaticals and so on.

Althea: the individual strategy

Althea's first priority is to ensure that she has a publication plan for the next five years, an application for a sabbatical year, and that she has a strategy for raising grant income that will enable her to employ one or more research assistants. She also needs to recruit two or three PhD students in her research area. With PhD students and research assistants she will have the basis for building up her area inside the department and thus displaying leadership. There is a new young lecturer who works on a related topic whom Althea likes, so that person can also be involved.

So Althea's list is:

- plan publications for next five years;
- apply for sabbatical for three years ahead;
- apply for grants, with research assistant post(s);
- get three full-time PhD students.

To get three doctoral students Althea needs to do several things. She needs to seek out second- and third-year undergraduates and encourage them to apply for postgraduate study. There could be mileage in asking around her friends and colleagues in other universities to see if they have any promising potential doctoral students. Once she has found some possible candidates, she needs to encourage them to apply for funds, and help them to do so. Applying for grants is the subject of Chapter 4 and we have not gone into more detail here.

Applying for a sabbatical needs careful planning. Not all universities have an entitlement, and if there is no entitlement one urgent task is to get the AUT to campaign for such entitlement. A typical institutional arrangement for study leave is shown in Box 2.1 below.

Box 2.1
Study leave at Arlinghurst

Study leave with pay

Study leave may be granted as a privilege by Council to members of the academic staff, subject to the staffing needs of the University, for the furtherance of specific research projects, defined works of scholarship or specified publications, or for other specific purposes where this can be seen to be to the mutual advantage of the individual and the University. Study leave will not be granted to enable an applicant to work for a higher degree or prepare a new teaching course. Study leave is granted as an important part of staff development. It is also important that applications are in line with the research strategy of the department concerned and all applications are checked accordingly. Applications for periods of over four weeks shall be submitted to the Deputy Director of Personnel via the Head of Department for consideration by the Personnel Committee. The Committee will require that applications establish that the project or research cannot equally well be undertaken in the course of the applicant's normal duties; e.g. because it requires prolonged absences from Arlinghurst and that the vacations are insufficient or inappropriate.

Study leave will normally be granted only to an applicant who has served the University continuously for at least five years. The normal maximum proportion of any study leave to service will be one in seven. Thus, after seven years' service, up to no more than 12 months leave may be granted. For the purpose of calculating eligibility for study leave, any previous period of study leave (paid or unpaid) will not contribute to a period of eligible service.

In exceptional circumstances, an applicant may be permitted to anticipate study leave provided that he or she undertakes to return to his or her post at the end of the leave and serve the University for at least the minimum period to earn the full allowance for the leave anticipated. An applicant will be required to establish that he or she has a satisfactory research record that may be enhanced by the award of study leave.

A member of staff to whom study leave has been granted shall at the end of his or her leave submit a brief report for consideration by the Committee. The contents of this report will be taken into consideration by the Committee should any future application for study leave be received from the same candidate. A member of staff who wishes to vary the purpose of study leave from that described in his or her application form shall give details, in writing, to the Deputy Director of Personnel describing the proposed change. In the light of the new information, the Council may vary the terms on which study leave has been granted.

The conditions for study leave at Arlinghurst are essentially similar to those at most old British universities. Box 2.1 shows the purpose – to further research – and excludes leave to complete a higher degree. Applicants have to prove that they cannot do the project during normal academic life. When Althea reads these rules, given her plans (which are shown in Box 2.4), she feels confident that she is eligible. She has been at Arlinghurst long enough, her plans involve going to New Zealand, and she has a good enough research record.

Assuming there is entitlement, the first thing to do is to get the offical paperwork, and find out the schedule for applications and what is needed to get one awarded. A typical procedure is set out in Box 2.2.

Box 2.2
Procedure for making applications for study leave

Applications should be made to the Deputy Director of Personnel who will be able to give advice on the method of application should it be required. Applications should be submitted via the Head of Department who should attach his/her comments as outlined below to the application. Applications should be no longer than two pages of A4 paper and contain statements to cover the following:

1. Dates and locations(s) of proposed leave;
2. Purpose of proposed leave;
3. Purpose of project work or publication proposed to be undertaken;
4. Financial statement of any earnings, expenses or grants it is expected that the application will receive during the proposed leave as outlined below;
5. Declaration that any changes in the financial statement, subsequent to the application will be disclosed.

The applicant will be required to make a financial declaration (relating to financial resources available to him or her during the period of study leave) at the time of application and to undertake to disclose any changes that may arise subsequent to the application.

The Committee will require that each application be accompanied by a statement from the applicant's Head of Department, who will be asked to comment on the applicant's research and publications record, to give an assessment of the proposed project or research, the degree of support given to the application by the academic staff of the department and indicate that appropriate arrangements to cover the applicant's duties during the period of the absence can be made and that they can be funded from within the department's own resources.

Return from leave of absence/study leave

On return from leave (paid or unpaid) for periods in excess of two weeks, member of staff shall submit a brief report for the attention of the Personnel Committee. Whilst it is accepted that any fees or other earnings may be used to defray incidental expenses, the report should contain a statement of substantial employment (lasting say more than a week) and the University reserves the right to review the position should there be substantial employment and additional earnings during the period of leave on full salary.

Inside Althea's department at Arlinghurst there will probably be a committee to scrutinize potential claims, which will expect a detailed research plan, a justification of why those plans cannot be carried through during normal working terms, and some detailed account of how teaching will be covered. Such a committee advises the head of department, and provides an opportunity for the applicant to have the proposal scrutinized by a supportive group before it goes out to the wider university. The procedures inside Althea's department are set out on the department's website as shown in Box 2.3.

Box 2.3
Study leave in social and political studies

Staff are encouraged to make use of study leave, for which any member of the academic teaching staff on a research-based contract, whether permanent or temporary, may apply. All eligible colleagues are encouraged to consider applying for study leave at a time that it is appropriate for their research plans. The School would normally not expect to support more than four members of staff for study leave each semester. Study leave can only be granted where:

1. A specific research project and/or publication will be carried out/completed that could not normally be undertaken during working time;
2. This activity contributes directly to the School's research strategy;
3. Adequate provision can be made for teaching and other departmental commitments.

Study leave plans need preparing well in advance, at least a year, and the Research Committee will only consider study leave proposals on two occasions each year: a) at its December meeting (normally for periods of study leave commencing the following autumn; and b) at its May meeting (normally for periods of study leave commencing the following spring).

   Members of staff wishing to make an application for study leave should follow the procedure described below:

1. Have a preliminary discussion about what they would like to do with their appraiser or mentor;
2. Discuss their proposals with their Research Group convenor, and make a case for how the work they propose to do will contribute to the interests of the Group and the strategy of the School (following the headings set out below):

Name:

Dates for proposed study leave:

Rationale:
Give the rationale for your proposed study leave, including details of what you intend to achieve – number of papers, books, conferences and so on.

Teaching:
Give details of your current teaching commitments and your proposals for how these can be covered. For each course that you teach, you will need to provide a signed statement from the course convenor that the arrangements that you have made are satisfactory. The normal expectation is that you will arrange cover for your teaching by your colleagues at no additional cost to the School. Where funded replacement teaching cannot be avoided, please give full details of estimated costs. NB. Staff on study leave are normally expected to continue supervising graduate students. If this is impossible (for example, if you are working overseas) you should discuss appropriate arrangements with the Director of Graduate Studies and provide details in your application.

Administration:
Give details of your administrative responsibilities and your proposals for how these will be covered.

Submission dates:
Applications should be received by the School Administrator one week prior to either the December or the May meeting of the Research Committee.

1. The Research Committee will consider the merits of the application: in arriving at its decision the Research Committee will be particularly concerned that what the applicant is proposing to do could not have been done anyway. Where too many applications are received at any one time, the Research Committee will prioritize those it wishes to support.
2. The Research Committee will make a recommendation to the Head of the School, who will make a decision in the light of teaching and administration needs.
3. In the event of a positive decision by the Head of the School a recommendation will go to Personnel for final approval.
4. Following a period of study leave, colleagues will be expected to provide a written report outlining their achievements. Reports should be submitted to the Research Committee within three months of the completion of the period of study leave.

Once Althea has read these departmental rules, she needs to organize herself to get her application into the Departmental Committee in time for it to get through, and on to the University Committee in time for her to make her plans to take the leave. With both sets of requirements in mind, Box 2.4 shows an application Althea might write.

Box 2.4
Althea's study leave application

Study leave application: Dr Althea Scandler, School of Social and Political Studies.

Year applied for: 2006–2007, that is 1.10.06–30.09.07

Rationale: I have been invited to be Visiting Fellow in Women's Studies at Otago University, Dunedin (New Zealand): there is no salary, but they provide an office with PC, an air fare to New Zealand and back, and some funds to enable me to travel inside New Zealand. My research on women in rural areas facing change will be strengthened by an international comparison with New Zealand. The views and position of the rural women in Wales and the West Country will be compared with data on women in New Zealand. At Dunedin, Dr Janine Yeudall is an expert on feminist political movements and we would be able to collaborate on a book, and several papers.

Research students: Two current part-timers will have finished by 2006: the only one still working – Sam Tuttle – is a joint supervision with Kieran Marcable, and he is willing to be sole supervisor. I can be unavailable for MA thesis supervision for one year.

Teaching:

1. Kieran is prepared to teach all of the Year One course, if I do all of it in Year 2007 2008.
2. The Year Two course on Political Theory, to which I contribute eight lectures, can be covered by the team.
3. My Year Three option can be suspended: Rural Societies is not a core course. The MA option in feminism can be suspended, or department could hire Jenny Stallard to teach it: the board needs to discuss this.

Administration: I am due to finish doing admissions in August 2006: if I pick up being MA course organizer in 2007 (September) that would be fair.

Research career: I attach a full CV and my publication plans for 2002–2008. I had a term's leave in 1997, which I spent at Wedmarsh in their oral history archive working on the data that I published in *Sociologica Ruralis*, in 1998.

The material on the work to be done in New Zealand would appear in both the departmental and the university application. The material under the headings 'Research students', 'Teaching', and 'Admin' are only needed inside the department. they would not appear in the application to the university. For that, a simple statement from her head of department that her teaching and administration can be covered inside the School of Social and Political Studies is required. Both the school and the university need the curriculum vitae, and the note about the one term of leave taken in 1997. Althea's publication plans are set out in Box 2.5.

Box 2.5
Althea's publication plans 2002–2008

In press:

1) *Feminism Today* to be published by Snipcock and Tweed in 2003
2) 'Farming in Crisis' (with K. Marcable) accepted by *Sociological Review*

In preparation:

1) 'Rural Feminism': chapter for *Handbook of Rural Affairs* (edited by Welbeck and Whitford), Pettifer and Polegate
2) *Mrs MacDonald's Woes* (with Lalage Hunstanton) for Arlinghurst University Press – to be delivered in 2005.

Intentions:
Book with Janine Yeudall on rural feminism – we are seeking a contract with Snipcock and Tweed to appear in their feminism list: this would be written during study leave in New Zealand (2006–2007). Two or three journal articles on research done in New Zealand, one for *Rural Studies* or *Sociologia Ruralis*, one for *International Women's Studies Quarterly*, one for *Political Quarterly*.

Thus Althea organizes herself a study leave. She also has to apply for grants and build up her group of research students with full-time candidatures for her return from New Zealand. Grant applications are discussed in Chapter 5. If Althea's plans work, she will have three books published as a basis for her application for promotion to a senior lectureship, in 2005–2006. She should also be raising enough money to employ at least one research assistant, and angling to get a lectureship that expands 'her' area – in gender or rural affairs, or perhaps food, or the impact of GM crops, or tourism – so that she can increase her influence on the research of the department.

Without pursuing the interests of our fictional Althea any further, we need to take note of several things that are already apparent. First, her own research plans cannot be achieved without collective effort and support. Clearly study leave is not always the first thing to think about. But it is a clear example of how time and resources need to be *planned* not just by the individual academic, but by the department or division, and by the institution. Institutions that do not have normal study leave entitlements for their academic staff are missing out on an important aspect of collective strategy. Moreover, such an absence implies that the university is not giving sufficiently high priority to the development of individual research careers and productivity. However, even where the university has such a regular scheme, it will be up to the department to ensure that it is used and is used to the best effect. It requires planning. Our fictional account assumes that the department has a research committee. Our purpose here, then, is to highlight the necessity for mechanisms of collective action and responsibility for research development. The role of such a committee is, of course, much wider than just scrutinizing and approving individual study leave bids on a one-off basis. Individual research plans and timetables need to be incorporated within a collective strategic plan. The mentoring of less experienced colleagues in research-related skills should be a commitment of this committee – or some equivalent grouping.

It is no good Althea developing her plans unless she gets some sort of support and advice in putting it into practice. Collective decision-making needs to go into the promotion and preservation of research time and resources. Some groups – especially those in 'new' universities and those with lower research income – may find that planning for research feels like an unattainable luxury. When teaching loads are high, and staff–student ratios are also high, then it may seem difficult, if not impossible, to create the space for sustained research to be undertaken. But this situation – which is frequently encountered – is all the more reason for a sustained collective approach to the research development of individuals and their colleagues. Scholarship and research all too easily are treated as something that gets done *after* all one's other commitments have been met. The problem with such an approach – which is often a symptom of a *laissez-faire* attitude towards research – resides in the fact that most academic work expands to fill the time available, and more. Teaching undergraduates and postgraduates is a greedy undertaking. Virtually all academics find that their time and effort are pressured, and find it difficult to allocate their time productively between their various obligations. It is a collective responsibility – as well as a managerial one – to try to ensure that research has its proper place in the timetable of academic colleagues. This may mean managing the timetable to try to avoid messy and incoherent teaching schedules, finding periods of time when staff can devote themselves to scholarship, research and writing. It might mean making collective agreements about a sensible rota of study leave. It can certainly mean a shared commitment to alternating light and heavy teaching semesters or terms. It should probably mean a departmental commitment to arranging for regular 'office hours' when staff are available to students, rather than a disruptive stream of student inquiries at unpredictable hours. And so on. We shall be returning to many of these themes in the course of this book. Our point here, to repeat our message, is that the development of a research plan for individual staff members involves collective decision-making and shared responsibility. Consequently, academics in managerial positions – heads of department, deans and the like – need to foster collective interests and commitments to research development. Further-

more, people like Althea need to feel that they are not struggling alone to
realize their personal research plans and ambitions.

Leaving Althea for the moment, Lalage's problems as head of department are bigger, and are the subject of the next section.

Lalage: the head of department

Lalage, as a new head of department, parachuted in to try to 'save' geography at Wedmarsh, has some hard choices to make, both personal and
departmental. If she stays at Wedmarsh but fails to turn round the
department, then her own career will be harmed. However, if her new
colleagues think she is going to move on elsewhere, they are unlikely to feel
very committed to her rescue plan. One thing she needs to do is read the
official RAE report on Wedmarsh, and the published report of the geography panel on the discipline as a whole. (This is assuming she was not,
herself, a member of the panel.) It is also common for universities to ask
one or two distinguished subject specialists, again ideally with RAE experience, to inspect the department and provide a report. If Wedmarsh has not
already commissioned such a report, Lalage should ask for one. Geography
is a broad discipline, with sub-specialisms overlapping with geology and
earth sciences at the scientific end, a social science sub-specialism in which
quantitative and qualitative researchers are found and, in historical geography and cultural geography, some scholars who are closer to humanities
colleagues in style of investigation. If Lalage is a physical geographer she
may have great need of help from an outsider who is a distinguished human
geographer, whereas, if that is her area, then she will want a physical geography perspective.

Lalage needs to get a clear picture of how departments are funded at
Wedmarsh, and what income, outgoings and looming expenses she is
facing. In the USA there was a course in higher education management for
women that required, as the entry qualification, a detailed breakdown of
the university's financial systems: if you were not allowed access to them, or
could not grasp them, then you were not ready for the course. The same is
true, in miniature, of departmental headship: Lalage has to grasp how
Wedmarsh channels funds and posts to departments. In some universities
the funding mechanisms are very transparent, based on formulae. So, for
example, there will be Teaching (T) money for every undergraduate, taught
postgraduate, and research postgraduate; Research (R) money for every
staff member who was returned in the last RAE; plus money from overheads
on research grants. Others are very opaque, with budgets held at the centre
and dispensed with little transparency. In some systems most costs are
charged to the centre and departments have small funds but small costs. In
others staff costs, room hire, even heat and lighting, are paid for by
departments. The scope a head of department has to change things may
depend on the budget arrangements.

If Lalage is going to raise the research achievements of geography at Wedmarsh, she needs to diagnose what has been wrong since 1992, and change the culture of each individual, each group, and the whole department. Lalage cannot know until she has done some investigations how far the problem lies in a poor research performance, or a good performance poorly represented to the panel. If the performance is poor, then it needs improvement. It is possible that Lalage will find that her new colleagues are doing too much teaching, teaching inefficiently, spending too much time and emotion on teaching, and/or having too many meetings, wasting energy on quarrelling and/or spending too much time and energy on administration, and/or spending too much time and energy on pastoral care.

Pastoral care is like housework – it can consume as much time as staff have. There is often duplication between departmental and central facilities – staff may be counselling students, giving careers advice, dealing with health problems – when there are specialist staff to do it better. She needs to see each lecturer, senior lecturer and other colleagues separately, with a CV and a research plan, to find out what they are, and are not, doing and what barriers they see to raising their game. We can imagine that Lalage had asked all her colleagues to prepare for the meetings by completing a form shown in Box 2.6, on which she had asked:

Box 2.6

1. Assuming there is an RAE in 2007, please list all the publications you hope to have, with the four you would expect to list marked (RAE).
2. Please list the grant applications you plan to make over the next five years.
3. Are you satisfied with (a) departmental support and (b) university support for your publication and grant applications? If not, please tell me what the impediments are, and what I can do to remove them.

In Boxes 2.7 and 2.8 there are research plans from one colleague, Eirian, who is clearly research active, and therefore does not present an immediate difficulty for Lalage, and another, Gregan, who presents an urgent problem for Lalage.

Box 2.7
Research plan of research-active lecturer (Eirian)

Publications

(RAE) *European Fisheries* (Beauminster UP) to be published 2004 (title yet to be fixed: manuscript to be delivered in 2003)
(RAE) Chapter in *Festschrift* for Richard Munton on fishing (Arlinghurst UP)
(RAE) Paper in *Int. Jnl. Pop. Geog.*
(RAE) Paper in *Transactions of the IBG*, 2005.
Paper in *Journal of Teaching Geography in HE* on PhD supervision

Grants

The ESRC grant I have (£272,000) runs until December 2004.
   I plan to bid in 2003 for a project on the social impacts of fish farming in three European countries.

Dept support

1. We need a dedicated research secretary or administrator who will prioritize circulating potential funding opportunities, costing and typing our applications, checking our research accounts every month, do our conference bookings, run our conferences here, help the post docs start applying for stuff – even demonstrate costings to the PhD students and new staff. Current situation is too messy: never clear who will help with these chores.
2. Move all the basic admin. onto the non-active: admissions, school liaison, exams, quality, prospectus, open days – all the grott.

University

Wedmarsh does not signal clearly that it wants all schools to be research active. V-C seems only interested in Chemistry, Chair of Res. Committee 'disses' everyone except Engineering. When Todd got that big NERC grant it was not even announced in University News, or at Senate: when a Chemist got half the amount it was on the front page of *UN*. I am not surprised he went to Arlinghurst – *their* V-C has a non-scientist as chair of the research committee, and signals he wants everyone doing research.

When Lalage reads this it gives her a good basis for her meeting with that staff member, and gives her useful ideas for changing Wedmarsh geography. Box 2.8 is equally revealing, although much less constructive in tone.

Box 2.8
Research plan of problematic lecturer (Gregan)

Publications

The Geographical Association have suggested a chapter for a book for
A level students, but I cannot be arsed.

My son suggested I wrote up that stuff on alluvial fans he did for his
MSc at Castleton now he has gone into industry, but there are not any
journals to put it in.

Dept support

What support?

University support

Get Todd back from Arlinghurst: we need him for the cricket team,
and the squash ladder.

Grants

None – Nobody funds my kind of research.

This sort of response is very revealing, because it shows a lecturer who has
given up, and apparently resents all aspects of the regime. Gregan is clearly
a problem. Lalage could consult his personal file and CV in the head of
department's office and discover whether he is burnt out after a good start
or someone who was never good enough to be in a top department, and
perhaps should never have been appointed. His age is also relevant – this
response from a 27-year-old would need very different treatment than the
same response from a 57-year-old. You may think that this is something of a
caricature of a disaffected and unproductive lecturer – but it is not all that
far from realities that we have encountered and had reported to us from
various quarters.

If we look at the two responses, it is clear that Eirian and Gregan give
Lalage different problems. Eirian is probably not a problem at all –
although she may need to be encouraged to apply for bigger grants; publish
in more 'difficult' journals, that is journals it is harder to get into, such as
the major international (often American) ones. She has the base from
which to be more ambitious and aim for larger and better things. She also
has reason to be confident in her abilities to succeed in those aims. Gregan
on the other hand is a real problem. First, there is an attitudinal issue:
Gregan is not taking Lalage or the inquiries she is making seriously. The
tone is offensive, retrospective and ignorant.

Gregan has no publication plans: his two suggestions are not likely to
become publications, and even if they did, he seems unsighted on the RAE.

The Geographical Association is not the research-led body (that is the RGS/ IBG), it is the body for school teachers, so anything it produced would not be listable in an RAE return. It might be a good idea to publish the chapter because it could help publicize Wedmarsh among teachers and sixth-formers which could improve recruitment. Such work needs to be done. But it is not *research*. The possible paper on alluvial fans could be an RAE item, but as Gregan says he does not know of any journals it is a long way from becoming a publication. If Gregan really does not know about the journals in physical geography and earth sciences, then he needs to have some rapid staff development. If he is pretending to be ignorant, then Lalage has to either get rid of him or change his attitudes. The retrospective complaints about the loss of Todd, if they are not 'really' about cricket and squash, suggest that a new Todd, that is a new professor in physical geography, *might* be able to turn Gregan around. However, it is not at all clear that the best candidate for a chair, in terms of grant getting and group building, will be interested in turning 'dead wood' around. Some Gregans are so stuck into being resistant to change that their whole identity has become bound up with objecting to the RAE, to the TQA, to change. Some valorize their teaching or pastoral care, some are just wastrels who avoid all work, some are very scared. Perhaps they were research-active once and have run out of steam and are not clear how to start again in case they cannot hack it. Perhaps they were appointed long ago, and given tenure, when even leading universities appointed staff who were not trained or even encouraged to be researchers, and failed to give them any staff development, or even clear signals that they had to bootstrap themselves into research activity.

It is a common joke, made recently by two vice-chancellors, Martin Harris (2002) and Roderick Floud (2002), that when they were appointed standards were low. They state that a lecturer appointed in 2002 is far, far better qualified than equivalent appointees in the 1970s. In 2002 it would be hard to get *shortlisted* for a lectureship without a PhD, four publications, some teaching experience and a plan for grant income and research culture building. There are exceptions, such as accountancy, where it is hard to recruit lecturers at all, because salaries and perks are so much better in the outside world. Any field in which the university is training people to work in a specific vocation, such as pharmacy, law, nursing and accountancy, needs staff who are professionally qualified, registered with a professional body such as the RPS, Law Society or Bar Council, RCN, or ACCA, have some recent and relevant experience doing the job (for example, a university pharmacy lecturer might need to do some locum work regularly to stay abreast of practice) perhaps to have a consultancy portfolio to show that one is a competent practitioner whose services are in demand, and then to be a lecturer and to publish and raise research funds. Many of the tensions in vocational/professional schools arise from this multi-tasking. When all academic staff in university departments of education were required by a quango called CATE (Council for the Accreditation of Teacher Education) to demonstrate that they had 'recent and relevant' (R and R) experience of teaching in schools or higher education colleges this problem was made very obvious. Universities that wanted the staff in schools of education to be research-active faced a particularly difficult task. Given that the PGCE year is 44 weeks, not the 30-week undergraduate teaching year, once staff had taught for 44 weeks and done their R and R, there was little time for research and publication. The traditional route into university teaching for schools of education was from schools: if you wanted a person to train chemistry teachers you recruited the head of chemistry from a successful school, who might have an MEd but would not be an active researcher. Many lecturers had little research background, or training, so it was particularly hard for them to reach RAE standards as well as teach, keep up their 'recent and relevant' and actually support students.

It is unlikely that Gregan was recruited like that as a physical geographer, but he may well be an old lag who got tenure long ago, and if Lalage had been appointed head of accountancy, law, education or social work, a Gregan-type response could be *expected* from a substantial chunk of the staff. One solution is to *institutionalize* a career structure for people who are not able to be research-active, but are useful to the university. Cardiff University has an employment category of 'Professional Tutor', with a promotion route to Senior Professional Tutor. Some staff are recruited to such posts *ab initio*, others were translated across from lectureships. For some of those so translated it came as an enormous relief: in music, for example, a person who runs the orchestra and choir, which are vital parts of the work of all music departments, may be sacrificing her own research time to ensure that there are concerts and operas, recitals and carol services. To be recognized for that work, and therefore have it given an imprimatur, is motivating and empowering.

If Wedmarsh has such a post, Gregan might *like* a translation: he might prefer a new job with a new title, new responsibilities. Such jobs are necessarily different – in particular, such a person has to work 46 weeks a year, and do administration when there is no undergraduate teaching going on. If an ordinary lecturer works a 39-hour week, in term time this would probably be 13 hours teaching, 13 hours administration, 13 hours scholarship. In the undergraduate vacation it should be 3 hours teaching (of PhD students) and others 3–6 hours administration, and 30 hours of research. A professional tutor needs to do 19 hours of teaching and 19 hours of administration in term, and 39 hours of administration in the vacation. Not all staff offered a professional tutorship are prepared to recognize that necessity: it seems to be seen as a type of school teaching with 'holidays'. (This is not an accurate reflection of school teaching either, of course.)

Lalage is going to have to see Gregan, and confront him with her agenda. She may discover his questionnaire was a bad joke, but if it is a genuine reflection of his plans, then she has to get rid of him, change him, or change his post. It is probably sensible to see him with a witness, to prevent accusations of harassment, and to have a longstanding Wedmarsh person present to challenge any claims that Gregan's behaviour is acceptable 'here'. If Wedmarsh has a system of departmental research mentors, then Lalage could ask one of them to see Gregan with her – if Gregan is a difficult man, she might find it helpful to have a male scientist with her. In Cardiff the University Research Committee allocates one of its members to a set of departments to advise each on its research issues and agenda: if Wedmarsh did not have such a system Lalage could propose it, and/or ask the vice-chancellor to give her a couple of leading researchers, one a scientist and one a social scientist, to advise her and to talk to key colleagues – both the ones who she needs to inspire to aim higher and her worst problems. Some of the issues raised by Eirian need attention. Lalage needs to find out if Eirian's claims that the vice-chancellor only values research in chemistry are true, and why Todd's big NERC grant was not reported in *University News* or at Senate. Sometimes departments are their own worst enemies: they fail to publicize their achievements inside the university, in the local paper, and with adroit press releases. If Wedmarsh did not value Todd, then his successor may feel equally unappreciated and not stay. Research leadership often means orchestrating publicity.

The away day

One of the devices that is often used to communicate new missions, or reinforce existing missions that are not understood or from which people have drifted away, is the away day, or even residential away 'more than' a day. Many universities use it for senior managers. Lalage might use it as part of her rescue package of geography at Wedmarsh: taking the whole department, or the research-active, or the research committee, or the highest earning staff, or whatever. A typical away day is in a university's own conference facility or an hotel. There is usually a mix of lectures and small group discussion, which may be genuinely intended to discover what colleagues really think. Sometimes it is intended to change people's minds towards the leaders' goals. Sometimes an away day is used to get a task done: for example, to get module descriptions rewritten into a standardized format, to get research planned, to draw up new structures. At Mallingford, for example, the new head of social work took the staff to a hotel, and once there, revealed that everyone was going to produce the first draft of a journal article and a plan for a grant application by the end of the weekend. The staff dispersed to their study bedrooms and were instructed to, for example, produce the abstract of a journal article, and then return to a small group to share it, then back to their rooms to write the opening paragraph, and so on. The shock was that the staff had been told that the weekend was about something else, and so the non-publishers had come, and were then forced to write. Such ambushing can only be done once: the next time the ones most in need of such shock tactics would absent themselves. Box 2.9 shows a plan for an 'away day' that Lalage could run, to see if she can enthuse geography to turn itself round.

Box 2.9
Away day at 'The Pines'

10.00 Coffee
10.30 Introduction: Lalage Hunstanton
10.35 Research Strategy Wedmarsh 2010: Prof. Saul Mollenstein (Pro Vice-Chancellor Research)
11.00 Coffee
11.15 Small group discussion of the report from Geography 2001 RAE panel
12.30 Lunch
13.15 Research groups
14.15 PhD Students and Post Docs: Dr Theo Beatock (Director Graduate School)
15.00 Tea
15.30 Creating a wish list (Delphi Groups using PCs)
16.15 Anonymized feedback to PVC (Research)
16.30 End

From this it is clear what Lalage's goals are: first, she has wheeled out a big gun, the Pro Vice-Chancellor Research, to tell everyone what Wedmarsh's goals are. Geography could have been closed down, it is in the 'last chance saloon'. If there is to be a future for geography, then the slide has to be halted, and a climb back up achieved. The staff have to understand *why* they got a 3A, and what they need to do to improve, that is what a 4, a 5 or a 5* looks like, and how to emulate one. The answer is more grant income, more and better publications, more PhD students and more postdocs, more equipment and technical support, and recruiting some 'stars' – ideally people with grants and a research group they can bring. There are other things, such as having the RGS/IBG to Wedmarsh, having regional meetings and more specialist national and international meetings, ensuring Wedmarsh people go and give papers (but ensuring that they are good papers, rehearsed and well delivered). One of the problems of a declining department is that as the QR money declines, the grant income falls, the number of PhD students funded drops, the number of postdocs falls, there is less conference money and so on. Lalage needs to produce a recovery plan and get it funded by the vice-chancellor or the Finance Committee, or whatever body in Wedmarsh University can provide such funding.

It is also clear to us that Lalage will not get anywhere unless she can convince her departmental colleagues that it is in all their interests to introduce step changes in their collective behaviour. She certainly cannot afford to alienate them. There are all sorts of ways in which she can make her colleagues feel disaffected and can inspire resistance. People who are brought in as potential research leaders can undoubtedly cause resentment unless they manage things sensibly and sensitively. The head of department can create problems if he or she merely lays down the law and expects people to change and improve their performance as a consequence. Nagging people about research is no way to improve their productivity. Leading by example is obvious, but important for all that. One cannot expect people to respond to 'leadership' if they do not respect the leader(s). One should not be asking or expecting colleagues to do things one cannot do or has not done oneself. Part of changing and improving the culture of your own department may well involve changing your own behaviour and performance too: and even more importantly, it may involve acknowledging that and doing so in an open manner. (This does not mean the equivalent of a public self-degradation or confessional, but academic colleagues are likely to withhold respect from senior colleagues who do not recognize their own strengths and weaknesses.)

If Lalage is experienced and has a successful track record in attracting research funds, for instance, then she will need to display and deploy that experience, actively helping others to develop their research bids, collaborating where appropriate in developing research programmes and projects. The aid and support of senior staff need to be mobilized if the entire department is to swing behind and endorse the new research ambitions. It is no good having events like away days, or generating things like strategic plans for the department, unless they are translated into everyday actions and collegial relationships.

Junior staff especially need to be nurtured and brought 'on board' with the research mission. We have already seen from the case of Althea that a lecturer needs to develop a personal research plan, and that needs to be integrated within the collective plans. It is easy for senior and more experienced members of a department to overlook the possibility that more junior staff can easily be made to feel marginal and under-valued. They need to be mentored and protected, as far as possible, made to feel central to the department's mission, and part of a collective enterprise that is going forward. Less experienced staff do not need to be pestered and harangued about their performance. Equally, however, they do not thrive by being left entirely to find their own way. The competing demands of teaching and research, and of publishing, coupled with any other demands of departmental and university administration, professional service and so on, can leave inexperienced colleague feeling overwhelmed and confused. They need to be integrated within peer groups, and that includes the possible role of research groupings in the department.

Research groups

Somewhere between the individual head of department's planning and aspirations, and the personal research plans of the individual lecturer, there is the organizational level of the research group. Research groups are entirely taken-for-granted in the laboratory sciences. Historically they have not been common in the humanities, and relatively uncommon in the social sciences. In recent years, however, they have received much greater attention in all disciplines. This trend reflects institutional pressures to concentrate research and present it to the outside world selectively, capitalizing on departmental and institutional strengths. It reflects the logic of the Research Assessment Exercise, in which critical mass of researchers in sub-fields of research has been important. It should and could also reflect the benefits to be gained from collective commitments to research and its planning.

Research groups in the natural sciences are fundamental to their organization and reproduction. We have documented this ourselves elsewhere (Delamont, Atkinson and Parry 2000). They are defined by shared research projects, with continuity over time, and with a clearly defined inter-generational transmission of research topics, techniques, skills and craft knowledge. Senior academics – professors and readers – are group directors. They are responsible for setting the agenda, raising the external research funds, and managing the research enterprise. Within the group, post-doctoral researchers (postdocs) are key members. Having completed their own PhD, they are responsible for a great deal of the practical work of the laboratory and carrying out the research project. Experienced postdocs do a lot of day-to-day supervision of postgraduate research assistants and doctoral students. The research effort of the group cascades through them, and is reproduced through the recruitment of postgraduates and more postdocs.

Colleagues in the humanities and the social sciences are fond of asserting that much of their most significant work is a matter of individual scholarship, and does not lend itself to organization in terms of research 'groups'. There are, however, merits in undertaking research planning and development on a group basis, even if the research itself is not conducted collectively or directed the way it is in a laboratory setting. Research groupings do not have to be based on joint research projects, but should reflect common interests and purposes; reflecting disciplinary fields, research methods, or other dimensions of common purpose. They should provide one mechanism whereby all the relevant people – senior and junior academic staff, postdocs, research students, technical and support staff – can all come together to develop and further the research that is in their common interest.

Research groups provide major mechanisms through which mentoring and staff development can take place. We are going to discuss issues of mentoring and the encouragement of careers later in this book. At this point, we want simply to emphasize that 'staff development' and 'mentoring'

are not *events* that are embedded only in a round of bureaucratic obligations. Obviously, staff development and training events are important, and
institutions with research aspirations or pretensions need to include a
steady round of research-oriented staff development activities. But in the
greater scheme of things, development is a *process* of everyday, routine
engagement with one's colleagues. Younger and less experienced staff learn
craft skills and internalize attitudes from working regularly with more
experienced colleagues. Equally, the older members of the team can often
learn a lot from working with their juniors: if nothing else, they have to spell
out what they normally take for granted. So the work of the research group
is all about working and interacting together – formally and informally – on
a variety of things.

Research groupings need to work together on the preparation of
research bids and the design of research proposals. This is a crucial set of
activities that Lalage is going to have to promote, and staff like Althea are
going to have to get involved in. A collective response to Research Council
initiatives, to European Framework Programme calls, to invitations to tender from central and local government departments, or new research
opportunities from the major charities will be much easier than a lone
academic struggling to get it done. It will be much likelier to be successful
too: major research developments are likely to need teams of investigators
to collaborate.

So Lalage probably needs to establish research groups, or to ensure that
existing groupings are working effectively. There will be no benefit if she
merely imposes these groupings from the top down. Consequently, she
needs to think about and talk to her colleagues about what shared interests
and commitments already exist, which members of staff are most compatible, where there are shared or complementary skills and knowledge.
Research groups that exist only 'on paper' – for the purposes of research
assessment exercises or departmental reviews – may temporarily achieve
their symbolic or ritual functions, but they are very unlikely to promote real
research enhancements and lead to sustainable research. Equally, if she is
trying to build and enhance a research culture, then a head of department
like Lalage need not assume that large groupings are better than smaller
ones. If the department has an under-powered research culture, then going
for large-scale developments probably will not work. She and her department will probably do better to establish smaller groupings of people who
can genuinely work together: who can write publications together or at least
act as friendly critics of each other's written drafts, who can prepare and
present joint conference papers, and can attend the major conferences
together, to ensure that the university has a visible presence there. Larger
and very formal groupings can prove daunting to younger lecturing and
research staff. Smaller and less formal groupings can help to empower
them, and help them to integrate with the intellectual and social context of
the department. (We return to the theme of isolation and marginalization
of junior staff later in the book.)

The tone of Althea's study leave application suggests that she already feels confident in her colleagues, and feels part of a supportive group. From Lalage's point of view, on the other hand, Eirian's response seems more negative. Eirian does not give the impression that she has that same feeling of colleagueship and support. Lalage and some of her senior colleagues need to work at supporting staff members like Eirian. Heads of department, directors of research centres and other senior research managers normally have a lot of demands on their time and effort. Ironically, they are often distracted from important aspects of research. They can often give direction and take the lead in projects, but often find that day-to-day activities get squeezed out, and writing papers can often become difficult to manage. They often benefit from a group – or even one enthusiastic collaborator – who can help with everyday aspects of project management, and drafting papers. Likewise, the more junior partner can gain enormously from the more experienced partner's leadership – in terms of broad perspectives and 'big ideas', intellectual networks, skills in drafting proposals and outlines and so on. Both partners can benefit, therefore, from a division of labour between them. Such a productive relationship can be expanded to the context of a research group. The benefits are generated by a division of labour within the group: members pooling their time and competences in order to achieve more than they might separately. Note that such a productive array of relationships is quite different from the essentially exploitative situation in which the research group leader or the professor just dumps work on the junior members, expecting them to do things he or she cannot be bothered with, or clearing up after their failure to complete tasks. Again, top-down imposition is entirely counter-productive to successful research development.

Lalage also needs to think about groupings beyond her own department. Geography has potential affinities with other disciplines and departments. (The precise configuration of which will, of course, depend on her own university.) Physical geography has obvious links with other sciences, such as earth sciences or geology, or oceanography. Human or cultural geography has links with a range of social sciences – sociology, anthropology, cultural and media studies, urban and region studies, town planning, architecture, and so on. Research developments are increasingly achieved on the basis of interdisciplinary, and hence inter-departmental, collaborations and teams. If her university does not already do so, therefore, she needs to get together with research leaders in cognate departments, and put together some potential working groups who can explore mutually beneficial research collaborations. They do not have to try to establish major research programmes all at once. Lalage and her colleagues need to be realistic, not over-ambitious. But a series of joint seminars, some individual collaborative links, perhaps a jointly organized conference – these can all be the basis for establishing some longer-term and larger-scale collaborations.

The crucial thing about all and any such groupings, whether they be within or across departmental boundaries, is that they should be focused on practical activities. They may have some formal recognition, of course, but what they *do* is more important than what they are called.

Staffing strategy

The vacant chair and the vacant lectureship will have to be filled astutely and strategically if Lalage is to transform Wedmarsh geography. The chair Lalage can fill will have to be either in physical geography *or* human. The two halves of the department will contest how it is to be filled. If 'Todd', the professor who has gone to Arlinghurst, held a NERC grant, then he is a physical geographer, and the physicals in the department will expect, want and need a physical geographer as a replacement. If the staff of Wedmarsh is as follows:

5 professors (1 vacant): Lalage, Prof. Verlaine, 2 others, 1 vacancy
1 reader: Dr Parslow
5 senior lecturers: Dr Hendren and Dr Farrar + 3 others
8 lecturers 'B' grade: (including Eirian and Gregan)
2 lecturers 'A', including 1 vacancy
1 technician, 3 secretaries

The physical/human split is:

5 Professors: Prof. Lalage, physical; Prof. Verlaine and 2 others, human; vacant chair to be decided
reader: human
5 senior lecturers: 2 physicals, 3 human
8 lecturers 'B' grade: 4 human, 4 physical
2 lecturers 'A': 1 human, 1 vacancy to be decided

Lalage is going to need to keep the physical *vs* human geography balance, and to keep her research-active staff from leaving for Beauminster or Perth. There are also tensions inside the physical *vs* human division. Human geography is deeply split between quantitative and qualitative researchers: between the sort of research that uses advanced statistical techniques and that which celebrates ethnographic approaches. So recruiting a 'human geographer' is not unproblematic – the quantitative researchers will probably want a quantitative person, the qualitative researchers a qualitative person. The advocates of feminist geography will want to strengthen feminism, and so on. There are also issues about what other disciplines exist at Wedmarsh. It is possible that any physical geography appointment should be carefully coordinated with the staffing and research strategy of the geology department, particularly if it is strong in research, to maximize the possibilities of getting grants and publications collaboratively. If there is a strong social science or humanities discipline which could provide collaborations, that might also be a good basis for staffing geography in a particular way. A well-regarded Centre for Medieval Studies might welcome an appropriate historical geographer; a famous group of experts on Latin America would be a good partnership for a specialist in the geography of that region, and so on. Lalage needs to get to know her new university, and what its strengths are, so she can draw on collaborative links and establish good networks.

All disciplines have such internal divisions, and different factions. Any head of department has to reconcile all staff to decisions made about where new and replacement posts are to be located inside the department. Staff can be reconciled to appointments if they can see sound financial reasons for them, but that does mean *all* staff understanding how the money comes into Wedmarsh and into the department, what it is spent on, where there is flexibility and how it can be increased. Anthropology at UCL, for example, had decided in the early 1990s to appoint one part-time personal tutor/ pastoral care expert to provide all the support and guidance to all the undergraduates, and not to have a technician for the biological anthropology lab, but just to buy regular time from a graduate student to set up and clear up after the undergraduate practicals. This freed all staff from pastoral care, and provided a graduate studentship in biological anthropology. The Psychology Department at Cardiff funds four graduate teaching assistants on four-year contracts to do all the Year One tutorials while they undertake a PhD: this provides four PhD students to add to the department total, but also frees up the staff from a chore, *and* improves the Level One tutorials because all four deliver classes explicitly related to the Level One courses.

Other departments might choose to employ an administrator or a technician rather than a lecturer: someone who did all the administration of exams, admissions and so on could lift a burden from teaching staff – someone who does X can lift the burden of X from Y. In Cardiff when we ran the School of Social Sciences we decided to appoint some tutorial fellows to do a half load of teaching, administration and pastoral care, and do a PhD. We took people with an MA, from which they could publish a bit while their PhD research got going. Most of the people we recruited did PhDs, got lectureships, published, became RAE returnable, and were appointable to lectureships. They had a salary, and pension contributions, and a clear career structure. In general, the people we appointed could not have taken a studentship, but were enthusiastic about the half and half route into an academic career. If Lalage were to use the vacant lectureship to create two tutorial fellowships, or four studentships, she could reduce the teaching loads of staff like Eirian, with the clear expectation that they would apply for more grants. Alternatively, she could appoint an administrator, to deal with admissions, timetabling, open days and so on, and require that the research-active staff devote the time released to raising grants.

If possible Lalage needs to release or redirect some other departmental resources towards research. A research-led institution, and a research-active department within it, needs to provide support for research activities. At the institutional level, there is need for a properly resourced and staffed administrative division that has responsibility for research initiatives, research grants, contracts, consultancies, patents and spin-offs. If the university is not providing that, then it is clearly not serious about its institutional commitment to research. No university would admit students without having a registry of some sort. No university should be without an equal commitment to research management. Equally, no department should try to develop major research plans without making available support services. This means at minimum an office where there are staff trained and available to help prepare research bids, who can receive and distribute information about research opportunities, who can help prepare and manage research grant budgets, who can provide the necessary up-to-date information on salary scales, overhead rates, equipment costs, the university-approved rates for travel and subsistence, and the purchasing consortium's costs for consumables. In many disciplines this will also require input from a senior technician, whose advice will be needed on equipment specification and costs. The details vary from institution to institution and discipline to discipline. But the function is a vital one. Lalage may not feel that her department is yet big enough and secure enough in its research mission to be able to afford such a facility. Then she should sound out other departments with similar interests – such as those she is building strategic research links with anyway – to think about funding a shared research office. She and the other department heads can think about developing their own departmental offices as and when the shared facility bears fruit.

The positive outcomes

If Althea and Lalage are successful, what will have happened by 2010? Althea will be a professor, having got a senior lectureship in 2005, and then a chair. Arlinghurst will be famous for its political science research on gender, or rural society, or food, or tourism. Lalage will have handed on the headship of a revitalized geography department, from which Gregan is long gone, which has an RAE grade of 5 and is valued for its research as well as its joint degrees. Of course, such outcomes will not come about simply because either of our two characters will it to be so. And the things we have just outlined will not bring about these desirable ends. There are many practical issues that need to be addressed, and many activities that need to be undertaken to reach such an end-point. Research grants need to be bid for and the research projects managed. Books, journal papers and other forms of dissemination need to be generated. Research groups need to be built up, and their staff managed. A good deal of staff development and monitoring needs to have been accomplished, with successful outcomes, and staff members need to be given a fresh lease of life.

In the chapters that follow we look at some of these specific kinds of activity and reflect on how they can be promoted and enhanced in today's increasingly demanding and competitive higher education institutions.

3

Supervising and mentoring: 'taken under the wing'

When Duncan Pattullo, a successful playwright, returns to his Oxford college as a fellow in drama, he is frequently unsure of how to behave. He comments that: 'Nobody was going to do anything so obtrusive as to take me under his wing' (1976: 9). This chapter deals with why novices need to be taken under someone's wing, and what, if you are the owner of the wing, you should provide for those you are mentoring. We can see why mentoring is necessary if we imagine two young lecturers.

> Roger Clatworthy, who has a temporary post at Beauminster meets his friend Dermot Garrowby, who was a PhD student with him, and now lectures at Wedmarsh, at a conference. During their evening together, Dermot mentions that he has a probation mentor, a research mentor, is enrolled on a diploma in teaching and supervision in higher education, and is part of a research group which is writing two grant applications. Roger is amazed: he was offered a half day seminar on teaching and he thinks he is supposed to have a mentor but has never met him. His contract runs out in another year and he does not know what will happen next.

We will meet Roger again in later chapters: he is an archetypal case of how new and temporary staff even in elite universities, or perhaps especially in elite universities, can be left to sink or swim. We meet Dermot again in Chapters 6 and 7 to 9: he is in a lower status but more supportive environment. In this chapter we address the supervision of research students, the training of staff to do that supervision, mentoring new staff in teaching and in research posts, the findings on how research staff are treated, project management and the policy context.

There are many ways in which new staff are superior to old lags, such as use of IT, knowledge of fashion, rapport with undergraduates, and experience of debt. However, a long career in academia does provide useful experience which new colleagues have a right to hear about. They can always reject advice: in ignorance they cannot make rational judgements.

The desperate need many PhD students and young staff have for mentoring was revealed in an article in the *Times Higher Education Supplement* (20 September 2002) by Simon Francis, a newly graduated PhD in politics with some temporary teaching at Bristol University. He began teaching apparently without any training or support, and ends his piece:

> Somehow, I have to find the time and inclination to write journal articles. These are unpaid and I just do not feel like burning my brains out for nothing anymore. (p. 21)

This piece has considerable similarities with the views expressed by young staff in the investigation undertaken by the Standing Conference on Arts and Social Science in 2001 (Delamont 2002). It reveals the desperate need for supervision, training and mentoring during the PhD registration and in the early years of employment, and its absence in many universities and colleges. For a man not to understand how academic publications work, and not to want to share his results with the research community, is a sad reflection of failure in the academic community. Academic publications in journals do not provide an immediate cash return, but they are a good financial investment. Initially they get young scholars jobs and tenure. In the longer term, if we imagine two people who work until they are 55, the person who gets promoted to be a senior lecturer or reader at age 40 in an old university will earn £138,000 more (using 2002 pay scales) than the person who remains a lecturer. Such a sum is certainly not 'nothing'. In 2002 the top of lecturer scale, without discretionary points, was £32,537, the top of the senior lecturer and reader scale, with discretionary points, was £41,732. Fifteen years on that higher scale is worth a lot of money. After the 2002 pay rise, the same calculations produce a difference of £140,000, so the gap is widening.

Most young scholars are not as clueless as Dr Francis purported to be in the *THES* about academic realities, but there is much they cannot know. William Tierney (2002) stresses how important mentoring is for women faculty and faculty of colour. In the USA black faculty report a lack of mentoring, and that lack of mentoring is a factor in attrition. Books of advice for women academics stress the importance of good mentoring: that is, they advise women to search out a good mentor (for example, Caplan 1993; Toth 1997; Cooper and Stevens 2002). Toth's book is set out like a problem page in a magazine, with queries from beginning academics and mid-career ones about the perils of American university life. It is a wonderful read, and full of terrifyingly realistic advice about higher education. It takes the reader from graduate school through job hunting, conferences, the first year, tenure, and the mid-career years. It is aimed at women, but could be read by anyone who feels unsighted about higher education.

We can take two concrete examples, one specific to men, one which particularly affects women. The female example has been discussed by Tescione (1998). If a woman changes her surname on marriage or divorce she damages her career. Her publication list becomes cumbersome, and her citation count is destroyed. A woman's publications can vanish from the cumulative record, become invisible, if she uses different names. This is a particularly acute problem if an appointing, tenure, or promotion committee uses citation counts, as many universities in the USA do. As citation indices are readily available on line, any member of any committee can decide to check citations. However, there is no way to unite, or reconcile, entries to the same person under different names, or different variations of the same name. If, for example, Jessamine Hyde starts publishing as Hyde, then marries and publishes as Phillips, then decides she had better publish as Hyde Phillips, and then divorces and reverts to Hyde, by the age of 40 large slices of her publications will have vanished from the record. In anthropology, for example, it is much easier to track all the publications of Michael Herzfeld than of Rayna Rapp Reiter, who has published as Rapp, as Reiter, and as Rapp Reiter. Similarly, in the sociology of education it is easier to accumulate Sara Delamont's publications than Madeleine Arnot's, because she began her career publishing as Madeleine MacDonald. Senior staff need to be aware of such potential pitfalls, and warn about them, so their junior colleagues can respond in possession of that knowledge. Alongside the changing names issue is one for men: ties.

In academic life ties can carry messages: especially messages about school attended, universities attended, and memberships of learned societies. If, for example, the Royal Linnaean Society has a tie, wearing it means something. This is mildly problematic for women (what, if anything, fills those functions for females?), and can be exclusionary. When Cardiff had a new Vice-Chancellor in 1988, Paul was head of sociology, and was summoned to meet him. What tie? Not his old school tie – Watford Grammar School was academically a fine state school, but no one would recognize an Old Fullerian tie (boys from Watford are Old Fullerians because the Fullers Livery Company founded the school) except another Old Fullerian, and the new Vice-Chancellor had been to Winchester (that is, he was a Wykehamist). Not King's, Cambridge because the new Vice-Chancellor had been to Oxford, and it could look adversarial. However, Paul had a PhD from Edinburgh, which had celebrated its 400th anniversary in 1983, and produced a wearable blue tie which had 1583 and 1983 woven into the silk, and a small Edinburgh University crest. We had bought it, along with six mugs and a silver pendant, as a small contribution to the appeal. The new Vice-Chancellor had taught at Edinburgh as a young man. Sorted. Paul had never worn the tie before, and never since, but it earned its price that day. The new Vice-Chancellor said 'Edinburgh – I taught there in 1950', and told some long stories about his early career! More recently we invested in a tie to celebrate the benefit year of the Glamorgan cricketer Steve Jones – but so far Paul has not found any occasion to wear that one. If there is a tie for a learned society or the university you did your PhD at, invest in it, and keep it for such an occasion. It will be useful when visiting potential funders, when negotiating research access or meeting parents. Wear it to make a bridge.

Having mentioned two very specific issues, one for each sex, which new scholars such as Roger and Dermot might never have considered for themselves or *their* graduate students or research assistants, it is time to focus more widely on mentoring and supervision. In the rest of this chapter we deal with the responsibilities of mentoring and employing staff: the legal position, the need for transferable skills, the Concordat, and the Roberts Report. We then move on to project management and address how those holding grants need to complete the research and achieve all the relevant goals.

Mentoring staff

In our fictional university of Wedmarsh, it appears that new staff are provided with a good deal of specific mentoring. Dermot has a probation mentor, a research mentor, is enrolled on a course and in a research group. The course provided for all new staff at Wedmarsh by the Teaching Support Unit leads to a Diploma in HE Teaching. It is not called a mentoring system, but the lecturers who run it are *de facto* providing a supportive environment in which Dermot can learn to teach and supervise research students, reflect on his learning and raise problems. Obtaining the qualification, a diploma in HE teaching, makes him eligible to join the ILT if he wants to. Because Dermot is not a lecturer in the Teaching Support Unit, it provides support for him, given by older and wiser staff who are not involved in judging him or managing him. This is a contrast with a probation mentor, who will be an established member of his department and makes official reports on his work. His probation mentor will observe him teach, discuss his achievements over the past six months and his plans for the next half year, and check he is clear about the Wedmarsh probation procedures and schedules. At Wedmarsh, because the institution has been falling behind in the RAE of 1997 and 2001, a new system of research mentoring was introduced for all staff below the level of professor. In this system each department was required to appoint one or more successful researchers to work with their colleagues to prepare individual research plans. These needed to include planned grant applications and publication plans. In Dermot's department there are five research groups, and the convenors of these groups are the mentors for the rest of the group. Each research group is required to have a five-year plan, scaffolded up from the individual plans.

Assuming that these interlocking systems actually happen, a new lecturer such as Dermot should be clear what Wedmarsh expects of him, on what schedule. He may not achieve it: he may become fed up with academic life in general or life at Wedmarsh, he may fail to teach adequately, do his administration, apply for any funds, or write anything for publication, and if so he will not pass probation/get tenure. However, he could not claim that he did not know what the Wedmarsh goals were, or how to attain them in his own personal career. If Dermot becomes fed up with academic life, as Charles, the boyfriend of heroine Robyn Penrose, does in David Lodge's (1988) novel *Nice Work*, he leaves from an informed position. If he leaves Wedmarsh for another university, he will be well trained for his next post.

All this mentoring will, of course, only work if Dermot and his mentors take it seriously. The probation mentor needs to understand the tenure process, and help Dermot meet a series of targets or goals they have set together to enable Dermot to gain tenure. The research mentor needs good ideas about how to raise grants, and how to publish, and needs to invest time in helping Dermot acquire that knowledge. The Committee of Vice-Chancellors and Principals (CVCP 1987) produced a code of practice about academic staff training, and universities were asked to implement it by the summer of 1988. They suggested the establishment of informal cross-disciplinary staff groups (on things like computer-assisted learning and teaching statistics to non-mathematicians), induction for all new staff, followed by greater help with teaching, pastoral care, administration, grant application and conference presentations for staff in the early years of their careers. They also presented a checklist of 33 topics for staff development courses and seminars, which they argue could be offered in regional consortia. The topics range from research supervision to preparing for retirement (p. 9). The CVCP also proposed that senior staff had courses in academic management and leadership.

In our imaginary Beauminster, it appears that 20 years after the CVCP report its modest aims are still not being met. Our fictional Roger is a temporary lecturer, and such staff are particularly likely to miss out on mentoring and training. A postdoctoral fellow, quoted in *THES*, protected by the pseudonym of Ian Brookes (27 September 2002: 12) complained that 'I need to have proper training but then I hit a brick wall because there is no interest in paying for any staff training or development.' It should not have been possible for anyone to be making such a statement in 2002. There is a Concordat between the Research Councils, and the Vice-Chancellors' organization which used to be called the CVCP but is now called Universities UK (UUK) designed to ensure that research staff are managed appropriately. The elite university employing 'Ian Brookes' should have been investing a proportion of the overheads on the grant employing him in his training. It is, of course, possible that they are, and that he does not recognize training he is receiving. It is also possible that the university which employs 'Ian Brookes' is training him in areas which he does not value, and failing to train him in the skills he wants. One lesson is to be very explicit about staff development and to encourage research staff to keep a Continuing Professional Development (CPD) log so that they recognize training when they get it.

In 2002 the Higher Education Funding Council for England published the Roberts Report, which dealt with the supply of people with skills in mathematics, engineering, science and technology. It excluded medicine, agriculture and all the social sciences and humanities disciplines. The focus was on schools, undergraduate and postgraduate university degrees, and the supply of teachers. The section relevant here dealt with employment in higher education, especially at the intermediate career stage of the post-doctoral researcher.

Over one-third of those who have done a PhD in science and engineering take up a postdoctoral research post in higher education or in a public sector research institute. Roberts concluded that the career stage is marked by demotivating uncertainties, uncompetitive salaries and a lack of career guidance or well-structured training. Roberts recommended that all grants employing contract research staff should contain earmarked funding for training and professional development. His proposals that the salaries of contract research staff should be raised, especially in subjects where it is hard to recruit staff, and that clearer career structures – with more per-manent contracts – should be developed would mean, of course, that the training would not be 'wasted'. Roberts was discussing a large number of people. In the United Kingdom there are about 30,000 contract research staff at any given time. In science and technology they typically make up 40 per cent to 50 per cent of the full-time staff of the discipline. Two-thirds of them are aged 34 or younger. About 12 per cent are women.

Staff in this category are covered by the Concordat between the Research Councils and the universities, originally produced in 1996 and revised in 2001 (CVCP 1996; UUK 2001). The Concordat 'sets standards for the career management and conditions of employment' of people employed on grant income for fixed terms. Its functioning is monitored under the terms of the Research Careers Initiative (RCI). Its aim is to 'manage the tensions' between the lack of long-term career prospects for most researchers and the need to invest in the career management of research staff at a time of declining resources. Central points in the Concordat are a commitment to good personnel management and regular career review for staff on fixed-term research contracts. There is supposed to be 'research training and continuing development for researchers', including 'in-service training'. The signatories in 1996 agreed to review implementation every two years. Hence the existence of the RCI. The RCI monitoring has found that there is more generic training available now than there was in 1996, but the take-up is still below 60 per cent. Some funding bodies still do not allow any part of their grants to be spent on training. As far as career planning is concerned, Roberts (2002) found that only half of contract research staff got a regular appraisal, even on an annual basis.

If you are a grant holder with staff under your management, then you need to read the Concordat, and ensure your staff have read it too. If you are employed on a research grant, then you should get hold of the Con-cordat (from the university's personnel department website) and put it on the agenda of a meeting with your line manager.

There are also evolving legal frameworks governing temporary employees in British higher education, particularly because of changes in employment law in the European Union. Academic staff and administrators in the UK are certainly becoming increasingly aware of the employment rights of fixed-term staff – researchers and lecturers alike. The fact, for instance, that an external research grant is for a fixed period (two or three years, say) does not preclude the fact that at the end of that period, if their contract is not renewed (on a new grant, say) they are being made *redundant*. The employer's legal obligations for the proper management and care of such staff are as pressing as any other aspects of employment law and good practice. Moreover, the good management of fixed-term staff, such as postdocs, is a crucial aspect of research group development. In many contexts the postdocs and the postgrads *are* the research group, plus the leader/director. Their intellectual and social welfare is, or should be, one of the prime concerns of departmental and group managers. In many contexts, however, the reality falls far short of good employment practice, and good working relationships. As one postdoctoral researcher put it, in an informal inquiry:

> There needs to be a fundamental re-evaluation of exactly what groundwork is laid for the future of contract researchers while they are in post. This is largely with respect to their long-term careers. If you fail to find anything more stable in higher education, emerging from a series of research jobs in your late twenties leaves you well behind in the job market.

And another summed up a common pattern of response to the lack of structured career development, mentoring and training that many research staff describe:

> The universities' indifference to the livelihoods of postdoctoral researchers must not go on. Not only is it completely demoralizing to go 8–10 years beyond your PhD without a secure job, home, country. Short-term contracts are very rarely sufficient to build an individual research base on which to secure a permanent position anywhere.

Research on contract researchers in education, from the work of Dooley, Graham and Whitfield (1981) to that of Freedman *et al.* (2000) suggests that the plans outlined in the Concordat have not been implemented. There is little evidence of change between the 1981 and 2000 surveys. There is ample anecdotal evidence, at the very least, across the board and across institutions to suggest that research staff do not feel well managed and well looked after. Sometimes such feelings erupt into individual or shared grievances, sometimes they fester in more subterranean resentments. Either way, they neither reflect nor promote good practice. We have encountered postdocs in various disciplines (not our own for the most part!) who have felt themselves marginalized and exploited in various ways.

Postdocs repeatedly report that they are not made to feel part of their department, and find they have no properly defined positions within it. Their formal position is often vague at best. They report not being treated as 'real' members of staff, and of not having access to departmental facilities. We have heard of postdocs reporting that the principal investigator for 'their' project denies them proper entitlement to annual holidays, expecting them to be available for research work virtually seven days a week, fifty weeks a year. In some departments, it appears that postdocs are expected to take on major responsibilities – such as supervising postgraduate students – for which they have not been trained, and are certainly not paid. (They are probably not supposed to have such reponsibilities under the Concordat, or according to most University quality procedures.) It is also important to make sure that research staff are not inadvertently excluded from the informal channels of mentoring and advice that are a normal part of departmental and research-group life.

There is, for example, a good deal of research that shows how women in science and engineering can miss out on patronage, advice, gossip, and on basic understandings of fundamental phenomena, because they avoid informal gatherings, especially those centred on sport, alcohol, cars, computer-gaming and even, perhaps, strippers, belly dancers and lap dancers. There is research on this phenomenon from the USA and the UK over the past 40 years, such as Reskin (1978), Rossiter (1982), Gornick (1983), Fox (1995), Sonnert and Holton (1995), and Etzkowitz, Kemelgor and Uzzi (2000). This is not the place to discuss the rights and wrongs of this male culture, or to outline the research on female avoidance of it. Here we only want to alert the reader to its existence and its consequences. Women who choose to work rather than socialize are common, and they damage their careers. This is a real dilemma: the talk and camaraderie at such events is a central part of science culture. However, for women offended by lap dancers, bored by sport, wanting to follow other hobbies, choosing to see other friends, or feeling the need to care for dependants and do domestic chores, the consequences can be damaging to their career. This is not due to conscious prejudice or exclusion, but rather a very male, laddish, clubby culture that is not aware of its own nature. Women scientists either need to stifle their boredom and join in, or make conscientious efforts to catch up when they are around or fight the culture: it is possible to suggest that the research group meets in different pubs without strippers, or that as well as cricket the team might go for a hike, or a cycle ride, or swimming, or ten-pin bowling or to a skittle alley.

Young women cannot risk absenting themselves *and* failing to catch up with the talk they have missed. Women scientists and engineers need to understand what 'DSc' and 'FRS' mean, and how and why people get them: too often they do not. Candace Pert (1997) reports that she had never heard of the Lasker Prize, and knew nothing about how nominations for its award functioned, until she discovered her former boss had been nominated to receive it for work she had conducted as his student. When she created a public fuss about her exclusion, she broke the rules of hierarchy, loyalty, and secrecy, with negative consequences for Pert and her former boss.

The care and maintenance of postdocs and the research group more generally should, by contrast, be seen as a major responsibility for senior academics and managers. The effort that goes into attracting the funding that supports them, into designing, equipping and conducting the research, into publishing the results, and so on, all represent enormous investment on the part of the university and its academic staff. Likewise, the time that postdocs devote to research represents a very considerable investment on their part. It is an investment that some younger and well-qualified people may feel reluctant to make. The higher education system does not offer substantial material rewards to young scientists and other researchers. If they are not treated well, and are not made to feel part of the overall research enterprise, then there are few extrinsic rewards to inspire them or hold them in the job. But the considerable investment on all sides means that research supervisors, heads of department, deans, vice-chancellors, directors of human resources and the like should all feel that the cadre of postdocs they recruit to the university should be seen as among the most vital resources within the institution.

Fixed-term research staff – research fellows and research associates or assistants – are not just dogsbodies. They need to be nurtured and looked after as much as possible. They need to be incorporated within the work not just of the research group, but also of the department or division. They need to be given the kind of staff development and experience that will help them develop – not just as research workers, but more generally. This will include helping them to develop their careers and their prospects as academics. But not all research fellows and associates will become academics, and not all of them will wish to do so. Their prospects outside of higher education will depend upon their discipline, but there are many opportunities for experienced reseachers to develop and further their careers in both the private and public sectors. Obviously for scientists there are career openings in research and development, and design and the like in commercial firms. For social scientists and arts specialists there are employment prospects in the public sector – in central and local government research, in museums, art galleries and other sectors of cultural work. The government statistics service is often in need of numerate researchers, as are polling and market research companies. There are, in short, many domains – many more than we have mentioned – in which our postgraduate and postdoctoral colleagues might well find their career destination. Consequently, postdocs need to acquire general research experience and skills in the course of their contract(s).

Employers who engage people who have completed a PhD and may even have done postdoctoral research sometimes say that the most important attribute such people have as recruits is the fact that they have experience of undertaking and completing a major project. After all, there are few projects more demanding than undertaking and finishing a PhD successfully. Most academics will agree that there is nothing else in the course of an academic career that is ever quite so hard again. More importantly, it represents a significant exercise in project management. Planning and conducting research, analysing one's findings, presenting the results at conferences and writing them up – these are all eminently transferable skills. These are also the skills that postdocs ought to be able to bring to a research team and a research group (CUDAH 2002). Postdocs need to be helped to value those skills, to value themselves by virtue of having them, and to take them further. Staff development should build on and enhance those skills.

Postdocs, then, need to develop their experience of project management. They need to be full members of the research team. Of course, the principal investigator and other senior staff members need to discharge their responsibilities and exercise ultimate control over the research they direct. But the research staff themselves need to develop and feel responsibility towards the overall success of the research. They ought to understand the research process and its management. Some experience and understanding of research funding is important. So too is the opportunity to collaborate in writing research proposals. There is a career progression, from postgraduate research associate, through postdoctoral research fellow to senior research fellow, who is also principal investigator. This is one way in which a research group grows and develops. If the group is always dependent on just one senior person constantly designing research and writing grant bids, then it can become limited to her or his vision, and by her or his energies. The activities of a research group can grow if it cascades through generations of postdocs, who become leaders in their own right. But that does not happen overnight, and it does not happen 'naturally'. One's colleagues need to be encouraged and developed. Leadership by example and close personal mentoring needs to be accompanied by structured development programmes. Whether or not long term research only careers and contracts will ever be widespread in universities, researchers themselves need to feel that theirs is a long-term engagement with the research group, and that they have a positive stake in its future.

In the vignette at the beginning of the chapter Dermot's rich environment at Wedmarsh was contrasted with Roger's impoverished one at Beauminster. However, Roger does not need to be a victim of Beauminster's lacunae. Roger does not need to have a formally endorsed mentor: he can search out someone and adopt them informally. Universities are full of people who love to help talented young people. He could find a person who is respected for his or her teaching, and ask to observe them, and ask them to observe him. He could find a sympathetic colleague and seek help with his first book review, article, conference paper and so on. He could also stay in touch with his PhD supervisor(s), and use the links with his PhD examiners too. He is, by virtue of being at Beauminster, in a position to help others: Beauminster has far better libraries and bookshops than most universities: he could offer his futon to coevals who want to come and work or shop in Beauminster and pick their brains while they visit.

There are some staff development programmes just for women. In Australia, at the University of New South Wales in Sydney, there is a scheme called Women Research 21. This lasts a year for each cohort, and is intended to help women become research active. Each woman who joins nominates a research project that is her focus. She is allocated a research advisor, and a small sum of money to spend on things related to their research plans. Extra support comes from an email list, a website and practical help. There are seminars, participants are asked to keep a research journal, and they have to make a formal application to release their small 'grant'. The organizers hope that participants change their self-image and make the concept of the 'research active academic' transparent (Devos and Casson 2002).

Cue-deaf colleagues

In the early 1970s a project was carried out on how fourth-year students in Law at Edinburgh understood their final assessment and how, if at all, they reacted in the run up to their finals. The researchers described the majority of students as cue-conscious: that is, if a lecturer said that a thorough knowledge of Rex *v* Bourne was a good idea they revised Rex *v* Bourne. A small minority actively engaged with the process: asking carefully planned questions, reading the external examiners' recent articles in the journals, analysing past examination papers, and so on. These were the cue-seekers. At the opposite end were the cue-deaf: who did not 'hear' the guidance the lecturers gave. Subsequently Jim Eggleston and Sara Delamont (Eggleston and Delamont 1982) used the three-part classification to differentiate PhD students in education, and then Delamont, Atkinson and Parry (1997c) used it in our guidance to supervisors.

It is equally applicable to junior research staff and new lecturers. The amount of mentoring they need, and perhaps more important, will accept, varies a great deal. Some new recruits are eager to learn about their new occupation, and want to pick up all the wrinkles. Others, perhaps overwhelmed by the tasks, or out of arrogance or ignorance, refuse or fight back against all advice, staff development or mentoring. For every Dermot, attending all his classes and seeing all his mentors, there will be another young lecturer skipping the classes, or not even bothering to register for the higher education teaching qualification, and avoiding seeing any of the possible mentors, or taking any notice of them.

The impostor syndrome

Just as mentors have to be aware of the possibility that the people they are advising are cue-deaf, so too mentors have to watch out in case their junior colleagues suffer from the impostor syndrome (Koch 2002). Briefly, there are people in universities at undergraduate, postgraduate, and all staff levels, who believe in their hearts that they have no right to be there. They have an irrational fear that someone will expose them as a fraud, that a hand will fall upon their shoulder and a voice say that a mistake was made: they were admitted in error, someone of the same name was meant to have the place, the degree, the job. Women frequently admit to having this syndrome but it is probably common among men as well, especially men whose class of origin or race are different from the majority of the students or staff.

Aisenberg and Harrington (1988) reported such feelings among women who had actually gained tenure at Ivy League universities, *and* among those who had failed to gain tenure. Success does not dispel the mists of uncertainty. Anyone who has to mentor a young staff member who is female, or from the working class or an ethnic minority, or who does not 'fit' the institutional profile, should be alert to the possible existence of deep feelings of inferiority and fraudulence that may be preventing them from performing to their potential. They may need more explicit goals with explicit criteria, and they may need more explicit praise, encouragement and reinforcement. With the cue-deaf things may need to be said repeatedly, and, to protect the employer or mentor, put in writing. With the impostor syndrome, there may need to be more reassurance and praise than the mentor feels to be 'normal'. It is all too easy for experienced research leaders and managers to think that clever colleagues, who are manifestly competent, are fully aware of their own competence and are therefore entirely self-confident. Experience suggests otherwise. Many less experienced members of staff in universities need and benefit from encouragement and praise. Recommending the positive reinforcement of their achievements may seem like obvious advice – but like a lot of obvious things, people do not practise it often enough, and some younger colleagues' self-esteem (and hence their productivity) suffers as a result.

Supervising and mentoring higher degree students

The supervision of higher degree theses is a big topic, which we have written about elsewhere (Delamont, Atkinson and Parry 1997c). There is now a research-based literature on all the stages from selection to examination, and a range of advice for students on all the phases, neither of which existed thirty years ago. We have not attempted to recapitulate the book, but have concentrated here on the supervision of these higher degree students who are planning to be academics, and are working in cognate areas to one's own. Other students, such as those from overseas who are returning home and those who already have non-academic jobs they are happy to stay in, are important, and deserve the best supervision, but they are not part of the future of the discipline, or of your research culture. These students who might be part of the future need to be supervised with

your eye on the future. Supervising a higher degree student who is potentially a future scholar in your area is rewarding, but it does need particular
care too. It is important to ensure that these students are fully socialized
into the vagaries of academic life. Whether the student is full time, or is
employed and doing the PhD part time, there are several ways in which
good mentoring can help them learn the rules.

Among the issues are topic choice, keeping up the pace, using the PhD
topic to build a reputation and start the career, and the choice of the
external examiner. The choice of the external examiner, or examiners, is
particularly important for students who hope to have an academic career:
they need prominent or up and coming figures in the discipline who will
help them publish their research, be a referee for them, sponsor them at
conferences, and in the job market. They should not have an external who
is already retired or burnt out: they need someone who is gatekeeping for
publishers, running symposia at conferences, editing journals, and generally being active. As far as topic choice is concerned, it is sensible to
encourage, even steer, the candidate to do a manageable topic: not to pick
something vast and unwieldy. Then, they need to keep an eye on getting on
with it – acting expeditiously – so that their CV shows a registration period
at the shorter end of the spectrum. Such candidates need to be taken to
conferences and introduced to people, such as leading figures in academia
and publishers. They need to start publishing and giving papers while they
are doctoral candidates: perhaps as joint authors with you or with a relevant
colleague. All these things will benefit other types of student too, but they
are much less vital if the candidate is clearly aiming to stay in an existing
job, or enter some other field when the PhD is completed.

Training PhD supervisors and examiners

In the past decade there has been an increased emphasis in Britain on
training those who are entrusted with the supervision of PhD students, and
the theses of those doing professional doctorates. There has been less
interest in the training people need to be internal and external examiners
of higher degree theses, but a debate has begun about the nature of that
examination (Tinkler and Jackson 2000; Mullins and Kiley 2002; Morley,
Leonard and David 2002). Staff development for teaching and examining is
not a central purpose of this book, but, we would argue, sessions on how to
supervise and examine higher degrees are a good arena in which more
general issues around mentoring, modelling, and responsibilities to junior
colleagues can be raised. Many people will attend a session on PhD
supervision and examination, and so will engage in a debate about wider
issues. Staff mentoring issues, like cue-deaf students, the impostor syndrome, the need to understand the procedures and rules of the university,
and the importance of timetabling so that the product gets delivered on
time, can all be covered in sessions on higher degree supervision.

In the sessions we run in Cardiff and elsewhere, we have different stimulus materials for science and engineering from those we use with social science and humanities staff, because all the research shows considerable disciplinary differences (for example, Clark 1994; Delamont, Atkinson and Parry 2000). In both we sketch in the policy context from Swinnerton-Dyer (1982) through Winfield (1987) to Harris (1996) and the current QAA policy (see QAA 2001), and mention the policy issues at institutional, departmental and personal levels. Here we typically suggest that everyone present can use attendance as part of their ILT submission or CPD. Typically most people present have never heard of Harris, never seen the QAA guidelines on higher degrees, and do not recognize the initials ILT, nor know what it is when we say 'Institute of Learning and Teaching'. When we are running courses away from Cardiff we ask everyone to bring their institution's higher degree regulations: and it is usual for most people to admit they have never read them, or have not read them for many years. In Cardiff we take the university rules and the guidance issued by the Registry to sessions: most people have never seen either before. (It is always salutary for an observer from Registry to be present at that point.) We are not pointing out these experiences to criticize anyone, but to emphasize that many people in higher education do not remember (or perhaps do not ever learn about) major policy issues, nor do they know the regulatory frameworks that govern their working lives.

In the staff development sessions we move on to small group discussion of vignettes of problems that can occur between staff and research students, and then use the feedback to draw out some of the key themes, such as cue-deaf students, the impostor syndrome, and student writing blocks. In the sessions on examination we go through a similar sequence, also with vignettes of examining problems. The main value of either session appears to be an increased sense of reflexivity, coupled with a realization that many problems have hit colleagues even though they have never been publicly articulated before. A similar pattern can be used to run staff-development sessions on project management, which has many similarities.

Project management

Project management, if there are any staff employed, can produce a tension between the need to get the research done and reported – on time and on budget – and the need to provide a rich, stimulating and career-developing environment for the staff employed on the grant. Like many other areas of academic life, one partial solution is to make that tension explicit. All the staff, including clerical and technical people, need to know why the timetable has to be adhered to, and what the consequences of missing deadlines would be. Having the key dates posted on the walls and in everyone's diary, for example, prevents anyone claiming they did not know what was required.

Regular team meetings, with decisions written down and circulated (usually by email today) are essential. It is particularly useful to agree things when they are some way ahead, before the decisions are critical. Scheduling the drafting of the three-monthly, six-monthly, annual and final reports – allocating the drafting of different sections so everyone is involved early on – is sensible. So too is organizing the publication strategy, long before there are any publications or conference papers. On the first ORACLE project which ran from 1975 to 1981, there was a clear agreement that no one had their name on a publication unless they had written some of it. The writing was not equally divided, but everyone was supposed to draft some of the parts of the planned six volumes, in order to have authorial credit on one or more of them. (See Delamont and Galton 1986: 267–70 for a complete list of publications up until that date.) The core team was Prof. Brian Simon and Maurice Galton, John Willcocks, Paul Croll and Anne Jasman, with Sara and Deanne Boydell as linked scholars. The covers of the six books reveal how unequally the eventual work of writing the books became. The six books were authored and edited by Galton and Simon (1980), Galton, Simon and Croll (1980), Simon and Willcocks (1981), Galton and Willcocks (1983), which has three chapters with Sara's name on them, and Delamont and Galton (1986). Deanne Boydell's name and Anne Jasman's name are not on the cover of any book. One reason for regular meetings is to ensure that everyone is actually doing what they are supposed to be doing. So, if Phil is supposed to have set up and conducted ten interviews, a meeting should receive a report of progress so far. If Jo is meant to have done ten all-night sessions in the low temperature area running liquid helium, then a meeting can log if she has. If Janice should have got her visa to travel to Albania on the geological field trip, then a meeting can log that she has applied, and a later meeting can record that the visa has arrived.

There are several common problems. Sometimes the junior researchers are preoccupied with getting their doctorates finished. It is better to have their thesis completion built into the project schedule, and part of that person's development plan, and an agreement that time taken for the thesis now will be made up to the project later, than to have staff sneaking off to work on their theses, believing they have to lie about their work. As team leader, the sooner they have their theses done the better, but their time allocation needs to be public. Research assistants and associates can be cue-deaf, and can suffer from the impostor syndrome, just as research students can. Sometimes researchers develop, or reveal, writer's block. Paul experienced this in the 1980s when a researcher who had done an MPhil perfectly competently, proved to be totally unable to write about the fieldwork he was undertaking on a funded project. He could neither provide written-up fieldnotes for the team, nor could he write anything analytic about the field setting himself.

The worst thing is the research worker employed on a project who simply fails to collect the data, *and* lies about it, or the fraudster. Serious illness, mental or physical, and maternity or compassionate leave, disrupt a project, but are not as bad as a dishonest researcher. There are two kinds of dishonesty – failure to collect any data is bad, but a researcher who commits fraud is even worse. One of our former students, Polly, told us about a fraud she discovered on a project where she was one of two junior researchers. Her opposite number was not tramping the streets of Scunthorpe and Grimsby interviewing young unemployed men. He was telephoning those of the sample who had phones in their homes, and inventing the data on the rest. She reported this to the grant holder, who, to her horror, colluded in the fraud, because he used the invented data in the final report.

Some of the worst cases of scientific fraud have occurred when the senior researcher was clearly not supervising the data collection closely enough. Broad and Wade (1982) are science journalists who open their book on scientific fraud with an account of congressional hearings chaired by Al Gore when he was a young congressman. Broad and Wade discuss a series of scandals including the case of John Roland Darsee, a biomedical researcher at Harvard, who invented data for experiments he had not done, and published 100 papers with the name of his team leader, Eugene Braunwold, on them. In 1981 Darsee was exposed as a fraud. Braunwold had not set up enough probity checks in his labs: one fraud was exposed by other junior researchers, the majority were eventually discovered only after a full investigation by the funding body, the National Institute of Health (NIH). Braunwold's reputation was therefore compromised. A parallel case reported by Broad and Wade is that of Mark Spector. He worked on cancer and enzymes, under a distinguished biochemist, Efraim Racker. Spector invented a dazzling set of results which Racker published. They were all fraudulent. When exposed, it was, of course, Racker whose career was destroyed: he had been a favourite to win a Nobel Prize. Broad and Wade devote a whole book to a series of highly coloured exposures of scientific frauds like those of Darsee and Spector. Similar lessons for good project management can be drawn from a more recent scandal, which has been thoroughly investigated by a respected scholar. Kevles (1998) is a serious historian of science, and has devoted a large volume to the Baltimore case. David Baltimore had won a Nobel Prize at 37 in 1975, and at 52 was President of Rockefeller University. In 1991 he was accused of publishing as a co-author a fraudulent paper, based on research done by Thereza Imanishi-Kari. Baltimore offered his full support to the validity of Imanishi-Kari's research and she was, in the end, vindicated. That is, there was no fraud. However, it is clear that Baltimore had not established a routine and regular system of data sharing that enabled him to defend Imanishi-Kari on the basis of his own knowledge of her results or a well-established audit system, against what, in the end, were malicious accusations by two unhappy junior colleagues. At the heart of the Baltimore case was a lack of care about the recording of results and no procedures for the group scrutiny and sharing of the data. Imanishi-Kari apparently kept very messy lab books and the readings from the gamma radiation counter were not systematically catalogued or shared with the team. Prof. Baltimore had not, apparently, seen the results regularly.

Failure to collect data is almost as serious. The worst experience we have ever had was a freelance researcher who was supposed to be doing a case study 150 miles from Cardiff. Zak came to meetings and said he would do the work 'next month', 'next week', but never in fact did it. Because Zak was supposed to be (a) earning his living by doing research, and (b) had been very warmly recommended by a colleague, we let the empty promises run too long. As we were only going to pay when invoices were submitted, and no invoices ever were, this did not cost us any money from the grant, but it left us trying to do a different case study far too close to the deadline. However time-consuming it is to have meetings and to check the probity of all stages of data collection and analysis, the damage to the careers of the senior persons who did not spot their staff's frauds was so catastrophic that the time invested in precautions is a wise investment.

Regular meetings, at which data are shared, are one insurance strategy against these problems. Regular meetings, with an agenda and a constructive atmosphere, can also help dispel bad feelings, accusations of favouritism and even prevent gossip about the (imagined) consequences of illicit affairs. One of the prime movers in the Baltimore case, Charles Maplethorpe, had already been unsuccessful in a previous post because, as well as having scientific problems, he was obsessed with the idea that his line manager Michael Bevan was having an affair with one of the other postdocs. Such emotions can fester and impede the project.

Alison Lurie's novel *Imaginary Friends* (1967) includes an account of a dysfunctional research team, in which the naive research assistant is deceived by a mentally disturbed professor. Although heightened for its impact in the novel, the consequences of poor project management in real life are often nearly as severe. There can be long-standing legacies of bitterness from projects where the team are at cross-purposes. In the 1960s a team employed by Swansea University on an ESRC grant set out to do a restudy of Banbury, a town in Oxfordshire. When one member of that team, Colin Bell (1977), wrote his personal reminiscences of that project a decade later, the other team members were extremely unhappy with his account, and protested. Newby (1977) provides an analysis of their views and their rejection of Bell's account. There are discussions of other British social science teams reported in Platt (1976).

Ownership of the data, and the related question of where they are kept and who has access to them, are potentially problematic. Professor Lucien Bex had an ESRC grant to study the careers of naval officers. His research assistant, Bruce, had sole charge of all the survey data – and the coding frame, and the many recodings he had done on the data. When Bruce vanished to Australia, the data went too. Professor Bex had not kept any copies himself, nor had he any coding frames or recoding guides – so even if Bruce *had* left a copy of the data Professor Bex could not have used them, without repeating a year's work on them. A final report for the ESRC was written, but *no* publications came out of the project. Bruce left academic life. In a parallel case, Prof. Chester and Prof. Whipsnade at Forthamstead had a grant and employed Dai ap Llewllyn as their research associate. They were writing the book of the project, which they intended to carry their three names, when, to their horror, a book appeared by Dai. He had taken copies of all the data, and written a book without ever discussing it with them. They took his name off their book, and ever since they have written him very bad references.

Depositing copies of all the data in a shared 'archive' – on paper, on tape, on mini disc, on floppy discs or whatever – has three positive functions.

(1) Making backups and storing them safely is good practice anyway – to reduce the risks from theft, fire, hard disc crashes and so on.
(2) Making data deposits available to all the team members allows for unobtrusive, routine probity checks and reduces debates about ownership, and prevents 'theft'.
(3) A common pool of data should build team morale and encourage everyone to see the big picture, the whole project in the round, and to think analytically about the totality of the research.

If any staff member is expected to get a PhD out of the project, then it needs to be crystal clear what data are 'theirs', and how they can do an 'original' piece of work built into the bigger project. If there are other staff not doing PhDs based on the project, they need to understand what has been agreed about how the PhD is to be 'carved out' of the project. Similarly, if the PhD supervisor is not part of the research team, he or she needs to be clear about what the project is about, and how the thesis fits into the bigger picture.

There is no reason for research staff to understand the pressures on the grant holder, unless they are kept in the picture. The grant holder should not moan or whinge, or appear to be a martyr, but the staff deserve to know the bigger picture of the grant holder's working life: it is part of their career development. We are assuming that no senior academic would expropriate the intellectual property of lowly paid researchers: but such accusations are made. Sometimes there are intellectual thefts. Much more frequently, however, there are failures of communication. People have not made explicit the conventions and rules of the research group, the lab, the department; or they have not discussed and planned what will happen about publications written long after the end of the grant; or the 'hired hands' – a useful phrase from a classic paper by Julius Roth (1966) – do not 'recognize' the contribution of the senior people at all; or they do not understand academic courtesies. We are not claiming to be exemplary employers here, but to illustrate what we consider a reasonable distribution of authorships on a set of publications we have used one set of our own.

Between 1989 and 1992 we had two ESRC grants on PhD students on which we employed Odette Parry, who moved on to other universities in 1993. We are still drawing on the data in 2003. So far there are two books, five journal articles, and three book chapters which report the data, and a methods book in which some of the data are used to illustrate a range of different analytic principles (Coffey and Atkinson 1996). Between 1989 and 1999 all three names appear on all the publications. However it is not just the appearance of the three names, there is also the issue of name order, particularly because only the first author appears in citation counts. The two books were substantially written in Cardiff and so the author order is Delamont, Atkinson and Parry (1997, 2000). The journal articles reflect the responsibility of the team member who dealt with submitting them, and dealing with the referees' comments. So there are, in reverse order of appearance: Delamont, Atkinson and Parry (1998) 'Creating a delicate balance'; Delamont, Atkinson and Parry (1997a) 'Critical mass and pedagogic continuity'; Delamont, Atkinson and Parry (1997b) 'Critical mass and doctoral research'; Parry, Atkinson and Delamont (1997) 'The structure of PhD research'. The book chapters similarly reflect the division of labour in their production and revisions: Parry, Atkinson, Delamont and Hiken (1994) 'Suspended between two stools?'; Parry, Atkinson and Delamont (1994) 'Disciplinary identities and doctoral work'. Since 1999 we have written and published two articles without Odette Parry. One is an article in a journal of science studies (Delamont and Atkinson 2001), and the other based on a conference paper given by Delamont and published in the book of the conference (Delamont 2003). Odette Parry therefore has her name on two books, and three journal articles written in Cardiff, and is lead author on the one journal article and two book chapters which she did most work on.

If there is any possibility of earning any money from publications, then it is even more important to agree how that money will be distributed before it arrives. Sometimes the principal investigator ends up getting all the money, paying tax on all of it, and distributing it after tax. Sometimes there are rumours about money being unfairly distributed. It may be better to put money into a project fund, and use it to pay for things the whole team benefit from, such as travel expenses, rather than share it out as cash. If a team are pooling resources to buy things, such as lottery tickets, it is also sensible to have a written agreement. Money, like sex and academic glory, can cause deep feelings of grievance, and it is much better to plan a good system before any problems crop up.

Problems do not end when the funding does. Atkinson, Bachelor and Parsons (1996, 1997) studied a research group in genetics who had made a major breakthrough and followed the group for a year after the discovery was announced in a paper in *Nature*. They found that initial elation and excitement was readily overtaken by other emotions. The research group's success went a bit sour when messages of congratulation were replaced by more bitchy comments from rival groups, who wanted to claim a greater share in the glory than they felt they had had. Furthermore, once the group had published their results – and in effect 'won' that particular race, then the rest of the research community knew as much as they did. (They came equal first with two other research networks: all three papers were published simultaneously.) They were thus faced with individual and collective decision-making that amounted to 'Where do we go from here?'. Of course, they were not devoid of ideas, but all the successful research groups that had converged on this well-publicized discovery had to re-position thcm-selves in the field, find new research problems, possibly re-tool the laboratory and so on. Moreover, some of the more junior members of the research team felt that their part in the research process and its ultimate success made little difference to them personally. The esteem seemed to flow to the senior team members, and they did not feel that either their career prospects or their personal worth had been enhanced by the team's collective success. Consequently the initial elation was followed by a certain amount of post-publication *tristesse*. Members of the research group drifted away to other jobs. Now that has not meant that the department has declined, nor that it has lacked for success in other fields. But the social-science research does suggest that research groups – their managers in particular – nccd to bc prcpared for 'what comes after' as well as focusing on the immediate tasks in hand in bringing a current project to a successful conclusion.

There is also a set of issues about the relationships between project staff and the permanent, and teaching, staff of the academic departments in which the projects are based. Project staff in a department without a strong track record in getting grants can feel very marginal. In sociology there are three autobiographical reflections from the three staff of one research project which expose such feelings of marginalization (see Scott 1985 and Porter 1984). Scott was appointed in 1979 to work with Mary Porter as the contract researcher on an ESRC (actually, in 1979, SSRC) project on part-time postgraduate students. Scott reports that: 'There were tensions between the department and the Project from the outset' (p. 117). She suggests that: 'no-one in the department had ever held a large grant with attached staff before' (p. 117) and that there was a 'widespread view' that the Director, John Wakeford, was 'empire-building', particularly because he 'had had the nerve to organise the research unilaterally with the support of the BSA' rather than as a departmental project. The whole department was involved in appointing the two researchers, but disagreed about choosing Mary Porter. Scott and Porter were not housed in the department, but on the other side of the campus, and they never felt properly intellectually integrated into the department. Wakeford (1985) confirms the depart-ment's disquiet about his big grant which was £40,000 in 1979. (In 2003 an equivalent project would cost about £220,000 to fund.) The day the appli-cation was to be submitted to the SSRC he found half the departmental staff in his office objecting to his application, and cross-questioning him about it. Formally, the objection was that Wakeford had not put the proposal onto the departmental staff meeting agenda for discussion. He interprets the objections as doubts about a projcct on part-time postgraduates damaging the reputation of the department. There were subsequently protests in the form of circular letters in the department about Wakeford's authoritar-ianism, and about appointing two women to the posts (p. 134).

In departments where large grants and contract research staff are normal and commonplace it is unlikely that anyone would have time to circulate petitions about one professor's management style or the sex of shortlisted applicants, but that does not mean that there are no tensions between permanent staff, contract teaching staff, and contract researchers. However, there are issues in all departments about how staff employed on contracts are plugged into the department and to the university, formally and informally. Such people may miss induction sessions (especially if they do not start work in October but at other points in the year), or not be eligible for them. They may not have access to the governance mechanisms, not be invited to meetings and left off circulation lists, not be encouraged to join the AUT, not be offered any teaching, or whatever.

All these activities may seem to be time consuming. However, they are like insurance policies: if nothing goes wrong then the principal investigator may feel they were a wasted investment. However, if a serious problem occurs, clearing it up will be far more time consuming, stressful and career-damaging.

4

Research funding: 'the maieutic instinct'

Duncan Pattullo, facing a recalcitrant young man, reflects on his Oxford colleagues: 'conscientious ones with the maieutic instinct' (Stewart 1976: 55). A maieutic instinct is the desire to aid the birth of something: in this chapter we look at raising grants to bring research ideas to birth.

Raising research income is a preoccupation in many spheres of academic life. We can imagine a Wednesday afternoon in April, around about 2.15, when the minds of many academics have turned not to pilgrimage, as in Chaucer's England, but to research grants.

> Roger Clatworthy is on the train back to Beauminster after the conference where he met Dermot. He is somewhat depressed because he feels his contemporaries are doing better than he is: they have permanent jobs and seem to have career plans. He does not expect to have his contract renewed at Beauminster and his CV does not seem to be moving forward. Perhaps he should apply for a grant – he muses – but he does not really know how to begin.

> Meanwhile at Beauminster Dr Desterro is sitting staring at her PC screen, on which there is a blank ESRC grant application form, which she needs to complete to try and get money for her project on the textile industry in Brazil.

> At Castleton: the research committee is having its first meeting of the year. There is only one item on the agenda: raising research income.

An outsider might notice that it is April – the lack of an active research committee that addressed these issues in September is probably one of Castleton's problems.

> At the same time there is a meeting of the Research Committee at Arlinghurst. There are two agenda items: raising the research income and allocating some university funds for research fellowships.

At Wedmarsh Lalage is chairing her first staff meeting: there is one item on the agenda: improving the research status and income of the geography department.

In the current climate, it would not be at all surprising that two universities, a department and an individual are all focused on raising research income, while a new recruit faces the need to get his research career going with a grant. In this chapter we deal with the benefits of getting grant income, then with finding a funding source, and then with preparing applications.

There are big differences between the disciplines around research funding. In arts disciplines and in some sub-specialisms in the social sciences and in pure mathematics and theoretical physics, it is possible to be very research active, have renown as a scholar, and not hold any grants. Of course people in those fields can get money, and some do, but grant income is not essential. In the empirical social sciences, sciences and engineering, external research funds are necessary, even essential, to fund the gathering of data by field trip, by experiment, or whatever. In those disciplines and sub-disciplines where grant income is not essential, the scholar often wants to raise funds to buy time: to be released from teaching, pastoral care, administration, examining and so on, so they can do the research themselves. In fields where funds are essential they usually pay for staff, for materials, for travel, for computing and for data analysis.

In both types of discipline, however, there are similar reasons to apply for grants. First, holding a grant is a way of building your career. It looks good on the CV in the university newsletter, on the website of the department, in the RAE return, in the acknowledgements of the publications. Second, the deadlines imposed by the funding body provide a discipline, and a schedule, to help you focus on getting the project done. Third, grants validate the refusal to do other tasks. Fourth, they are rewarding: a grant means some committee values your ideas. Fifth, many funding bodies other than charities pay overheads, that is a fee to the university to have their research done in that institution. So every grant increases the university's income. In some, the individual researcher gets some or even all of the overheads to spend on library books or conference travel; in others the department gets them; in others they are kept centrally. Overheads (indirect costs) pay for the institutional facilities that make research possible: the office and lab space, the IT network, the telephone system, the central computer system, the library with its skilled librarians, and the administrative structure of the university: its personnel, finance, safety, security and estates divisions, its infrastructure.

The most important reason to apply for and to get grants, however, is to legitimize the allocation of time for research. It is too easy to feel that research is a form of self-indulgence, of selfishness, of pleasure, of escape from the 'real' work of teaching, listening to students' problems with academic work or their family lives, making assessments, ordering library books, even attending committees. When research is unfunded it is too easy to push it aside: once there is a grant, then the project has to have some priority. Given that time is the most precious commodity in higher education, having a legitimate reason to prioritize research is itself precious.

Grant income does provide some freedoms. Grants can provide money to attend conferences, visit archives or distant libraries, buy stationery or extra library resources, clerical or technical support, equipment (new computers, tape recorders and so on), and postdoctoral assistants and/or doctoral students. These are all scarce resources, which can be tightly controlled by the head of the department or a powerful clique, and therefore a grant providing resources also provides freedom from control. Or, if you are lucky enough to be in an egalitarian department, the extra resources of the grant for you allow bigger shares of the general resources for everyone else.

So, the best reasons to get external funding for research are the reinforcement of your sense of efficacy as a researcher, and the increased autonomy it gives you. However, the prestige it brings your university is also important. Universities are ranked by the amount of grant income their staff bring in. Every pound you can raise helps your institution up the league tables, and your department up the internal 'grants received' ladder. Of course, there can be a down-side. Colleagues may be jealous and resentful, especially if your grant includes money to buy you out of teaching, or there is no tradition of grants in your department. The only rational response is to smile, stress the longer-term benefits to everyone, and encourage the envious to apply for their own grants. Developing mechanisms to support and encourage grant-proposal writing and vetting is the most positive response one can make.

There are many good reasons for applying for a grant, but of course applications can be rejected. There are three things. One, be prepared to be rejected and to have to try many funding bodies. Two, think about how to use the work that goes into the application for other purposes too – put the research into an article, a conference paper, a lecture. Third, put in the work to find a *range* of possible funders and to make your application as good as possible to maximize your chances of success. It is to these aspects that we now turn. Many successful academics only ever apply to a very small number of funding bodies, and remain blissfully unaware of the enormous range of bodies that provide money for research and research-related activities.

There is a regular UK publication *Research Fortnight* which carries a few news items but also contains a list of deadlines by which applications have to be submitted and then announcements of funding opportunities of all kinds. In the issue for 2 October 2002, for example, there is a notice of British Council funding to pay for exchanges with Slovenia (£300 from London or £350 from elsewhere), the Jacob Blaustein Institute for Desert Research calling for scientists to join their programme, and invitations for bids from those who want access to the free-electron laser-user Felix in the Netherlands. There are 10 pages of funding possibilities across all kinds of fields, from sperm membranes to American Indian studies. There are opportunities to do research in the Newberry Library in Chicago, or to go to Japan. Some are very specific: The Royal College of Physicians has a fund (The Lewis Thomas Gibbon Jenkins of Britton Ferry Memorial Trust) to finance research on 'physical diseases prevalent in Wales'. Others are very general. The Leverhulme Trust fund research in almost all areas except school education, social policy and welfare, and medicine. They encourage applications which are for interdisciplinary work or 'which fall outside research councils' terms of reference'. Funds are available for travel, to run conferences, for individual fellowships, for small grants, and for larger projects and programmes. Charities do not pay overheads to the university, so university bursars and directors of research prefer money from government departments, research councils or commercial bodies which *do* pay overheads. However, funds from charities can be very high status, and highly regarded.

The first step is to think about what you want a grant for, and why you want it. If, for example, you needed to make a preliminary visit to Slovenia then that £350 travel fund from the BA is ideal. However, if you want to be relieved of teaching for a year, then you either need a fellowship that will pay your salary, *or* you need to apply for a grant to a body that will pay teaching replacement for the principal investigator. Most funding bodies have websites where their basic terms and conditions can be found. Roger and Dr Desterro need different types of grant, because he is a beginner and she is established. She has a salary, so needs money for a research assistant, and travel and research expenses and subsistence in Brazil. Roger probably needs a small grant to give him some research expenses, *or* a grant to pay his salary for a year to prolong his time at Beauminster. Lalage, however, needs to persuade everyone in geography at Wedmarsh to apply for something: the senior people for big programmes (grants of £500,000 to £4 million) and the more junior staff need to be getting smaller grants (£100,000) to employ one research assistant, or getting themselves teaching buyouts, fellowships, conferences, or all three.

At the institutional level, Castleton and Arlinghurst need to find ways to get individuals to apply for grants, and they may need to think about their institutional infrastructure, if there is one. The former polytechnic, Penbury, would have a harder task still, and it is the beginning of that task which is presented in Chapter 9 in our fictional case of Tom Kentallon. If Castleton is sliding downwards, then it is likely that the incentives and infrastructure are not right: and it may be that Castleton has got caught in a vicious circle, where a declining number of staff are increasingly struggling to cover the teaching, and lack energy to get grants or publish. The most research-active leave for other universities where there is better support for research, and so on.

In this chapter we have drawn on our experience of applying for grants, coaching others who have drafted applications, refereeing proposals, and sitting on commissioning panels. We have refereed for British, Belgian, Canadian and American funding bodies, predominantly in the social sciences. Our knowledge of science grants is based on discussions with similarly experienced scientists.

There are concrete, practical things that Lalage can do to raise the number of applications going in from geography at Wedmarsh, which will be staff development and consciousness raising. A head of department can organize:

1. Getting the relevant person from central administration to come and explain how Wedmarsh checks costings, what the procedures are, and how the contracts office or its equivalent works to help academics. This needs to be done about every 18 months, with PhD students, postdocs, and research associates present, so that new people are regularly informed, and old lags reminded, and younger colleagues encouraged to think ahead about the continuity of research.
2. Regular demonstrations of how to fill in the forms of the main funding sources – in geography they would include NERC and ESRC. These can be done as a pair of sessions about a week apart. In the first, the forms are explained, then everyone is sent away to draft a proposal, then a week later these are shared and examined. If there is no one in the department with the relevant expertise, then someone needs to be borrowed from a cognate department.
3. A panel of the most experienced grant holders, or research council referees, can be established to help less experienced colleagues sharpen their applications: again, if there are no such people in the department, such a panel needs to be set up at faculty or university level.
4. A folder of successful applications to every conceivable funding source, ideally with notes from the applicant, should be kept in the relevant secretary's office, along with the latest brochures and newsletters from these sources, hard copies of the forms, and any annual reports from these bodies. The AHRB, for example, produces an annual report, and these are useful for potential applicants.
5. A subscription to the *Times Higher Education Supplement*, to *New Scientist*, and to *Research Fortnight* and a collection of the back numbers filed carefully is sensible. If that is too expensive for an individual department, then perhaps there should be a faculty resource, or the library should be involved. The big issue is that all staff, postdocs and PhD students need to be enculturated into looking at each issue and following up leads.
6. Browsing websites: because lots of research opportunities are posted on websites it is productive to get everyone into the habit of checking the relevant websites, and sharing what they find on them. A department, faculty or university research office also needs regularly to check the most important websites (Research Councils, major charities, government departments) in order to provide regular up-dates and briefings on research opportunities, deadlines, changes in procedure (such as new application forms) and general horizon-scanning.

One potential problem is that by the time initiatives are announced the deadlines are close: the insiders, the 'core set', will have known about the plans for some months. Institutions that have never been research leaders, or which have fallen out of the race, will not have staff in the relevant networks. One of Lalage's tasks is to re-connect her new colleagues to the networks. Her own contacts will have come with her arrival, so she can spread the word at Wedmarsh about what she knows. As Lalage is a physical geographer oriented to NERC, her expertise will not help all her new Wedmarsh colleagues. Those whose research is suitable for funding by the ESRC or the AHRB will need to be encouraged to find out about those agencies, and to connect themselves to relevant networks.

If any of the funding bodies a department might apply to require user involvement, then a department can build up panels of 'users' ready to wheel them out when required. A school of education will regularly need users who are teachers, so there can be a standing panel of local teachers: perhaps those who have done higher degrees in the department. A school of social work similarly could have a panel of social workers, of probation officers, of charity officials. A department of planning could have a panel of housing officers and representatives of housing associations. Lalage could brainstorm about which 'users' her social science colleagues might need to invoke, and empanel them. User panels deserve to have at least a departmental newsletter, and an annual invitation to a buffet and seminar on the department's research projects, so they feel cherished and in touch. If they are people who have done their own higher degrees in the department they should understand something of the research process, and be able to offer informed user advice when it is needed. In many fields of strategic science and applied research, users and beneficiaries are likely to include industrial users (such as research and development departments, or commerical laboratories). Working relations need to be established and maintained with such potential users, and their managers should be ready to provide appropriate letters of support for appropriate research grant bids.

If Roger does not have access to any resources of this kind at Beauminster – and it is possible that all these things are happening but he has not noticed them, or has not realized what they are and why he should participate – he can, and should, start them himself. It is perfectly feasible for a group of temporary, junior and postdoc staff to ask for, and indeed arrange, the events and activities 1, 2, 3, 4, explained above. They can also browse websites regularly, and pool their own money to buy the *THES* and *New Scientist* every week. If the department does not take *Research Fortnight*, or it vanishes into the head of department's office, they can ask to have it placed in a more public place. If Roger really does not have any mentoring from the person allocated, then seeking help with getting a grant is a good pretext for a meeting. Equally, an experienced grant-getter is usually flattered to be asked for help, or approached with a good idea for a collaboration. A keen, enthusiastic person who makes an appointment armed with material about a potential grant application is rarely thrown out of an office.

Researching the funding body

There are various things you need to know about any potential funding body. Are there specific closing dates, or do they take applications throughout the year? In *Research Fortnight* 18 September 2002 the Particle Physics and Astronomy Research Council (PPARC) called for bids to support the subsistence and travel costs of visits to telescopes with a deadline of 1 October 2002, the US National Institute of Child Health and Human Development invited bids for research on poverty and child development with deadlines specified as 'every 1 February, 1 June and 1 October until 1 July 2003'. The American Museum of National History offered postdoctoral funds to study their snake collection with a deadline of 1 November 2002. If a body has deadlines, then it is vital that you and anyone in your university who needs to sign your application know what they are. Aiming to be ready a month ahead of the deadline is sensible.

Do applications go in by post, or electronically? Are there specific forms or not? If there are, are they available on line or do you have to get hold of them by post in hard copy? What information is required in the application? Some bodies want the applicant to collect testimonials from referees and include them, some want the application to come from a referee, who has already provided their confidential views.

What will that funding body pay for, and what is excluded? For example, is there the possibility of teaching replacement to free the time of the principal investigator? Are PhD studentships normally included in research grants? What equipment is allowable? What is expected and what is allowed for travel (for example to national and international conferences)? Do not apply for anything that the funder excludes: it only makes you look careless or cavalier. Equally, it is important to *include* all the allowable costs of the research: failure to do so will make an application look under-specified, and therefore unlikely to succeed at a practical level. These are the sorts of things that research-active staff and a research office ought to have a sense of, as well as having the formal documentation for. They are the kinds of things that regular staff-development sessions on research funding ought to cover. While one would not expect every research-active academic to have all the regulations for all the grant-giving bodies at her or his fingertips, one would expect them to ask the right questions and to know where to turn to for the right answers – official documentation and personal expertise.

Eligibility can be tightly specified: in July 2002 the National Ataxia Foundation in Minneapolis offered money to allow someone with at least one year of postdoctoral research, but not more than two years, to spend a year studying ataxia. Award between 35,000 and 45,000 dollars. Their aim would be to help young scholars 'establish an independent ataxia research programme'. Clearly there is no point in applying for this as a 55-year-old full professor who wants study leave: such a person is not eligible. Similarly the Society for Endocrinology will fund members to go to overseas conferences, but only if they earn less than £30,000 per annum, have been members for a year, and attended the society's last annual meeting. For those eligible, such funds are very useful, and the award can be put on the CV. For a non-member, or someone who earns too much, an application would be a waste of time.

If you spot a possible funding source when the deadline is too close, or has just passed, it is sensible to find out if that body regularly calls for bids to that deadline. If they do, you can be ready for the following year. Start work on that application, and on some other application with a deadline within the next three months you can hit. We find it productive to have a number of research ideas 'on the go' within our research groups. Sometimes an idea can progress quickly and smoothly from initial discussion to final application. Some other ideas take longer to come to fruition, and have a less even gestation period. That does not mean that they are less productive ideas, or are half-baked. But they can 'simmer' while more pressing ideas and bids are formulated and submitted. But having a small number of longer-term ideas means that one is never starting the process 'cold'. It is easier for group members and individuals to chew over and refine some ideas that they have been sharing, rather than all coming together and facing a blank sheet of paper, or computer screen, and trying to come up with fresh ideas.

Initiative or response?

There are two basic types of funding offered: open-ended, where any sensible proposal within that body's remit will be considered; and initiatives or programmes, where a funding body has a particular topic in mind and calls for bids on that topic. For example, in 2002 the ESRC and the AHRB had a joint programme on 'Cultures of Consumption', and during the period 1998–2002 the Wellcome Trust had a programme on ethical and social aspects of the developments in genetics. In 2002 the Leverhulme was asking for 'major research undertakings' on 'the changing character of war' and 'the nature of evidence'. Each could last five years and cost £1.25 million. Grants that size are not suitable for a novice like Roger Clatworthy on his own, although he could get an established senior scholar to bid with him. They are, however, exactly what Lalage needs her colleagues at Wedmarsh to be getting, to turn the department around. In September 2002 NERC called for applications for its 'standard' research grants, which is 'an open competition for curiosity-motivated, basic, strategic or applied research'. This is a major source of funding for geographers, and Lalage needs to be urging all her colleagues to prepare NERC applications.

In the social sciences the ESRC initiatives are harder to get money out of than the ordinary responsive mode. The publicity, the excitement and the deadlines flush out proposals in greater profusion than the responsive mode. There is also the attraction of a two-stage process. Most ESRC initiatives have a phase 1, when only an outline is required, with basic costings and a short description. Only those proposals that are shortlisted to be submitted for the second round have to be produced in full – with a full-length proposal, detailed costings, and all the other paraphernalia of a complete Research Council bid.

The initiatives we ourselves are most familiar with, those funded by ESRC, are highly competitive. They attract very large numbers of outline applications. Even getting through to being shortlisted is tough, and – in purely numerical terms – the odds are against success. Programme grants have many advantages: they are part of high-profile activities; they have a collective presence in the research community, often greater than that achieved by a one-off grant from the responsive mode; programme directors can provide value-added contribution, in terms of national and international publicity; they plug you into a national network of individuals and groups. They do impose further obligations on award-holders: you are required to participate in collective events for all or part of the programme network; programme directors will need to extract surplus intellectual value from the research project in order to inform general overviews, syntheses, reports and the like. This is not a down-side of participating in research programmes and similar initiatives or networks. It is merely an additional set of undertakings that an applicant and hence potential principal investigator needs to be aware of and prepared for.

The fact that there are from time to time new funding programmes and new programme initiatives on the part of many research funding bodies – and not just the Research Councils – does not mean that one should put all one's eggs into those baskets. They tend to attract a good many applications, simply because they are advertised and attract high levels of interest. Bids in responsive mode that precisely reflect the strengths and interests of an applicant or a team will have much greater chances of success than an over-ambitious bid that stretches the local resources and capacities too far.

For a department, a group, or an individual trying to raise their profile and develop a track record in funded research, then very big grant applications may be too ambitious at the outset. Smaller bids should not be overlooked. Often awarding bodies have programmes specifically designated as 'small grants', which may be administered separately from larger grants or programmes. Sometimes they may come under 'chair's powers', which means that they can be awarded (provided the referees clearly recommend it) without having to wait for the entire cycle of full committee meetings. Such smaller grants can be remarkably useful. There are often relatively small so that specific problems can be addressed without the full panoply of long-term postdoctoral appointments. A particular analytic issue can be addressed using existing data (such as national statistical data-sets), from a small-scale exploratory study, or a specific experiment. This may not require huge amounts of staffing, or the collection of substantial volumes of new data. Smaller grants can appropriately be targeted at such problems.

Smaller grants can be used to help develop a track record. While funding bodies do not just give money to the better-established researchers, they, their referees and committees are – if only implicitly – reluctant to make major awards to applicants with little or no experience of directing funded research. Smaller grants can help build a portfolio of successful research (provided the projects are successful!) that are a springboard to more substantial and longer-term awards. Younger colleagues, and researchers who want to move from doctoral or postdoctoral work to become fledgling investigators in their own right often do well to work towards smaller grants in the first instance.

Irrespective of whether you are going to apply for a grant in your own right, whether you are putting together a research team, there are various things you need to know, and it is best to become acquainted with these things at an early stage.

Your institution

You need to know what support and procedures relating to grant applications is available in your institution, and what approval you need to seek before you submit. Do you have to have all your costings approved by someone in an office? Does your computing or information services centre have to agree your bid for PCs and software? Does your head of department sign it, or do you have to see a dean or another senior university manager? Do you have to clear the plans with an ethics or human subjects committee before you can bid? These are the sorts of questions that Dermot will have had answered at Wedmarsh by his mentors, and Roger will not have had answered at Beauminster. He would need to find out what the procedures are at Beauminster, and doing so as soon as possible is a sensible first step towards his application(s).

Sources of help

There are some books which offer help with writing research proposals, such as Punch (2000), Locke, Spirduso and Silverman (2000), and Peters (2003). Peters is a British writer, who worked closely with Dr Janet Lewis, an experienced researcher who was Director of the Joseph Rowntree Trust, in compiling her book. She therefore covers many of the ways in which applicants fail to provide the necessary information, or otherwise ruin their chances of getting a grant, drawing on Janet Lewis's own experience. Published books of advice on how to prepare research bids will not give you the bright ideas that are turned into successful research. But they will provide many useful tips concerning the practicalities of preparing research bids. It is remarkable how few people seem to have read up on research funding and applications. Academics are, or should be, very good at using the relevant literature when it relates directly to their own research topic. They seem to be much weaker when it comes to consulting published work that can help them in other aspects of their working lives.

As we said earlier in the chapter, it is not a good idea to embark on preparing a research proposal without careful scrutiny of the funders' regulations and requirements. Again, this is so obvious that it should not need re-stating. But we are constantly surprised to see research proposals that are not compliant with basic requirements, eligibility and so on. There is a danger in tossing aside the instruction book in order to play with a new gadget: the same applies to research proposals.

Proposals that work

Neither we nor any general source of advice can instruct you or your colleagues in how to have a winning idea in your discipline. But there are some general guidelines that help in most cases. They can sound awfully like 'motherhood and apple pie', but we frequently see proposals failing, or at least not being greeted as enthusiastically as they might because applicants have not followed basic precepts. The overall guiding principle should be clarity. If the proposal is not crystal clear, then referees and committee members will not be convinced that the applicants have really sorted out precisely what they will do, and why. Clarity applies at several levels.

First, there should be *clarity of purpose*. The aims of the research and the specific objectives should be transparently clear. That does not mean that they cannot be technical, or clear only to other specialists, but they must be clearly explicated. The objectives of the research are among the most important elements in the overall application. It should be very clear why the research is of significance: why it is timely; whether its specific focus is of more generic relevance and application; what problems you are going to solve; what ideas you are going to explore, test or extend; what past research you will be building on. Of course, not all disciplines and projects lend themselves to tightly specified hypothesis-testing or problem-solving research; not all are based on experimental research designs. But the fact that research might be more exploratory, more open-ended, or more speculative than that is still no reason why one's purposes and objectives should not be as clearly expressed as they can be.

Second, there should be *clarity of design*. Irrespective of what the research design is to be – exploratory fieldwork, laboratory experiments, large-scale social surveys, secondary analysis, or archival research – it should be absolutely clear to the referees and committee members just what you are intending to do. We have no doubt from our own experience in the social sciences that many applications fall because they do not specify with sufficient clarity precisely how the research will be conducted, what information is to be collected, how the analysis will proceed, and so on. The applicants may have thought that it was entirely obvious, implicit in their overall description of their proposed work. But implicit research designs and analyses do not suffice.

Third – and just as importantly – the objectives and the research design should relate precisely and clearly to one another. The application should be thoroughly 'joined up' and hence the underlying logic of the entire proposal should be clear to its readers. There should, therefore, be *clarity of logic*. These general principles should always guide any proposal for research funding. There are many funding bodies and opportunities that place even greater demands on clarity of expression. While funders normally seek reviewers' opinions from experts in the field, decisions are often made by panels drawn from different backgrounds. Depending on the body in question, the final decision may rest with committee members or trustees who have a substantial 'lay' representation. While scientific and scholarly work should not be 'dumbed down' for such people, non-technical summaries, general statements, indications of general significance and so on should be comprehensible to readers who are not among the very small number of fellow experts and enthusiasts in your highly specialized field.

Completing the application

Good applications often reflect collective effort – even when they are based on one investigator. It is usually sensible to show a draft to a couple of more experienced colleagues or colleagues with relevant experience on relevant committees, so that they can find the obvious mistakes we all make. It is a sign of strength and not of weakness to share drafts. It is good practice to offer one's colleagues a critical reading of their bids. In some departments this will be a formal requirement before the head of department will sign it, but even if it is not, informal help is priceless. In one department we know of it was a custom that all applications were shown to a colleague, and if the grant was awarded, a bottle of champagne was given to that colleague. Research groups are among the obvious mechanisms for discussing research ideas, and for the circulation of draft bids, before they are finalized for submission.

Like many tasks in academic life, it usually takes longer than one thinks: prices of equipment have to be checked and quotes obtained. Large items may have to go out to competitive tender and therefore several quotes may have to be sought. Letters of support may be needed from commerical collaborators, potential users and beneficiaries, or agencies from whom research access and cooperation will be needed. Nowadays virtually all substantial research grants need some sort of equipment component, if only a personal computer and/or laptop and printer(s) for research in the humanities and social sciences. For laboratory and field sciences, equipment requirements and technical support to go with them may be major elements in the overall costings, and require considerable planning and preparation. This is why potential applicants need to have proper support from within their department (such as senior technicians, or a research office) and also need to plan the timetable of preparing the actual proposal. If a major research term is to be assembled for the proposal, then that will add further time to the preparation process. Getting several academics together at the same time seems to be akin to classic problems in mathematics or quantum physics. There should be a conjecture (and a prize for its proof) that states that it is always impossible to get more than three academics together at the same time to work on the same task: this is the Delamont-Atkinson conjecture.

Travel has to be costed if it is that sort of research: the car mileage, the rail fares. Each university has its own rules, and so do funding bodies. Subsistence has to be costed: again this is normally requested on the scales used in that university. Salaries for any staff – technical, clerical or academic – have to be researched, and cleared with the appropriate office in your university. The costs you bid for have to include pension and national insurance payments. If the grant and the staff appointments are to run for more than a year, all the staff have to have an increment, and all the costs increase proportionately. If the initial appointment is made near the top of the scale, there may need to be provision for payment on the lower rungs of a higher scale further into the project. If the sponsors pay for them, then you will need to include the costs of attending conferences – national and international – in order to present the research and its findings.

In August 2002 the cheapest research assistant in an old university, on Research Grade 1B, earned £18,265 per year, rising to £19,279 a year later. To employ someone on £18,265 will cost at least £7,000 in pension and national insurance payments, so to employ one researcher for 12 months needs a grant of £26,000. That is before they have wordprocessed anything, gathered any data, travelled anywhere, put a staple into three sheets of paper, or dropped a test tube. If the funds are coming from a Research Council there need to be 46 per cent overheads on the full staff costs; if they are coming from a commercial firm, then the university will expect full indirect cost recovery, which will be at least 100 per cent of the direct costs – which may be negotiated up or down depending on various other factors, such as the relevance of the research to the university's mission. The cost of telephone calls, post, photocopying, stationery, floppy discs, tapes, minidiscs, laboratory glass, time on a big telescope, or whatever, has to be calculated, and the calculations approved by the appropriate authorities. Forgetting to cost something vital, such as the production of the final report, the dissemination process, the website, the conference presentations, a vital piece of equipment, is the sure sign of a novice. Such blunders are readily avoided if people share their outlines and drafts with helpful and knowledgeable colleagues. This is not, incidentally, something that should be seen as a 'favour', but as a regular aspect of collective commitment to the research effort.

The curricula vitae of all the applicants are needed, and this can take ages to gather up. Worse, they may all need editing to fit onto the application forms. Sensible planning means getting such information together at the outset, and having them stored electronically in readiness for completing applications. Well-prepared research teams have such information in the office, on their server, and ready to go.

The heart of the application is, of course, the intellectual agenda: the proposal itself. We have already made some suggestions on that score. We have stressed the overall need for clarity and consistency. You and your colleagues need to read each draft application with a very critical eye. Assume that you are a referee, or a committee member. Ask yourself: are there any weak spots I can find and probe? Can I find any obvious reasons to turn this proposal down? The harder you are with yourself at this stage, the harder you make it for a committee, whose funds are limited and who therefore have to make tough choices, to downgrade your proposal so that it falls below the line of the projects that are highly rated ('alphas') but remain unfunded.

In addition to the essentially intellectual tasks of constructing a sound research bid – with clear objectives, clear justification, explicit and appropriate research design, and the right analytic strategy – there are several positive and practical things you and your team can do that can help it get funded. They include:

1. *Self-presentation*: A badly proofed application is annoying for the referees, and gives a bad impression. Careful attention to the presentation and layout of the proposal itself can be advantageous. While referees do not give more points for style, the clear layout of aims and objectives, the specification of research design and timetable, and so on can all be enhanced by the judicious use of bullet points and similar enhancements or formatting. Things should stand out and be perfectly intelligible on first reading. Many referees are old, and their eyesight is not what it was – do not use a tiny typeface, or squash everything up so it is hard to read – redraft your prose to be more succinct, and make the text look nice.
2. *Good style*: It is worth reading through the proposal to check that it is crystal clear, and as well written as it can be. An opening sentence with ugly split infinitives, or, as one we once saw that opened 'Following having read', can put off the referees. Again, while grants are not awarded on the basis of artistic impression – unlike figure skating – anything that can distract or antagonize the reviewers should be avoided.
3. *Good current awareness*: While lengthy literature reviews are not necessarily possible for all types of application, and may not be appropriate in any case, your bid needs to make it clear that you are perfectly au fait with the current research. A proposal that does not appear to be based on a team who have kept up with the field gives a bad impression. You also need to indicate how *you* fit into the current literature and the current debates in your field.
4. *Timetabling*: The way in which the research will be scheduled, so that it is completed on time, with the data analysed, needs to be shown clearly. There is nothing more clearly indicative of a research proposal that has not been thought through than a timetable that manifestly leaves insufficient time for key aspects of the research process. A timetable that

is not easily interpretable is unhelpful as well. The judicious use of charts using timelines to plot key features of the research process (Gantt charts) can be very useful – especially where the sponsors' application form has no separate space for a timetable, or allows for only a very schematic one.

5. *Clear user engagement:* If the funding body require or desire user engagement then it is suicide to ignore that requirement in the bid. Plan user engagement and describe it. We have already made reference to this aspect of the bid. Too many colleagues treat things like this as annoying extras, to be filled in at the last minute. One consequence of that is that their plans for engaging users and beneficiaries become vague and generic, rather than targeted and specific.

6. *Dissemination and communication strategy:* If the funding body require or desire dissemination, then it is foolish to ignore that element of the bid. Have a dissemination plan, and include it in the application. Depending on the sponsor, this may well go beyond just papers in conference presentations, academic journals or a monograph. Your communication strategy might well include engagement with print and broadcast media, for example. If you can specify *which* conferences and *which* journals you will be targeting, and *which* publisher you will be trying to place your book with, then that looks much more purposeful and professional than more vague aspirations and generic indications.

7. *Website design and maintenance:* Many projects today have a website. If you plan to have one, then ensure you cost it, and that the websites of previous projects that the referees might scan are in apple-pie order, or have been removed. Nowadays referees and others are quite likely to look at applicants' web-pages and departmental websites – to get quick access to other research activites, publications and the like. So it is a good idea to ensure that they are accurate and current. ('Last up-dated' months ago looks really bad.)

These are all simple, but practical things that any small group can work on together in making research bids better. Moreover, they are the kinds of things that can be promoted through staff development sessions. Less experienced staff can learn a very great deal from going through a typical application form, or from role-playing being referees and criticizing a completed application (with the applicant's permission), and from trying to compose key bits of an application form.

Peer review of applications

The referees of grant applications are usually unpaid, and fit the refereeing into busy lives. Do think about the task of the referee when drafting the application. He or she will have a checklist from the funding body, and if you can discover what is on that checklist, do so. (A senior colleague who regularly referees will probably have a copy lying about or even neatly filed.)

Make everything as clear as possible: if you have asked for a lot of travel money, explain *why*. If the research associate has to be at the top of Researcher Grade 1A (£27,339), explain *why* someone at £18,265 will not do for this project.

Referees are not mind-readers: they need to have your proposal explained clearly. One should assume in this – as in all things – that anyone reading the application has insufficient time to devote to the task, has multiple calls on their attention, and would rather be doing something more enjoyable. This is one set of reasons why your submission needs to be crystal clear, explicitly structured and well presented.

Some funding bodies ask the applicant to suggest possible referees. Take advice from your network on names, and be sure to find out their full address with post code or zip code, and email. The funding body will not have the time or energy to track down a person from an incomplete address. Even more important, do ask the people concerned if you can nominate them, and ensure they have a copy of the proposal when you request their permission to be nominated. A busy person who is suddenly told by a charity or a research council that 'Dr X has nominated you to referee the proposal', when she or he has not been asked is likely to be less enthusiastic about it than the same person properly approached. Do thank them afterwards and tell them the result. Courtesy, good manners and thank you letters are always appreciated.

Referees of proposals are usually asked the same basic questions about applications they are reviewing. We have summarized the ESRC criteria here as they were in 2003, but in all disciplines the issues are essentially similar. ESRC send a letter explaining how it awards grants, why peer review is important, and giving a deadline for the report. Then there is a checklist, which explains the grading system. This is very British: there are three basic categories alpha, beta and reject. However alpha is itself subdivided into alpha plus, alpha, and alpha minus. ESRC states sternly 'an alpha grade should be awarded to an application felt to be of such merit, timeliness and novelty that it is likely to make a significant contribution to knowledge and the development of the research area'.

ESRC point out that 'normally' any application rated beta or reject from the majority of the referees does not go before the Grants Board. Those rated alpha minus or above are seen by the Board. However, it is very rare for the ESRC to be able to fund any projects which have not been graded alpha and alpha plus: only 17 per cent of the 'alphas' are funded. In the science and engineering councils there is usually enough money to fund a higher percentage of the alphas. All over the UK there are scholars with 'unfunded alphas' they need to redesign, re-present, and try on other funding bodies. By and large, only those proposals that are rated as 'high' alphas are likely to get funded. That is why we all need to learn to reduce to the absolute minimum any areas of ambiguity or lack of clarity that can give the reviewers the opportunity to mark us down. Apart from the grading, the referee is asked to produce a written judgement, which addresses:

1. Originality and potential contribution to knowledge
2. Research design and methods
3. Value for money
4. Communication strategy and planned outputs.

This last heading includes user engagement, to which the Research Council attaches considerable importance. Apart from the need to demonstrate the public benefit derived from the use of public money, it is one mechanism that ensures that the research and its potential implications have been thought through. While other potential funders may not specifically ask about the engagement of users and beneficiaries, it is still important to think about, and state explicitly when appropriate, who will benefit from this research if it is funded.

ESRC stresses the confidentiality of the process: the referee should not tell anyone that they are refereeing, and should not disclose the contents of the application, or the names of the applicants, to anyone, nor discuss the application with anyone except by prior arrangement with the ESRC. There is also an opportunity to state whether or not the applicants and their work are known to the referee, and to list any conflicts of interest. ESRC also ask referees to rate themselves as competent or not (on a three-point scale) to judge the four aspects of the project listed above. A conscientious referee can take several working days to produce a thoughtful response. This work is not only unpaid, it is also invisible. It is, however, part of the generalized exchange of service that constitutes good citizenship among the networks of the research active.

Presentations

Some funding bodies want shortlisted applicants to give a face-to-face presentation. If that is likely, it will probably be specified in the guidance for applicants. Sometimes the date or range of dates is given: 'Shortlisted teams will be required to make a presentation in London on Dec. 5th (*or* in the week of Dec. 5–8th).' That means you have to clear your diary, and ensure appropriate representatives are free on those dates. Then you need to think about who will do the presentation and what will be in it before you know if you are going to be shortlisted. The call to do a presentation is usually issued too late to prepare from scratch.

When you present, the same rules that lead to good conference presentations (and even good viva defences) apply. Dress needs to be layered, so you can stay cool if it is hot, or warm if it is cold: pouring sweat or gooseflesh are not attractive. Clothes and shoes need to be comfortable so you are not constrained or chafed by them, but smart and clean enough so they look as if you have dressed up. Junior colleagues with vivid hair dye and noticeable body piercing or tattoos are probably best left at the home base, unless the project is focused on gaining access to reach heavily pierced youth populations. The presentation should run to time, be crystal clear, use audiovisual aids professionally, and deal with the issues raised by the potential funders, however 'off the wall' they may seem to be. Do not *read*: speak with your head up, making eye contact with the audience. Do not repeat detailed material that is on the powerpoint or overhead or handout, summarize it succinctly. Practice conveying confidence but not arrogance. The aim is to look as if you and your team are keen to do the research, can do it if you are funded, and will deliver what the funders want. Peters (2003) suggests every minute of a presentation should be based on an hour's preparation.

There are two main types of panel. One sort know what good research is like, have a clearly defined research area, and are choosing the best applicants from the field who they can trust to go away and do the project. The other type are required to commission some research, or have some money left over, or have an inchoate problem, and are actually using the presentations to help them formulate exactly what research can and should be done. Pitching to such a panel is much harder: and the possibility of helping the panel to focus their thoughts so they give a clear brief to some other team is omnipresent. This has happened to us at least twice. Some nine months before the Welsh language TV channel (S4C) was launched, the relevant government minister had promised the House of Commons that its impact on the Welsh language would be monitored. In the August before the October launch the civil servants woke up to the need to meet this promise. They asked us to meet them to outline appropriate research. The terms 'the impact' of a new TV channel on 'the language' were impossibly vague. During a boiling hot August we wrote three research designs, all of which needed some data collection *before* the TV channel began. Each time the civil servants decided that what we had suggested was not appropriate. When we finally had a design they felt met the ministerial brief, they calmly announced that our research design would be put out to competitive tender. We collected our pre-launch data at our own expense, so we could make our bid. In the end, the grant was not awarded until November, went to a team elsewhere in Wales, and the government never made any use of the results. All our work had been helpful to the civil servants because it enabled them to decide what research they could fund, but did us no good at all.

We had a similar experience with a government agency, long abolished, the Manpower Services Commission. They wanted a study of unemployed youth in rural Wales. We met them, explained basic issues about sampling, about data collection in rural areas, about the Welsh language and about analysis. We eventually reached agreement on an appropriate design. We costed it, and the MSC were appalled. They put our design out to tender, and another team bid £50,000 less than we had: about £200,000 in 2003 prices. Six months after our rivals had been awarded the contract, they found their bid had been under costed by £50,000–£60,000, and had to go back for an extra top-up of funds. In this case too, we had educated the civil servants, done all the conceptual work, and even costed it accurately. However, our work was not rewarded by the MSC: our presentations had been useful to them, but we did not get the money.

In contrast we have made successful presentations to civil servants, and to other funding bodies. We have also been on commissioning panels. In 2001–2002 Paul was a co-leader of a team based in two universities that obtained a £4 million pound grant from the ESRC which included two appearances in front of a commissioning panel. Preparation for the presentations and interviews were as thorough as short notice allowed. The team tried to second guess each area of questioning and prepared answers accordingly. They tested out possible areas of weakness and rehearsed the justifications for their preferred position. They coached each other as best they could. This is not done in an attempt to pull the wool over the eyes of the commissioning panel, but to ensure that the research ideas and the organization of the research are presented in the best possible light, and that the case is made in the best possible way.

Making funding count

As we have said, neither we nor any source of advice can guarantee that your research ideas will impress reviewers and committees. Research funding can be something of a lottery. While committees may find themselves with proposals that are unequivocally endorsed as 'alpha plus' and can fund them with little ado, they will also find themselves dealing with a substantial proportion of bids that fall into an intermediate category. As a consequence, anything and everything you can do to give yourself a competitive edge may help lift your application out of the general run of 'alphas' into the 'funded alphas'. The general advice we have offered in this chapter is all aimed at doing just that.

When building research careers and research groups, therefore, such attitudes need to become part of the general culture of the department, the research group and the research team. Less experienced colleagues need to have the benefit of more experienced colleagues, either by structured staff development activities, or through the less formal support they can provide. They need to learn to become part of a culture of success. They also need to understand that even the successful can also experience failure. Even individuals and teams with high 'hit rates' with research proposals can rarely, if ever, be successful 100 per cent of the time. Rejection is disappointing, and may feel like a terrible waste of time and effort. Repeated failure can be especially hard. In the latter case, one has to ask if there is anything that can be done to improve proposals: Are reviewers' comments highlighting the same sorts of problems? If one repeatedly feels 'they didn't understand ...', then perhaps those aspects of the research are not being explained with sufficient clarity.

Equally, however, one cannot take these things personally. A rejected grant proposal does not mean that you or your colleagues are unworthy, or 'not up to it'. Success often comes after failure, provided one can learn from the problems, and does not lose heart.

5

Writing: 'superogatory contributions to scholarship'

Jenny Stallard sat at her desk in the front room of her terraced house in Arlinghurst and sighed deeply. She'd been sighing deeply for most of the morning. She had done other things too. She'd tidied her desk drawers and its surface once. She'd made herself two cups of coffee, and put a load into the washing machine. She'd waited for the post and looked through it when it had come. It consisted entirely of mail-order catalogues and invitations to take out credit cards and loans. What she hadn't done – and this was why she was sighing – was to write anything. She was supposed to be writing 'her' book. It was based on her PhD thesis and she had a contract from a reputable publisher to write a general book on her research area. It should have been straightforward enough. She knew her stuff, and she had already written 100,000 words in completing her thesis – so she knew she could do it. But every time she started to write she ran out of steam almost immediately. It was like having one of those annoying little viral illnesses. You don't feel much like doing any work, but you think that's because you're lazy, so you tell yourself 'I must try harder', and the harder you try the worse you feel. Jenny knew she wasn't actually unwell, but the thought of writing 80,000 words by next autumn certainly made her feel ill. She had the feeling that for the first time in her very competent life she was 'blocked'. She had never before failed to write an essay or a thesis. She'd prepared conference papers and given them very professionally. But now it wouldn't come. The problem was not just the lack of words on the page or the empty screen on her computer. The real problem was the guilt she felt as a result. And there didn't seem to be anybody she could really share her guilt with, or the fear that came with it, or the nausea that came with both of them. If she owned up to her line manager, her head of division who was responsible for her annual appraisal, she would look weak and incompetent. It would not go down well on her annual report. Everybody was anxious enough already, what with people trying to get a permanent contract, or promotion, or a job elsewhere, and the Research Assessment Exercise bearing down on all of them like an incubus.

In separate chapters we discuss some of the mechanics of academic publishing in journals and in books of various sorts. But a productive research career and a productive research group is predicated on a more general culture of writing. The mechanics of publishing are of no value whatsoever unless one has something to publish in the first place. Writing seems – oddly considering our work and our background – to be a problem for at least some academics. We think that it is one of the most important and fruitful areas in which to think about and act on personal research plans and the collective activities of a department or research group. Our research students will never complete their theses, let alone forge successful academic careers, if they cannot or do not write. Our own precious research will never see the light of day unless it is published: it cannot get published until it has been written. Careers depend on writing. Promotions depend on writing. Research assessments depend on publications. If the process is mysterious and daunting, then all those other things will be equally problematic.

Too many of us are haunted by an unhelpful set of images of the author. It is an essentially romantic image of the lone author striving for inspiration, struggling to get the words on the page, impatiently screwing up page after page of writing paper. The lonely garret existence of the author in this kind of mythology recalls the classic images of struggling bohemian artists, poets and novelists such as might be found in Murger's *Scenes from Bohemian Life* and immortalized in Puccini's operatic setting as *La Bohème*. Such views are unhelpful. They are also completely inaccurate representations of what most academic authors are up to. Writing is a craft skill, or set of skills. Unlike the romantic imagery, it is not a matter of inspiration, it is a matter of work. It is more a matter of routine, discipline and collective commitment than the *Sturm und Drang* struggle of a crazed genius. Admittedly not all academics think of themselves as tortured geniuses when they contemplate writing, but there is no doubt that too many find the prospect of sustained writing difficult. The development of a research career and the enhancement of a research group often depends on the promotion of a writing culture. Indeed, in many ways a research culture *is* a writing culture.

It is crucially important in doing so to break away from any implicit notion that writing is something that 'comes naturally' or is a 'gift', or that it is something to struggle with in private. If nothing else, it is important to transform writing into a collective activity, and remove any romantic notions about authorship. Collaborative work is one of the best ways in which one can demystify the processes of writing. Staff development activities and seminars – for experienced and junior staff – can be productive. There are several messages that can be got across, and that you need to appreciate if you are going to build a personal research career, and if you are going to cultivate productive research groupings.

We have a small number of maxims that we ourselves try to impress upon successive cohorts of research students we help to train. It is the same advice that we offer to those colleges we try to help through staff development seminars in our own university. The most important one, we feel, is: 'Write early and write often.' Writing is an activity that becomes easier the more regularly it is exercised. We were both impressed by the parallel offered by Phil Jackson, distinguished professor of education at Chicago. He runs every day and he writes every day. He says that they are much the same. If you set yourself to run *every* day, then you cannot think in terms of letting it go for a day or two and catching up at the weekend. If you plan to do it every now and again, it is always too easy to allow yourself to be diverted. Moreover, the more regularly you run, the easier it is to go on doing it. It is partly a matter of fitness, but also a matter of attitude. The same is precisely true of writing. Regular writing makes any authorship manageable and easier. It is certainly easier to keep writing than to start writing. Walter Mosley (2000) puts it very well. He also says that you have to write every day:

> If you want to be a writer, you have to write every day. The consistency, the monotony, the certainty, all vagaries and passions are covered by this daily occurrence. You don't go to a well once but daily. You don't skip a child's breakfast or forget to wake up each morning.

Many colleagues and students find ways of making things difficult for themselves. They harbour all sorts of myths that constitute displacements rather than getting on with the tasks in hand. There is a widespread sustaining myth that one needs to – and will – clear a long period of uninterrupted time in which to embark on major writing tasks. There is no doubt, of course, that uninterrupted time is beneficial. But in contemporary academic life, such 'free' time hardly ever materializes. There is the myth, for instance, of the summer period when we can all get on with our own research and writing. If you wait for that golden summer time, then it is easy to put off until then the difficult tasks of starting a new book, or preparing papers for publication. The problem is that the 'summer' rapidly disappears. The pressures of teaching and assessment increasingly encroach on the summer. By the time that all the assessments and examination boards are over, and periods of re-sit examinations, Masters courses and Masters dissertations to be supervised, and the preparation of the next year's paperwork, there is precious little time (or very little precious time). If you take any kind of personal holiday in that period, or catch up with any kind of personal life, then the 'summer' can dissolve altogether. Rather than allowing yourself and your colleagues to place trust in that period devoted to writing – and seeing it dribble away to just a very few days – it is more productive to regard writing as an everyday activity to be scheduled during a busy working week, along with other tasks. It is useful to remind yourself, your research group and your students that if you take out weekends, then there are probably about 200 working days in a calendar year. If we could all write an average of one page a day for that time, then we would all draft 200 pages a year, without committing extra time at weekends or encroaching on 'holiday' time. That modest rate of progress would provide the basis of a very decent level of productivity for most research students and academic staff. In reality one page of typescript a day is an odd goal. It is so very little, it would be like a slow bicycle race to write just a few hundred words at a time, and on a good day one can certainly write more. That makes up for those days when one is unavoidably interrupted. It is, however, a helpful benchmark against which to measure steady and productive output. It has the clear advantage that it does not sound at all daunting a target.

There are several books on writing, and we have put an annotated list in Appendix 1. There are two very different books we always recommend, Becker (1986) and Richardson (1993). Becker focuses on how to settle down and produce some usable text, and is very funny as well as inspiring. Richardson shows how she presented the same research findings for three different types of audience in three different formats: and thus makes targeting writing transparent. Peter Woods (1986) has an excellent chapter on writing, which is frequently neglected or skimped in methods textbooks. The reader will be encouraged to learn that Peter Woods finds writing hard, and throws away piles of drafts as he works. Too many people believe that productive scholars have a 'gift' which makes writing 'easy', when in fact prolific authors like Woods probably force themselves to sit at their desks from 9.00 a.m. to 12.30 p.m. and from 1.30 p.m. to 3.30 p.m. whether anything is being produced or not. Engagingly, Woods also admits that when he is trying to get started on writing something he can be bad-tempered! Equally delightful is Woods's self-portrait, when trying to write, of himself as an ancient Morris Minor 1000 which had to be cranked by hand before it would start. He has to crank himself up before he can write, and is explicit about how he does it, and how it can hurt.

In his 1996 book Woods returns to the topic of writing. In the gap between the 1986 and 1996 volumes he had shifted from writing with a pen and giving the draft to a typist to working straight onto a wordprocessor. He explores his shift, and illustrates his exploration with a wonderful range of quotes from academic, creative writers such as the late Iris Murdoch, and popular novelists such as Joanna Trollope. He argues persuasively for keeping the pen as an alternative to the keyboard.

Now colleagues sometimes find it hard to write on the basis of 'little and often'. They say that they need time to read over what they've done, and get themselves into the right frame of mind. They cannot pick up the thread. This is a smaller-scale equivalent of the myth of the long summer period. The trick is never to leave a writing session without having an idea of where the argument is going. If you have the problem of picking up the flow of the writing, then always leave a note outlining the next sentence and the next paragraph. By the same token, it is unhelpful to sit down at a blank page or at a blank screen without knowing how to start. It is a useful aid to think about opening statements and paragraphs *before* sitting down to 'write'. If we know how to begin, then it is always easier to find ways to continue.

Whether you and your colleagues want to sit in front of a pad of writing paper or in front of a computer screen is very largely a matter of preference. If writing is an everyday craft activity, it is also something which people approach in their own individual ways. Writing is not something that everybody talks about in public, but when they do it transpires that people – productive people in particular – have their cherished ways of going about it. We ourselves find this to be true when we conduct development seminars or talk to our research student seminars about it. For that reason we share our own idiosyncrasies with them. This often helps to open up a more general discussion of the practical, mundane and embodied work of writing.

We have always had completely different, but symbiotic, ways of working. Paul always preferred to draft in handwriting. He has always found it necessary to have a preferred pen and a fresh block of paper. It ought to have a printed margin, and narrow feint ruled lines. He writes on alternate lines. He likes to keep this manuscript clean and neat. Consequently he rarely, if ever, crosses out and changes while drafting. He likes to carry on writing as fluently as possible without stopping to correct the draft or re-draft at the first stage. If he does go wrong then he starts the page again, to keep it pristine. If he wants to quote directly from another author, he carefully draws a second margin in pencil, so that the indented quotes are kept neat and tidy. He finds it much harder to draft if it is scruffy. Sara is quite the opposite. She also likes to draft in handwritten manuscript, but she finds perfectly fresh writing paper dauntingly unhelpful. She does not like to sully virgin paper with preliminary draft. Luckily she does not have to. She can take the sheets that Paul has previously drafted on (after his work has been re-drafted and wordprocessed!) and draft on the back of the sheets. She has no problem about the manuscript getting scruffy or messy. If she changes as she goes along, then she is happy to scissor and paste bits of manuscript together. So while Paul's manuscript stays pristine, Sara's become a palimpsest of fragments. A lot of other people work directly on the PC or laptop, finding the wordprocessor a great liberator of writing, enjoying its flexibility. There is no right way to do it physically. What is important is to do what is most comfortable and helpful.

In the final analysis, of course, it matters not a bit how we produce our first drafts, or what they look like physically. By the time they are published the books and the papers come out the same. But the important thing is that we know how we work best, and we do whatever it takes to get started and get the basic materials written. It seems to be useful for academics and students to find out how best they work, and to stick with that. We all have different biorhythms, and they can affect how we write. Some people can get up and write a few pages first thing in the morning before they get on with the mundane problems that the morning post brings, before they teach, keep office hours and so on. Others cannot do anything creative first thing in the morning: they are best confining the administrative and the routine to the morning hours while they feel uncreative and they may find that the afternoon or evening hours are their most productive. It is better to find out how and when you work best and build a schedule around that. We find that when we lead staff development sessions and discuss these personal aspects of authorship, other people find it helpful to 'confess' their own personal styles and preferences. Talking – and often laughing – about these things can help to take away any anxieties about how one 'ought' to be doing it. It also helps to demystify the entire process.

It is, however, vitally important that once you have found a rhythm, you use it. Academic life is full of displacement activities. If you are not careful you can always find some task that seems more pressing than writing. Time management is something that is sometimes exaggerated in significance, and there is often a bit of a mystique about it. But there is no doubt that it is possible to find one's days being filled with tasks that take one away from the difficult and sustained tasks of authorship. It is a good idea, therefore, to pay some attention to one's own patterns of behaviour. Do you always turn on the computer and deal with your email messages when you first get into the office? You may think that this is an efficient way of getting 'correspondence' answered. But you may in fact be responding to non-urgent materials on a daily basis and wasting time that could be devoted to something like writing and editing. Likewise, you need to ask yourself if you are sometimes unnecessarily conscientious about other aspects of your job. The demands of even a modest teaching load can expand to fill all the time available. Now we would not want to advocate neglecting our students, or skimping on teaching and assessment. But the contemporary demands of paperwork, committee meetings and other things surrounding teaching can lead some people to spend virtually all of their time on teaching-related tasks. Like housework or painting the Forth Bridge, such work is never done, and is almost infinitely expandable. We do not need to engage in elaborate exercises in time management, accompanied by the higher mystifications of management consultancy, in order to recognize the corrosive effects of displacement activities or routine work that gets in the way of creative writing.

The other lesson we try to convey by talking about such things is that it is important to realize that writing is not a matter of getting it perfect the first time. There are processes of successive drafts and revisions. Consequently our second motto is: 'Don't get it right, get it written.' At least one research student in our classes has managed to misunderstand this maxim, so we shall spell it out. We do not mean that it is all right to get things 'wrong'. But we know that far too many students and inexperienced academics find themselves paralysed by the desire to get their ideas and their writing perfect at the first draft.

If we could all get things perfectly right the first time, then it would be wonderful, but it is rarely the case. Some people can become so proficient as academic authors that they can draft if not perfect at least well-advanced text at their first attempt. The majority – and especially the inexperienced – will not have that option. There is good experimental evidence on writing styles that addresses precisely this point. There do indeed seem to be two ideal types of writer. There are those who try to get their ideas sorted out and planned out perfectly before they begin to write, and there are others who use the process of writing itself to clarify their ideas. For the first, their mindset is 'I don't know what to write until I know exactly what I think', while the others are more like 'I don't know exactly what I think until I write'. Those who use the process of drafting to think are the more productive authors.

There is carefully conducted psychological research on prolific and unproductive academic authors (Torrance and Thomas 1994) which found that the prolific ones used drafting as a part of their thinking, while those who planned their publications before writing were much less productive. Now if your students or your group members include people who are productive and happy while writing in that first mode – working with very careful planning and painstaking first drafts – then it would be foolish to try to change their behaviour. On the other hand, it often seems to be the case that there are people who are not as productive as they might be and are being hampered by such a personal style. In that case it can be productive – indeed liberating – to engage in group development seminars and other collective activities, to encourage colleagues to try more provisional and tentative preliminary drafting, and to recognize that 'getting it right' can sometimes be a hindrance to 'getting it written'.

Writing – even straightforward academic writing – is normally felt to be a private matter. It is normally invisible work. We see the products, especially when they appear in print, but we do not normally see the processes. Colleagues do not often talk to each other about the conceptual and practical issues they are struggling with, or about their successes in solving them. Because writing is so often thought of, however implicitly, as a personal gift and a private struggle, people do not confess to one another that they are blocked, or are completely stuck over a particular chapter, or cannot find the right way into an argument. It is common to share papers among research group members, but that tends to happen when the papers have been finally drafted, accepted for publication, or finally published. By contrast, we do not always share rejection letters and the accompanying referees' comments. Outline book proposals are not always shared among colleagues.

For those kinds of reasons, because privacy seems to be valued in this context, collective work is not always easy to achieve. People get quite defensive about their work. Any attempt to encourage collective work can therefore feel threatening. One cannot expect one's students and colleagues necessarily to share their experiences and, more importantly, their work without building up relationships of trust. It is, therefore, helpful for more experienced supervisors and research group leaders to set an example. If they are fairly productive and publish regularly, then less experienced and more junior colleagues and students may think that they find it easier or are more 'gifted'. They will not think of their mentors as facing the same problems of drafting and revising, of getting blocked and so on. The sharing of collective writing experiences needs to be reciprocal and based on mutual respect, therefore. Mentors need to expose themselves just as much as they expect others to risk self-exposure.

Expecting others to join in a collective commitment to writing is something that cannot be imposed. If it looks like an imposition, it will be resented rather than welcomed. Resistance is the last thing a research group needs. Trust is best built up on the basis of small groups working together rather than trying to involve a larger group immediately. The emphasis on trust is an important one. We treat writing as a personal virtue. Consequently it is all too easy to respond to criticism as if it were a personal attack. To have one's writing commented on is stressful. To have somebody else point out our shortcomings is like an assault on one's moral worth. It is easy to fall into emotional double-binds about writing and criticism. 'Would you mind having a look at this?' can easily turn into 'Who asked you anyway?' if the response is negative. Even if you know that a piece of writing is not 'right', it is often hurtful to have that feeling confirmed by another. The benefits of involvement in a writing group are explored in the chapters by Valian and Hood in Fox (1985).

On the other hand, it is easier for many people to share work initially with one or two trusted collaborators before trying to open the process up to a wider network within the research group. If you can do so, then it becomes much easier to establish the kinds of relationships that can bear mutual criticism. Having one's work criticized never really gets any easier: it goes on feeling like personal criticism, and it goes on making one feel like kicking the furniture and giving up altogether. What does get better is knowing what criticism is for, what it can help with, and at least being able to anticipate that it is a pain. If you know you will not like being criticized, then it will not feel so bad. If it gets treated as part of a craft, rather than a matter of inspiration, then criticism itself will feel like part of the work process.

Jenny Stallard is coming out of a Faculty meeting. Her friend Althea Sclander is carrying a book [Fox 1985]. Over tea Althea enthuses about one chapter she's read. 'It's on writing circles. It sounds great. These women set up a writing circle to help each other get published. We could do that – we've nothing to lose.' Jenny is sceptical, but she's got to do something. 'What's a writing circle?'

'Well, you meet regularly and you all agree to be supportive but also constructively critical. And you set goals, and the group meetings give you a deadline, and you bring along what you've done, and everyone reads it and is supportive. And you share tips – like software and cake shops. If people submit stuff you share the feedback. It sounds good. We could ask people to come and share their secrets with us as guest speakers, but have a core of beginners like us as the regulars.'

Jenny is warming to the idea, 'All women?'

'Yeah, I think so. I'd feel better in a women's group'.

If one can build up relationships of trust between peers and between mentors and the colleagues they advise, or between supervisors and students, then it may prove fruitful to start to develop writing circles and similar collective activities. The functions of a writing group are various. A commitment to collective work can help to foster the overall commitment to a research culture. Or an existing research culture can be propagated though new recruits and successive intakes of research students. Such a shared understanding can also help group members to appreciate a strategic view of publishing commitments. The group can discuss not just how to write in general, or specific writing tasks, but also how to build up a writing plan for individuals and groups.

We share our own commitment to planning with our students, for instance. We ourselves always keep a progress-chasing chart of all publishing commitments from first outline idea to final publication. We can trace each publication from first draft through subsequent drafts, to submission and editorial verdict, through any revisions that are necessary and re-submission, to copy editors' queries, proofs and publication. This has entirely pragmatic functions. Obviously it helps us to keep track of deadlines and our progress towards hitting them. It helps to avoid forgetting to complete a commissioned piece (such as a handbook chapter – of which there seem to be more and more). It also helps to spread the load of writing, by reminding us of all the work that needs to be scheduled.

We commend such a progress-chasing chart to our junior colleagues and students. In this chart, (Fig. 5.1) the scholar is writing a book with nine chapters, plus the 'Prelims' (Preface, Acknowledgements, Table of Contents and so on) and the References. She has set out spaces for three drafts of each chapter, then a column for the submission of the book to the publishers, for the copy editor's queries (CQ), for the proofs, and then for its final appearance (OUT). She is also preparing four journal articles and a book chapter: with a separate line for each title (ANZJQ is clearly the Australian and New Zealand Journal of 'Q') and a parallel set of headings. For an article, she has 'Abstract' (which would include not only the Abstract but the keywords and other material journals need), two drafts, submission, the verdict of the journal, and, because most journal articles come back for revisions, a 're-submission' column, then copy editor's queries, proofs and out as in the section on books. Finally, she has listed, under 'other' a book review, and two conference papers she has to write and deliver, so in this section there is a heading of Submit/Deliver.

The progress-tracing charts we use are done separately for books (we keep one joint chart with all the book projects as single line entries, and one each where every separate book has its own page with all the chapters set out individually) and each of us keeps one for papers and 'other output'. However, what works for us would not suit everyone: adapt the basic idea to suit your style. You may have fewer commitments to keep track of, of course, but it will still help to stay on top of undertakings if they are kept physically visible. There is, too, nothing like the feeling of satisfaction when you can

Speciment Progress Tracing Chart

Books	D1	D2	D3	submit	CQ	Proofs	Out
Chapt 1	x	x					
2	x	x					
3	x	x					
4	x						
5	x						
6	x	x	x				
7	x	x					
8							
9	x						
Prelims	x						
Refs	x						

Papers	Abstract	D1	D2	submit	verdict	resub	CQ	Proofs	Out
BJQ	x	x	x	x	R	x			
RQ	x	x							
ANZJQ	x	x	x	x	R	x	yes	x	
Q Studies	x	x	x						
Phil's Book									
Chapter	–								

Other	D1	D2	Sub/Deliv	Proofs	Out
Book Rev RQ	x	x	x	x	
Aberdeen Conf	x				
Perth Seminar	x	x			

Figure 5.1   Specimen Progress Chart

tick off another item on the chart, seeing an article move from submission to acceptance, and from acceptance to proof stage and, finally, to publication. It is also helpful because it helps focus the mind on the fact that one can keep several projects on the go at once. Inexperienced researchers in particular need to get the hang of working on one task while something else is proceeding. The timetables of research and writing can involve long periods between different stages. There are time-lags between submission and editorial decisions from journal editors, for instance, and there are long lead times between acceptance and publication. Consequently authors need to have more than one project on the go, so that one is not left waiting, metaphorically twiddling one's thumbs while waiting for something to happen.

It is coffee time at Wedmarsh, on a July morning. The handful of staff in work that day are strolling across the campus back from the only café that's open. Dermot Garrowby, a temporary lecturer, is alongside Theo Beatock, a tenured lecturer he does not know very well. They get back to their department and go straight to the pigeonholes. Dermot's is empty and he curses. Theo asks 'What's up? Hoping for a letter?'

'No. I'm waiting to hear from the British Journal about my paper. They've had it five months, so I'm stuck and I'm fed up waiting.'

Theo says sympathetically, 'Oh well, you'll just have to get on with your other articles and – have you got a book contract?'

Dermot is surprised, 'I'm not writing anything else. All my best ideas are in that paper. I haven't tried to plan a book yet.'

Theo is even more surprised, 'Oh that's no good. You should always have three or four publication projects – a book, two or three journal papers, a conference paper. Otherwise it's all too dependent on the referees of one journal being sane. Usually they seem to send my papers to madmen who hate them. Why not plan a book, or draft some more papers?' . . .

Dermot is surprised – no one has ever suggested that before: it sounds complicated. Within the research group it is possible to develop a collective strategy for writing and publication. Shared research interests – not necessarily collaborative research projects – can lead to a shared sense of writing commitments. Members of the research group can develop a collective understanding of what and where to publish. It is useful to inject a sense of purpose to individuals' and groups' plans for journal papers, for instance. Different papers can be planned out among authors and co-authors, targeted towards specific conferences, journals or other outlets. Again, inculcating a craft approach to writing implies the development of a sense of different audiences and different outlets for one's work. While there is a place for writing something out of the blue, most of us do better to write something with a specific journal in mind, or a particular kind of readership. So we know we want to reach a specialist audience, or to reach professional practitioners and teachers, or methodologists, or theorists, or an overseas readership. These all imply a writing strategy involving different kinds of papers, with different styles, formats, editorial requirements and so on. In a later chapter we discuss the mechanics of publishing in journals, and we do not labour those points here. Our point, rather, is that we can all benefit from a joint research group approach to the planning of where and how to submit our papers. In Chapter 8 we discuss other kinds of dissemination – including web pages, press releases and reports to sponsors.

If there is joint research among the research group, the planned co-authorship is also a possible writing-related activity for the group. Should you be publishing single-authored journal papers or should you be publishing jointly? In part this will depend on your discipline. The conventions and the symbolic rewards vary enormously. Obviously in the natural and medical disciplines, co-authorship is the norm. Research is carried out in teams. Moreover, if data are shared between collaborating research groups, then those data have the names of the originating scientists attached to them, as it were. The long strings of authors that can arise out of large international collaborations signal participation in the research process by one means or another: they do not imply that all of the people named have simultaneously sat around the same table and thrashed out successive drafts of the actual paper. In those same disciplines it may be conventional for the head of the laboratory or of the research group to have her or his name on virtually every paper that emanates from the group. To some people in the humanities and social sciences, this seems alien, even immoral. It looks like an authoritarian style in which senior academics impose themselves and claim the work of more junior colleagues for themselves. The culture is quite different from that, however. Joint publication reflects the team approach to research. The laboratory director is responsible for ensuring the throughput of research funding, staffing and other resources. He or she sets the intellectual tone and the research agenda. Research problems and paradigms 'trickle down' between generations in the research laboratory. This is a completely different tradition, therefore, from the culture of authorship in the humanities, in which solo writing has been the norm, and where credit for authorship is a much more personal matter. Indeed, it is abundantly clear that 'authorship' means something quite different across the disciplinary spectrum.

In consequence, the development of research group cultures and the promotion of joint activity means that the academic in the arts and humanities needs to suspend taken-for-granted attitudes about co-authorship. So too do social scientists if they find it alien. While there is clearly no requirement to work together on publications, there is no stigma attached to collaborative writing either, and it is not based on exploitative relationships. We have talked about the necessity of seeing academic writing as a craft skill, and as something to be discussed within the research group, and not a private problem. This can be carried over into publication strategies too.

It is September in Arlinghurst. The archaeology of the Iron Age team are having their first meeting after the summer: they have had to come out of the field to attend an exam board meeting, and they are killing two birds with one stone. The team leader, Professor Renate Ingleson, calls for quiet and says they need to plan their publications for the year. Those present sort out their plans for two conference presentations, two journal articles and a report to their main funders. Each person has tasks – organizing the photographs and the maps, preparing the presentation of the geophysics findings, doing the first drafts of the articles. One person is missing. Paige Rimmell is on maternity leave. The rest plan the name order on the different publications and pre-sentations – including Paige on three of them – rotating the order so that everyone has their name first on something. They close the meeting and head for the pub.

Not everyone can plan collectively like our fictional archaeologists. Research groups may not have such closely shared responsibility for one major project. But if research groupings have any basis in genuinely shared intellectual commitments and are used as the basis for real collegiality, then there is no reason why some collective approach to papers and conferences should not be undertaken. After all, you know what major conferences are coming up on an annual, two-yearly or four-yearly cycle. Not everyone will want or need to go to every one. But you'll want to make sure that your department or your research group are represented at the appropriate meetings. So if you plan out who is going to present what at which con-ference, and when, then you can ensure that you are all represented: you can also plan ahead the research group's budget for attending the con-ferences.

Collective and individual planning of publications is, in the UK, given particular urgency by the pressures of the Research Assessment Exercise. We discuss the RAE and preparation for it in a later chapter, and we do not want to imply that everything to do with research development is or should be geared obsessively towards the RAE itself. The promotion of successful research cultures should be the ultimate goal, and the RAE merely con-firmatory of one's success. However, given the regular cycle of Research Assessment Exercises – and they are not unique to British higher education, although they are especially prominent and highly developed in the UK – it makes sense to gear one's publication plans to their requirements. More-over, the criteria for research assessment are the same as the criteria for personal research achievement, and so the personal and the institutional interests coincide in this respect.

Indeed, whatever else is taken into account, it is the quality of research output, in terms of publications, that really counts for the evaluation of research. It cuts little ice that one has attracted external research funding if it has not resulted in publications of high quality. Writing in general – whatever the medium of output – needs, therefore, to be seen as a craft skill that is part and parcel of the everyday work of any and all academics. Mentors and others need to find ways of encouraging and helping junior staff to write productively without making the whole process seem like an incubus. In other words, we should instil the sense that writing is something we all do more or less all the time. We do not need to build it up to be something special or especially demanding. In successful and research-active departments and groups, it *is* taken for granted that everybody is committed to writing. It is *not*, however, taken for granted to the extent that there is no shared interest or understanding of the processes. Patterns of co-authorship among active groups do not merely reflect the courtesies of putting principal investigators' names on papers. They also reflect the extent to which ideas are shared, turned into drafts that are also shared, and translated into publishable papers. The active researcher and his or her group will, therefore, have – at least implicitly – a sort of collective progress-tracing chart. It will identify conference presentations that need to be prepared and the relevant deadline for submision of abstracts and finished papers (if relevant); it will also indicate the target journals for those papers to be submitted to when they are written up; it will also identify who is going to take the lead in drafting each paper, and therefore map out the division of labour within the team. Not all papers will be produced on the basis of conference presentations, of course, and other papers will need to be prepared in the normal way: but these too need to be identified, potential journals sourced, and authorship established.

Work in the arts and humanities is often expressed in single-authored works. The collective commitment to high-quality writing and prolific outputs is not, therefore, expressed through collaborative writing. But that does not preclude shared interest in the undertaking. The preparation of a major monograph or major new edition of a work may be a major undertaking in its own right. A *magnum opus* may require the implicit collaboration of colleagues – possibly in helping the author have a light teaching semester, or a light exam-marking load while the volume is completed. Sympathetic heads of department may also provide support services – such as secretarial support – to aid the completion of such a major project, especially if there are no external funds available.

In all these ways, writing need not be a private matter. Research workers should not be left to struggle on their own to turn their PhD into good-quality publications, or to produce drafts of papers and reports for their principal investigator. Younger lecturers nowadays are all made aware of the need to publish work of high quality – not least because of external scrutiny like the UK's Research Assessment Exercise, and tenure reviews – but those pressures ought to be accompanied by positive support. Academic managers should not will the ends without willing the means to achieve them. As we have argued in this chapter, that includes inculcating a culture in which research-led writing is a shared commitment. It also means arranging relevant staff support activities – formal and informal – to help younger staff realize their potential. There are things that all academics need to know and to think about when it comes to publishing. In the next two chapters we focus on two modes of publication – journal papers and books. In Chapter 8, we turn to a consideration of other forms of dissemination.

6

Publishing journal papers: 'some marvellous things to say'

Collette Hallard opened the morning's post with more than her usual sense of apprehension. She recognized that one of the envelopes came from a journal she had submitted a paper to some months before. This was probably the editorial decision coming back to her. She put the envelope to one side while she quickly opened and tossed aside the flotsam and jetsam of academic life that the post had brought – publishers' catalogues, management memos, circular letters from learned societies and the like. Finally, she opened that letter. 'Dear Ms Hallard', it began, 'we have now received our referees' comments on the paper you submitted to this journal. They are enclosed for your information. I regret to say that ...' 'Oh damn,' Collette muttered. 'They've had the bloody thing for months, and now they've rejected it. The letter went on a bit longer, but she felt sick and couldn't bear any more disappointment. So she stuffed the envelope and its contents into the bottommost drawer of her desk, and made herself another cup of coffee, her hand shaking a little with pent-up emotion. She was about to submit her PhD thesis, and had tried out a couple of the draft chapters on key journals in her area. She had been advised to try to start publishing, and had conscientiously tried to do so. This was the first reply she had received. She felt crushed. If the work wasn't publishable, how could her PhD be of the standard required? She knew that Beauminster University's instructions to examiners for the award of a doctorate included the criterion that the work should be of publishable quality.

Later that week Collette plucked up courage to 'confess' to her favourite staff member (not, as it happened, her supervisor) that she'd had her first rejection. 'Oh, that's a pity. I'm surprised. I thought it was in pretty good shape,' said Dr Desterro. 'Where's the letter. What did it say?' Collette confessed that she hadn't actually read the letter properly, and was sent off to her office to get it. When she brought it back, Dr Desterro read the editor's letter through quickly, and then read through – more slowly – the referees' reports that had been included. 'Chump,' she said smiling, 'If you read it through properly, you'll see that you've been accepted, but you have to make a small number of sensible and straightforward changes. It won't take us too long to fix it, and it looks as if the editor is going to accept it without much more argy-bargy.' Collette looked sheepishly at the letter properly for the first time. The editor had indeed said that 'I regret to say ...' but it went on '... that we cannot publish the paper in its current form. You will see that the reviewers have suggested some specific changes that should be made in order to strengthen the argument, and I agree with them. If you feel able to undertake the changes we require we shall welcome the submission of a revised version. ...' And so on.

Collette's experience is a very common one. First, we all have to get used to being rejected, or at least receiving 'revise and resubmit' requirements from academic journals. A lot of people react with pessimism to such responses. Sometimes they really do get rejected, of course, and there are many reasons for such a verdict. In the course of this chapter we want to help the Collette Hallards of the world understand the process her paper has been through, the outcomes and the possible reasons for success and failure. We also want to help her understand more about the process of academic publishing she is trying to put herself through.

We know of one successful social scientist who has published relatively little, and who confessed to us that if a journal article came back with the commonest of editorial decisions – 'revise and resubmit' – he could never be bothered. He had, he claimed, always lost interest in the topic by the time the paper came back from the journal. For his generation – those who got tenure and promotion in the 1960s and early 1970s – that might have been a viable (if unusual!) way of operating. It isn't now. Today our acquaintance would really struggle to get a regular job, let alone promoted, in the absence of a steady stream of published papers. Today's aspiring academic has to make the extra effort to get her or his papers into the journals.

Why do you need or want to publish papers in academic journals? The journal paper is the primary outlet for scientific and scholarly work that reflects the 'peer review' process. It is not a mechanism to reach a mass audience. It is not the way to change the perceptions or the practices of your fellow academics or professionals. It is not the way directly to reach large numbers of students. It *is* the way in which your work will appear in the public domain with the guarantee that it has been reviewed critically by independent peer reviewers, and that it has passed that specific form of scrutiny. If you are thinking about developing your career, establishing your own presence in your discipline and building your curriculum vitae, therefore, you need to be thinking sharply about your strategy for journal publications. While they are not the only form of publication, they are the key to academic and scientific success. You can certainly be promoted on the basis of journal articles without publishing a book; publishing only books with no academic peer-reviewed journal papers will not carry the same weight. Journals carry more than just articles, including research notes, review articles and book reviews. These are all very useful ways of building up a CV, and keeping your name in the public realm. Anyone building up a research group should be encouraging research students, research staff and junior colleagues to do book reviews, offer review articles to journals, and try to publish research notes as well as the journal articles we focus on in the rest of this chapter.

The reason for publishing in academic journals is to communicate your research and scholarship to a relatively narrow readership of your academic peers. With a very few notable exceptions, academic journals do not reach many readers. The majority of copies of any given journal are likely to be found in university libraries. Personal subscribers and avid regular readers are relatively few. There is thus no absolute guarantee that anybody in a university will read any or all of the papers in a given issue. So your own papers are not going to be life-changing experiences for many people. You are not trying to reach out to the masses by this route. Your research may well have the capacity to affect public policy, or professional practice, but an academic journal article is not the place to do it. The journal is the place in which research and ideas receive a certain kind of public legitimacy. They have the warrant of 'peer review' and are in the public domain for anyone to inspect and criticize, replicate, cite and so on. In recent years there was a very well-publicized and notorious assault on work in academic journals in the sociology of education by James Tooley (1998). He took it on himself to criticize a substantial number of papers in the *British Journal of Sociology of Education*. Amongst other things he criticized the papers on the grounds that they would not help teachers improve their practice, and were written in terms that were not accessible to teachers. He did not seem to understand the principal purpose of such a journal. Its readers are not teachers in schools or post-compulsory education: the readers are sociologists of education. Consequently the language and concepts are those of academic sociology. If an author wanted to affect the teaching profession directly, or to intervene directly in education policy, there are other routes. We know. Although Tooley did not take us on (we wrote about higher education and he seemed only to be exercised about schools), we had a paper in the *British Journal of Sociology of Education* (Delamont, Atkinson and Parry 1997a). It was about the management of research students in British universities. But we did not think that a journal article was ever going to be the way to bring our research results directly to bear on practitioners. We had a completely different strategy for that. We wrote a book (Delamont, Atkinson and Parry 1997c) that was directly aimed at academics who wanted to improve their own practice, to be used in universities' staff development programmes and the like. The readership for the book is wide; the readership of a journal for the sociology of education is inevitably narrow. Of course we wanted to have an impact on the basis of our journal article – but we wanted to affect how a small number of fellow specialists thought about the sociology of education, not to improve their performance as PhD supervisors. So the general message is: if you want to change the world, do not think that a learned journal is the best vehicle to do that. (Here the social and cultural disciplines are different from the natural sciences. A paper in *Nature* can change the world. One need only think of the brief communication in *Nature* in which Crick and Watson proposed the double-helix structure of DNA, for instance.)

What is an academic journal? This is not quite as straightforward as it might seem. The origins and styles of journals vary quite markedly. Some are very old and well established. They represent the 'old aristocracy' of academic journals. Sometimes they are associated with particular academic departments, sometimes with learned societies. In our own discipline of sociology, for instance, the major American journals – the *American Journal of Sociology* and the *American Sociological Review* – have those two origins. The *AJS* is the main official journal of the American Sociological Association, while the *ASR* has its origin in the department of sociology at the University of Chicago (an early and especially influential department in the history of the discipline). Andrew Abbott (1999) has written a centenary history of the *ASR*, and this provides a detailed account of how submissions have been handled in different epochs since 1895. In the United Kingdom there are three parallel journals – the *British Journal of Sociology* has its origin in the London School of Economics, while the *Sociological Review* is associated with Keele University. They both have permanent homes, therefore. *Sociology*, on the other hand, is the main journal of the British Sociological Association. It does not have a permanent home; the editorial team changes regularly, being appointed by the BSA on the basis of bids from academic teams and departments.

The older journals tend to be quite broad in scope. As disciplines have expanded and as the culture of publishing has changed, there have been new demands and newer journals have been founded and developed. On the whole they have tended to be at the more specialized end of the spectrum. Whereas at one time the field of academic journals was restricted to a relatively small number of generic journals, now it is characterized by greater and greater specialization, with more and more niches in the market. There is nothing wrong with the more specialized journals. In many ways they provide the right sort of outlet for much scholarly work.

Academic journals – like books – are one of the domains in which there is a shared interest between academics and commercial publishers. Again, this is not universally true. Some journals are owned and produced by the relevant subject association and are not in the hands of a commercial publishing house. Some are published by commercial publishers on behalf of a learned society. Yet more are purely commercial publishing ventures. There are houses that specialize in journals, and have complete divisions within the company that deal with academic journals. There are some firms that are entirely devoted to the production of academic journals. Before it was taken over, the publishing house Carfax was entirely devoted to publishing journals. It is now part of the journals division of the Taylor and Francis group.

Now as a prospective author you may not need to know too much about the origins, background and management of all the journals in your field. (You will need to know more about these things if you ever want to edit a journal or start a new one: we return to that below.) But you do need to understand the more specifically academic side of managing a journal, and the management of papers that are submitted to it and are (or are not) published in it.

Irrespective of whether the journal is a learned society one or a commercial venture, the academic side is managed in much the same way in all cases. A journal stands or falls on its academic credibility – on that valuable but intangible commodity 'reputation'. That credibility is established and safeguarded by its editorial team and the editorial board, and the processes of peer review that it employs. Each journal has an editor or an editorial team. They in turn are advised by an editorial board. In addition there may be extra advisers, such as 'international' or 'regional' advisers. Now the editorial board is a key aspect of any academic journal. It is the collective standing of the editorial board that helps to warrant the quality and status of the journal itself. Board members of high international standing will not automatically convey prestige on the journal – ultimately that will depend on the quality of the papers that are published. But board members help to maintain those high standards by advising the editor or editors.

This is so by virtue of the process of peer review. Peer review is undoubtedly a very imperfect system – but as has been claimed for democracy, nobody has ever come up with a better system. Peer review of publications is the key mechanism whereby scholarly standards are established and maintained. It might be thought that peer review – the considered evaluations of other scholars in the same discipline – would be a conservative mechanism. By definition, one's peers are likely to represent the consensus view, and are more likely than not to endorse whatever orthodoxy is current. Almost by definition editorial board members are drawn from the more established figures, often drawn from older generations, so there is a tendency for them to reward the kind of work that they are most familiar with. Such a view of peer review has some merit, and to some extent it is something we live with. On the other hand, as the scope and variety of academic journals has widened, there is more and more scope for minority or innovative approaches to find their proper outlets. Any particular academic discipline nowadays is likely to have journals that will accommodate academic approaches that are not entirely traditional, mainstream or whatever. Within our own field of sociology, for instance, there are now plenty of outlets that are explicitly designed to publish not only highly specialized subject matter, but also publish papers from specific standpoints – feminist scholarship, postmodernist and poststructuralist accounts, phenomenological perspectives, culturalist analysis. Moreover, while the great majority require what one might think of as 'traditional' formats of authorship, others will publish 'papers' in alternative literary forms, such as auto-ethnography and autobiographical accounts, fictionalized narratives, even poems. They too have their editorial advisers and undertake peer review – but the people who review and the journal editors themselves will be committed to the publication of papers that are in keeping with the journal's editorial style.

In purely practical terms, how does the process of considering a paper occur? First, of course, an author sends a paper for consideration. The number of copies required and the format will be specified in the published 'Notes for Contributors' for that particular journal. (We shall say more about these requirements later.) The editor(s) will inspect the paper initially. They may undertake a preliminary 'triage' on the submissions. ('Triage' is a term derived from front-line emergency medical treatment, whereby cases are sorted in terms of their urgency.) Some journal submissions come from people who have not had the benefit of good advice and mentoring – or have not read this book! – and are manifestly inappropriate for the particular journal, and the editor may well undertake a preliminary review to weed out the completely inappropriate submissions. Indeed, the editor will need to do so, as she or he will need to decide which peer reviewers to ask to look at the paper on behalf of the journal. The choice of appropriate referees is a key part of the editor's work. It is also a matter of self-preservation for the editor: if she or he repeatedly sends papers to the 'wrong' people, then the result will be a collection of disgruntled advisers and a stream of papers returned unread. The editor wants the best advice about a paper, then. That advice will ultimately guide the editor as to whether a paper is worthy of publication in this particular journal. Journals vary in their specific practices. Some will send a paper out – initially at least – to two reviewers; others will send papers out initially to more. Five is the largest number we are personally aware of (*Social Studies of Science*). The editorial board members will be the first port of call for our editor. Some journals will always have a paper reviewed by members of the editorial board only; others will also go outside the board members.

The process of peer review is normally interpreted to be 'anonymous'. It is anonymous in two senses. First, the reviewers themselves will remain anonymous in that their identity will not be divulged to the author(s). Likewise, the paper itself will normally be anonymous, in that the author(s) will not be identified to the reviewers. For this latter reason, journals normally ask that the author'(s) name should only appear on a cover sheet that can be removed before the paper is sent out. It should not include other identifiers (so that running heads incorporating the author's name should not be used). Some will also require that self-citations by authors will be anonymized in the text and in the references. Otherwise, citations such as 'As we have described in more detail elsewhere (Delamont and Atkinson 2000)' rather give the game away!

It is mid-October in Arlinghurst. Althea Sclander is collecting her friend Kieran Marcable to go to lunch. He is editor of an inter-disciplinary journal of Latin American studies. She finds him in his office looking despairing.

'Look at this,' he says, 'This idiot has only sent one copy of his paper, and he's put his name as a running head on every page. How can I send that out for refereeing?'

Althea is brisk, 'You can't. E-mail him and say you can't referee it until you have four clean copies without the running head and without any other identification in the text. Send him the message now, and then come to lunch.'

'But...'

'No, your time is too valuable. Just do it.'

Referees are normally asked to do a small number of things. They are asked to write an opinion about the quality of the paper, including specific advice and opinion about any revisions that they think ought to be required. These are normally required to be in a form and style suitable for feedback to the author. This latter requirement is a useful one: it allows the editor to provide feedback to her or his authors, and it also helps prevent unnecessarily coruscating remarks. It also helps to focus the mind of the reviewer on providing a constructive and helpful reading where at all pos-sible. The reviewer may also be allowed to provide a confidential comment to the editor. This will help the editor to appreciate just how negative a reviewer feels, notwithstanding the more guarded feedback comments. It also helps the reviewer draw any particular peculiarities or problems to the attention of the editor. Some journals leave open the aspects of the paper to be commented on, while others provide a more detailed checklist of issues to be addressed. Most journals also ask the reviewer to provide a summary recommendation. In essence, and whatever detailed wording is used, these fall into four recommendations:

- Publish the paper as it stands.
- Publish the paper subject to minor amendments.
- Publish the paper subject to major amendments.
- Reject the paper.

There may also be a subsidiary category something like 'Suggest the author try a more suitable journal, such as...'

Dermot Garrowby wanders into Theo Beatock's office in Wedmarsh, 'Can I ask your advice?'

Theo saves what he is doing on his PC and swings round in his chair. 'Sure. What's up?'

'The *Journal of Narrative and Life History* has sent me a paper to referee, and I'm not sure what to do. What do they want?'

'That's nice. Let's see the paperwork – it probably tells you what to do.'

Theo reads the letter from the editor, which includes the following instructions:

'Please provide two sets of comments: one in confidence for the editors, which will not be shown to the author(s) and a second for the author(s). Please do not put your name on the comments for the author(s). Please try to be constructive in your comments to the author(s). Our aim is to try to help people to publish their work. The editors welcome candour; authors often need help to improve their work.

Please judge the following aspects of the paper, where relevant:

i)   Is the topic central to *JNLH*?
ii) Are the methods clearly described?
iii) Is the literature review adequate?
iv) Is the paper written in good English?
v)   Is the paper in the journal's house style and free from errors?
vi) Is the paper interesting?

Please provide a summary recommendation to the editors:

i)   Publish it as it stands.
ii) Return for minor revisions and then publish.
iii) Return for major revisions and then re-review.
iv) Suggest submission to a more suitable journal (please give examples).
v)   Reject.

Please do not write on the manuscript – just send us comments.

If you cannot reply within 24 working days, please send the paper straight back, ideally with the name and address of an alternative referee.

Theo looks up, 'Well that seems clear enough. Have you read it?'
Dermot nods.
'Is it any good?'
'It's quite interesting, on people who were called up for the Gulf War but who never got out there in the end.'
'OK, well, can you answer the questions in the editorial letter? If you can do that then the editor will be happy. Does it need revision, do you think?'
'A bit. There's a couple of American things not cited and a table that's not labelled clearly.'
'OK, so imagine it's your own paper and write positively about what needs doing in a style you'd like to get it in. Do a draft of your report and I'll look at it. But don't be afraid to say clearly what's good about it and what needs fixing. The editor will thank you for a clear opinion.'

The editor will read and compare the reviewers' comments once they have been received, and on the basis of that advice take some further decisions. It may prove necessary to take further advice. With the best will in the world, reviewers can disagree quite markedly, and the editor may want to consult one or more further reviewers before something like a consensus emerges. Otherwise, the editor will need to decide on the fate of the paper. If reviewers are enthusiastic about a paper, then there is little problem. The same is true if reviewers are equally in agreement that a paper is inappropriate. A great many opinions fall between the two extremes. The editor will then need to decide whether to encourage 'revise and resubmit', and if so, in what terms to feed that decision back to the author. Editors do need to make judgements at this point – reflecting on how extensive a revision is actually called for, the extent to which some revisions may be regarded as optional improvements and whether others are absolute requirements. (We shall reflect on how to interpret editors' comments later in this chapter.) From the editor's point of view, therefore, what is needed from a reviewer is a prompt and clear recommendation. What she or he does not want is a long delay followed by a short essay about the paper with no clear recommendations as to its revision, or whether or not it is worth publishing.

If, in bald outline, this is the process, what are the lessons for an aspiring author? First, one has to bear in mind that most journal work is done by hard-pressed academics who do it on top of the other calls on their time. Editors are normally full-time academics who are themselves trying to maintain their own research and publications. Members of editorial boards and referees are also academics doing this – and other – pro bono tasks along with all their other work. It is unrewarded work. Like external examining (which is virtually unrewarded in financial terms) and reviewing grant applications (which is also unpaid work) it is part of the general exchange of services that academics undertake for the general benefit of scholarship and of their own discipline. Membership of the editorial boards of high-status journals confers a modest amount of prestige, but it hardly compensates for the effort of reviewing papers. Journal editors may also gain some modest rewards from their labours, but they are essentially doing the work in their 'spare' time.

Given that it is a competitive business for any aspiring author to get her or his papers into print, it is obviously worth thinking about how to make the job of hard-worked editors and reviewers easy. It is relatively straightforward to get published in many journals, and the task is made even more straightforward if one follows some pretty simple guidelines. Some basic research and some sensible kinds of behaviour will go a long way towards securing successful outcomes.

For the purposes of this argument, we shall assume that you have got something worth publishing somewhere in your work. That may be derived from a thesis, or a research project you have worked on, or an especially interesting idea, or a novel perspective on an old problem. We shall think a bit more about what constitutes a 'publishable' paper a bit later, after we have discussed some of the more mechanical aspects of the process.

The first thing to think about is which journal to submit your work to. You might think that this went without saying – surely any research student or young academic would have some very clear ideas about the journals in the field, and where to try to place a paper? Well, you might think that but you would be wrong. When Paul was editor of the journal *Sociology of Health and Illness* he did an informal content analysis of referees' comments on the papers that had been submitted over a two-year period. One of the commonest reasons for the rejection of papers was the fact that they had obviously been sent to the wrong journal! Despite the published objectives of the journal, it was remarkable how many people sent in material that was not suited to it. Submissions included papers that were essentially celebratory pieces about particular systems of alternative or complementary medicine, or had nothing to do with sociology or cognate disciplines (such as anthropology or social history). It was clear that those would-be contributing authors had never seen a copy of the journal and have never consulted its published editorial statement about its scope and mission. So the advice to choose a *relevant* journal is not quite as self-evident as it might appear.

It is really quite noticeable how many people seem to spend years of their life undertaking research – for a higher degree or on a funded research project – and then do little or nothing to research the field for possible publications. But a relatively modest effort spent on such a task can save a lot of wasted time and heartache in the future. How might you tell what journals are likely to be relevant? Obviously there are no hard-and-fast rules here, but some rules of thumb help. First, if you have never had occasion to refer to work in a particular journal, there is a good chance that your own work is not going to be especially relevant to that journal – especially if it is in a specialist area. By the same token, if work you draw on and admire (or criticize) has appeared in a journal, then there is a much greater likelihood that it will be a possible outlet for your own work.

Equally, if a journal has recently had one or more articles that relate directly to your own work, then it may be that it will be advantageous to link your own work to those papers, in order to establish the relevance of your own paper to that journal. If you can position your paper as a contribution to a continuing debate or theme in the journal's pages, then so much the better. It will not guarantee success, of course, but it will establish that your paper is of potential interest to the editors and the readers of the journal. You will need to check whether the kind of approach you have taken is in line with the general intellectual style of a given journal. It really will be hitting your head against a brick wall sending a philosophical or epistemological discussion of something to a journal that is always devoted entirely to empirical research reports. Likewise, a qualitative piece of work based on a small series of intensive life-history interviews is probably not going to work in a journal that is always devoted exclusively to large-scale quantitative work. Again, you might think that this is obvious to the point of being trivial, but the experience of editors is that they receive a disproportionate number of papers that are intellectually unsuited to their journal and its readership.

Preliminary research in the university library is therefore advisable – and there are several things that you will need to find out about a journal anyway. But it is also worth remembering that there are probably more journals in the field than any one library will subscribe to at any given time. Some of the large publishing houses have quite bewilderingly long lists of journals. It is worth looking at the range of journals published by the main publishers: you may find that there is something that at least sounds potentially relevant. An inspection copy from the publishers (if they will supply one) or an inter-library loan copy of a recent issue will help you evaluate the journal in question. The journal may have a website, it may be possible to look at a recent issue electronically, and some ideas about the journal can be gained from inspecting abstracts of its articles from a print or electronic source. *Current Contents* contains the contents pages of dozens of journals, and is a good way to get an impression of what, and who, a journal prints.

Research should go beyond just identifying the name of a journal. There are other things you will want to know about it. You should look at the list of editorial board members. We have already mentioned some of their functions. Their collective identity is one of the ways in which a journal is 'branded'. The names of the board, and their own research interests, help to establish the corporate identity of the journal whose pages they grace. If you look at the editorial board and you have never heard of them, and have never referred to their work, then again this may be a clue to the likely relevance of the journal for you. This is obviously more likely to be true in the case of a specialist journal. When dealing with a very general journal, there is no reason to suppose that the editorial board members would be directly relevant to your own research.

Research will also go into deciding on the kinds of papers that a journal normally publishes. We have already mentioned some of the parameters here. You should pay particular attention to the 'Notes for authors' that journals normally publish in at least one of the numbers in an annual volume or that are otherwise available (from editorial offices, on journals' or publishers' websites). You will need to establish simple things like the normal length of a published paper. When Paul did his content analysis of rejections, he found that one of the commonest reasons was that the paper was the wrong length. If a journal specifies that it will normally seek to publish papers between, say, 6000 and 8000 words, or sets an upper limit of 10,000 words, it really is counter-productive to send in a submission that is 15,000 or 18,000 words long. But a lot of authors seem to think that such conventions do not apply to them. Perhaps they think that their own work is so important that the editor will devote the equivalent of two or three articles to their work. Well, they usually will not. Journal editors only have fixed numbers of pages to play with for any one number or annual volume.

They cannot expand their issue length indefinitely in order to accommodate over-length papers. Equally, a journal that is looking for substantial papers is not going to be attracted to a very short contribution, unless it counts as a 'research note' or a similar kind of brief contribution (of which more later). While brevity is the soul of wit, it is perfectly possible for a paper to be too short. It is too short if it does not develop an argument with sufficient depth, or does not ground it in sufficiently detailed commentary on the literature, or does not present sufficient empirical research to substantiate it. There is a world of difference between a paper that is just under-developed and a short research note that is brief and to the point.

Research on the notes of guidance for authors will also provide further information. They will provide notes on the 'house style', for instance. Journals and publishing houses more generally have their preferred styles for the preparation of papers. These can be very detailed. Some in the social sciences, for instance, insist on the style of the American Psychological Association, which has developed a hugely detailed and highly prescriptive style manual. Others may stick to a rather simpler set of guidelines, confining themselves to required formats for things like citations and bibliographies. In any event, you need to discover what those conventions are and use them for your submission. Complete failure to abide by the house style does little to suggest that you have prepared the manuscript professionally, or have targeted this particular journal for your work. It may result in delay if your paper is accepted, and you will have to do it properly in the end if the journal does decide to publish you.

At a more general level, journals may have preferred structures for their contributions. Some may have very formulaic structures for empirical papers, for instance, insisting on standardized sections for things like 'methods', 'findings', 'discussion' and the like. If they always do papers like that then they are not likely to make an exception for you, so you might as well get it right. Equally, if your own paper cannot fit that format, or if you do not want to make it fit, then those journals are not for you.

Of course these are primarily practical things about journals. You need to know about them and how to work with their conventions. But there are also many other things about journals that you want to find out about if you can and will use in making decisions about where to approach.

In this age of research assessments and tough promotions committees, just publishing is not the only consideration. We are all trying to publish in 'the best' journals. Now journals do undoubtedly enjoy different degrees of prestige, and getting published in a 'top' journal will do a lot for your career and for the notice other people take of your research. In some disciplines the ranking of top journals is quite explicit and there will be consensus about which 'count' as the 'gold standard' or 'blue chip' journals. They are the international journals in which the top academics from the top institutions publish their work (yes, there is an element of circularity here). They also have high impact values, meaning that papers in them are highly likely to be cited in other journals.

In one sense, therefore, it will seem self-evident that everyone will try to publish their work in such high-ranking journals. It is true that many of us will try to publish *something* in such a journal, but a productive academic cannot hope to publish everything in a very high status journal. A younger academic cannot necessarily expect to break into a top journal with her or his earlier papers. There is a danger of letting the best be the enemy of the good here. We have noticed from our own staff development activities that younger scholars have sometimes been so thoroughly mentored in the ways of research assessment that they can only think of publishing in the very best journals. But thinking about the blue chip journals to the exclusion of all else can be counter-productive. Almost by definition they are often very difficult to get into. They will have very high rejection rates. A high rejection rate is a kind of performance measure in its own right. It shows how selective a journal is, and therefore how competitive publication there is. A top journal may accept and publish only 5 per cent of the papers submitted to it. Obviously being successful in such a competitive context is a considerable achievement. It suggests that one's paper must be exceptionally meritorious to have got through such a stringent selection process.

So if we always aim at the absolute top international journals, then we are in danger of just adding to their rejection rate. There are in many disciplines plenty of excellent journals that are somewhat easier to get into. That does not mean that they will publish any old thing. But it does mean that if a paper is good then it has a good chance of success. Often more specialist journals will have such a function, with more manageable rejection rates – perhaps something more like a 20 per cent acceptance rate. So when we are building up a portfolio of publications and developing our curriculum vitae, it makes sense to think about a range of possible journals to which we might submit work.

Acceptance rates are not the only thing to be aware of in relation to journals. There are good reasons to be aware of the likely length of wait to have a paper published. The time lag for publication varies quite dramatically between disciplines and between journals. There are obviously many outlets for the natural sciences, where rapid publication of new results is of paramount importance, and they are published with great frequency. *Nature*, for instance, can publish scientific discoveries in a very short time. At the other extreme, there are journals in the humanities that have a time lag of several years. In between those two extremes, the majority of academic journals – especially those that appear three or four times per year – will have some degree of delay. It is useful for you and your research group colleagues to have a collective understanding of the sort of timescales we are thinking of.

At Arlinghurst Paige Rimmell is back from maternity leave. She bounces into Professor Ingleson's office waving a letter from the *Archives d'Archaeologie de Nimes*.
'They've accepted our article on the Nether Dumbleton dig.'

Prof Ingleson is delighted. 'Great. Do they say when it might come out?'

Paige is confused, 'Well, volume 92 which should have come out in 2000 hasn't been published yet as far as I can see, so they are about four years behind. I think we're accepted for Volume 94, which at the current rate of progress will have a 2002 date on it and will actually appear in 2006. Unless they fall even further behind.'

'Oh well, everyone in archaeology knows they're all behind. My husband's colleagues in Physics don't *believe* a journal could make you wait two years to appear in a volume that is up to four years late.'

This scenario may appear bizarre. However, there are several journals in classics and ancient history published in Europe that are running several years 'late', so that the issue that actually appears in 2006 is dated 2002. A long delay between acceptance and publication is also common in many humanities disciplines. If you are in such a discipline, the people who have direct influence over your career will probably be used to taking the letter of acceptance from the editor as solid evidence of forthcoming publication. The UK Research Assessment Exercise has, so far, given humanities disciplines a seven-year timeframe for publications, whereas everyone else has a five-year period. So in the 2001 RAE a scholar in Italian could list publications that appeared between calendar years 1994 to 2000. A scientist or social scientist would have to list only publications which appeared after Jan 1st 1996 and before 31 December 2000.

The processing of an academic journal paper is not very quick under normal conditions. It is possible, of course, for something to be 'fast-tracked' if there are pressing reasons to get something out in a hurry. But under normal circumstances, editors are dependent on their reviewers. Reviewers are asked to reply within a given time, usually a few weeks. Editors and authors would love reviewers to reply by return of post – and some do – but as we pointed out above, the entire system of peer review depends on the unpaid help of busy people. (If they are not busy, their opinion probably is not worth having.) So editors have to rely on reviewers returning their comments. Then editors have to make decisions and convey them. Often some sort of revision is called for. Then the ball is back in the author's court, and the overall process depends on the speed with which she or he can get the revisions done. Then a revised submission may have to go out to referees once more if the revisions are substantial. Then once the paper has finally been accepted, it may have to wait until there is a slot in the production schedule. Each issue of a journal has to be submitted to the publisher – for copy editing and typesetting – several months before the publication date. So the issue that appears in the spring of 2003 will have to be made up in the autumn of 2002. The papers that are included will have been accepted several months before that, and therefore submitted and refereed over a long period before that. If a journal has a large number of submissions, then it can develop quite a backlog. In consequence, you may have to wait a very long time between first submission and finally appearing in print – two years is not unusual in our own field.

On the other hand, there are journals with shorter waiting lists. New journals do not build up backlogs of papers in the same way, and may be 'easier' to get into initially. Even though they may not have lower standards, they are likely to have more room to publish papers fairly rapidly. There are new journals being announced and sending out their calls for papers all the time. Most of the academic fields are getting crowded, and although authors have to compete to get into good journals, it is sometimes the case that as journals jostle one another to get established they also have to compete for good authors.

You and your colleagues may, therefore, have to face protracted processes of submission and revision with the top journals. Given their rejection rates, the outcome may well be disappointment. Consequently, it makes little sense to put all your eggs in one basket and pin your hopes exclusively on a very small number of blue chip journals. There is nothing wrong with building up journal publications in the broad range of decent journals that are not absolutely outstanding. Most academics develop their publications across a range of journals. It is, therefore, realistic to think of building up a list of publications across a variety of journals and journal types: not only the absolutely 'best' outlets, then, but also some specialist journals, and – depending on the topic – something in one or more professional journals.

You and your research group might therefore want to start thinking strategically about how you are going to build the publications collectively and individually. Let us assume you have a joint research project between you. You might very well decide that there should be one journal article of record deriving from that project. And you might equally decide to target some specialized journals for specific aspects of the research project. If you want to get a rapid publication out, then something completely different may be called for, and something in a commercial or professional outlet will be appropriate. You will be reaching different kinds of readerships as well as spreading your publishing efforts. Not everybody reads all the journals. Even where there is overlap in terms of content, you cannot assume that there will be a great deal of overlap in terms of subscribers and readers.

Does this mean that you and your colleagues should be submitting the same paper to different journals and hoping that one of them accepts it? Certainly not. It is unethical. Journals explicitly require that a submission is unique, and that papers are not being concurrently submitted elsewhere. After all, editors and referees put in a lot of effort and cost: they cannot be expected to devote that amount of work if they then discover that an author has got a better offer elsewhere. On the other hand, there are few projects – whether individual or collective – that do not contain within them specific aspects and are covered within just one paper. There are usually detailed matters that are only of interest to a restricted and specialist readership. Equally, there may be technical matters like methodological considerations, or arguments deriving from literature reviews, that can be placed.

Many journals state explicitly that they only review a submission on the understanding that the author has not submitted it anywhere else, and they will immediately reject it if that is not the case. Others require authors to sign a statement that they have not sent it anywhere else simultaneously. (Trying different journals one at a time is fine, of course; a paper that has been rejected can be tried serially on other journals subsequently.) Multiple submission is a silly form of cheating anyway: the active referees in any given field are a restricted pool and so the paper may well land on the same person's desk from both journals. This is also an argument against repeatedly sending the same paper to different journals if it has been rejected. A referee who has recommended rejection to the *British Quarterly* is not likely to offer a very different opinion if he or she is refereeing it some weeks later for the *British Journal* (of whatever).

'Salami slicing' one's publications is also dangerous. This term has been applied a good deal in recent years to the perceived danger that career-conscious and RAE-driven academics will carefully parcel out their projects into smaller and smaller chunks, getting a separate publication out of each chunk and so maximizing the number of publications. A similar sharp practice is not dividing up the work, but publishing essentially the same paper in several different places with only minor variations. This is equally undesirable. Of course, that can work in the short term, and people can be impressed by the quantity of published work. But in the longer term it is the quality of what is published that counts. People who go in for salami slicing, or who keep publishing what looks like the same paper with just minor variations, end up with the reputation of being 'chancers' and damage themselves and their research groups. (This is one reason why the Research Assessment Exercise, of which more in Chapter 9, only asks for four publications per staff member over the assessment period: it is about quality of published work and not sheer quantity.)

Phil Bywood came out of his office at Penbury and bumped into his colleague Tom Freeson. 'Guess what,' he said, and continued without waiting for a response, 'I've had another paper accepted by the *Midlands Journal of Audience Research.*'

'Oh, very good.'

'That makes fifty I've published in the past five years.'

'Splendid.' Tom made to move on.

'And twenty alone from that survey of opera-goers.'

'Oh, I didn't know you were still getting papers out of that project. What's this one about?'

'The same stuff – constructing an index of postmodernist consumption cultures.'

'Haven't you published all that already?'

'Yeah, but I thought if I tweaked the data, tried some different proxy measures, fiddled with the scaling again, I could get another paper out of it.'

'Well, good luck to you. But be careful. Some authors are still using the first version you produced, others are using the second version. And a lot of people have given up altogether. They think if you can't get it right once, then they can't trust it at all. And if you just keep on turning out different versions of the same thing, then nobody is going to take any of it very seriously.'

'I'll still get promoted, though.'

'Maybe so.'

Salami slicing and multiple publishing is by no means a sensible response to the pressures of research assessment. The quantity of publications from any individual or from a department is not the issue. Since each individual is required to submit only a maximum of four publications in a five- or seven-year period, then Tom Freeson's fifty papers in five years are neither here nor there. If he has sacrificed quality for quantity, then he is disadvantaging his department's chances and its eventual reputation. A smaller number of major publications will count for much more in the long run. That is not an argument for publishing little. Rather, a decently productive, research-active academic should be concentrating on a steady output of significant publications, not on sheer quantity. Likewise, short-term career goals may well be helped by quantity. But in the longer term, one's reputation in the discipline and consequently the standing of one's department and research group will be determined more by the quality of one's published work. You will get noticed by publishing a lot, but if it is not all good, then you may be noticed for the wrong reasons.

Like all our advice in this book, we cannot tell colleagues how to have the best and most publishable ideas. But what we have tried to do is to give some pointers about how to think about journal publishing, and how to build it into a coherent strategy. 'Research' in the broadest sense does not just include conducting original scholarly work, or collecting and analysing data. It also means researching – paying serious attention to – the various ways in which that research can be published. That means knowing about the processes that lie behind academic journals; spending the time to find out about them, doing the sort of 'market research' that will identify the right readership for your research, journals that will form part of an excellent portfolio of publications; helping one's junior colleagues to build their curricula vitae with publications that will enhance their career, make them employable, worthy of tenure, or promotable. It means having the research group and the research team working collectively to promote the research they have been working on: reaching the *right* specialist readers for that research, covering between them a range of general and more specialized publications, and contributing to the collective dissemination strategy. Like everything else, therefore, it implies using one's considerable intelligence to make the publications system work to your advantage.

Many disciplines move forward almost exclusively through journals. Indeed, some move very fast through the circulation of pre-prints, even before the journal issue itself has been published. Other disciplines, especially in the arts, humanities and social sciences, also move forward through the publication of books. Scholarly monographs are among the most significant outputs in such intellectual fields. Again, getting one's book published – especially for a first-time author – is helped by an understanding of the processes and practices involved, and a sense of how to approach publishers. We therefore turn to that aspect of career building in the following chapter. We also discuss editing journals – especially founding a journal – in Chapter 8.

7

Publishing books: 'a kind of apocalyptic romance'

Reginald Povey sat in his 'study' at home in Penbury. (Actually it was a desk in the corner of an over-crowded family room.) He looked palely at the pile of paper in front of him. He looked at it as if he never wanted to have anything to do with it again. There it was, his *magnum opus*. His life's work. It hadn't actually taken him a lifetime to produce, but it felt like it. In fact it had taken him several years of full-time work to produce a decent doctoral thesis, and now it had taken almost as long to turn it into a monograph. He knew more than anyone else in the world about the discourse of medical instruction. If there was such a thing, then what he had in front of him was the definitive work on the topic. He should have been pleased and proud to survey this manuscript. Lots of people want to write a book, and by no means all of them manage to do so. Completing a book-length manuscript is an achievement. Reginald's was over 120,000 words in length. It had consumed long hours of wordprocessing, revision and editing. So why did it depress him so much? Because nobody seemed to want to publish it. He hadn't given it too much thought when he embarked on it. Proud of his PhD and having published several well-received journal papers, he had assumed that writing a monograph was the next logical step. He really needed to publish a scholarly book for the sake of his reputation, his career and his future promotion prospects. So he had started on it. For a while it was a good feeling. 'How's the book going?' friends and colleagues would ask. 'Pretty well, thank you,' he would say, pleased to be among the fellowship of authors and to share the academic grind of 'getting on' with a book. After a while people stopped asking, and Reginald stopped feeling quite so good. The job got boring. Moreover, the nearer he got to finishing the revisions to the book, the more pressing became one big question he had managed to shelve when he'd started out: Who was going to publish the thing? He consoled himself with the thought that the world is full of books, and the academic world is full of dull books. He assumed that just about any book can get published. He wasn't looking to be a commercial success. He knew that his research monograph was not going to challenge the kind of books that make the bestseller lists. Stephen Hawking or Simon Schama he wasn't. But he did assume that his modest ambition was reasonable. And so he had ploughed on and finished the work. He had then started sending copies of it to the major commercial publishers of academic books. In several cases he had not had to wait very long for their response. Rejection letters started coming back almost immediately. Not from everybody; sometimes publishers took six months and more to get round to rejecting him. People he'd never heard of kept sending him short letters, in which they found different – more or less polite – ways to reject him. They said that his book did not fit their current commissioning plans, or that they were not commissioning monographs. Some added that he should not take this as a reflection on the quality of his work; most did not bother to sugar the pill very much. In any event, the result was the same. No publisher. Worse, he had no coherent plan. He'd lost direction and he'd lost heart. What was worse, he felt ashamed of this apparent failure, so he didn't feel he could consult his colleagues in the department at the university. He could hardly expose himself to them. The only thing that he could keep asking himself was why on earth had he spent all that time and all that effort without a proper plan, without a contract from a publisher, and with so little idea of what he was doing?

The development of your personal research career, and the promotion of your research group, is probably going to involve the publication of books of some kind. Humanities and social sciences value the book as a mode of publication, and their disciplines lend themselves to book publishing far more than the natural and applied sciences. Indeed, there is a certain suspicion of books in the latter disciplines. The assumption is that any book must be a textbook, and therefore of secondary importance, and of no account in research terms. This is not true in the humanities and social sciences. Moreover, there is not the same sharp division between textbooks and research materials. Many works of synthesis and criticism are major and original contributions to a field without being entirely based on 'original' research (in the sense of being brand new discoveries). Obviously there are many kinds of 'books' – monographs, scholarly editions and translations, edited collections, textbooks among them – and we cannot cover every eventuality here. On the other hand, there seem to be some generic guidelines that can be followed that can inform a publications strategy, and that can save a lot of wasted time and effort if followed. Moreover, we shall suggest that there are several different kinds of value to be attached to book writing and editing. Unlike our colleagues in the laboratory sciences, we can place greater value on and reap more rewards from book publication. Likewise, it is not necessary to be bound too stringently by the need for purely research-driven exercises like the RAE to find value in writing books.

The writing and publication of books can serve a number of different functions, and one needs to have a fairly clear idea about what kind of book one is trying to produce at any given time, and what function it is going to serve. If everybody thinks they have at least one novel in them, most academics in the social sciences and humanities reckon they have a book in them: sometimes the problem is that they do not know what kind of book, and consequently they do not know what to do about it. For similar reasons people often have quite unrealistic ideas about books and publishers. Robin Derricourt (1996) demystifies publishing books, and starting a new journal. Each section takes the form of a letter from a very gentle and patient publisher to a potential author, explaining a specific aspect of accepting and producing a book. There are letters about indexing and cover design, about pricing, and about getting radio coverage, as well as whole chapters on different types of book (scholarly, trade, *Festschrift* and conference proceedings, for example) and other vital matters. Indeed it is an interesting coverage of everything in this chapter at greater length. Every potential book author would do well to consult the reasons for rejection on page 5 and the checklist for submitting a proposal on page 54, for example. Germano (2001) deals with a similar range of issues in a shorter, but less entertaining way. Powell (1985) conducted research in Apple Press, a small social science publisher, and Plum Press, a large publisher, with only a small social science list but a larger presence in other disciplines. Apple had 30 employees, Plum over 400. Powell's book provides valuable insight into the corporate cultures of the two contrasting publishing houses and their approaches to commissioning and selling books.

Indeed, before we begin to discuss 'what is a book?', it is probably wiser to start by discussing 'what is a publisher?' The production and marketing of books is one area where the academic reputation of a scholar is partly dependent on the symbiotic relationship with publishers. Publishers need authors and authors need publishers. Finding the right match, and finding what is of mutual benefit is the issue. Publishers come in different sorts and sizes. At one extreme are the large commercial publishing houses, often with several imprints and often in turn part of some larger corporate entity. There is no doubt that they are driven largely by market forces. Because these publishers are regularly merged, de-merged, sold and rebadged, we have not given examples here. If you consult *The Writer's Yearbook*, which is published annually, and should be in any large library, it lists recent mergers and changes of ownership. They have commissioning editors, of course, who are interested in the quality of what they publish in their lists, but the large commercial houses are increasingly driven by marketing and financial considerations. Books need to make money. Books that do not sell up to forecast sales will be dropped from the catalogue and allowed to go out of print. Some books go out of print so quickly that they are unobtainable by the time that the reviews appear in the major academic journals (often several years after publication date, because of the slow speed of some journals and a backlog of reviews and review articles). It is thus increasingly difficult for commissioning editors in these houses to take risks with apparently unfashionable and quirky books. It is also increasingly difficult for them to find books that are 'sleepers' – books that are not really expected to find a large market or to sell well, but that surprise everyone by turning out to sell in large numbers, perhaps because they are especially timely, or 'catch a wave' of interest that was not foreseen. That can still happen, of course, but it is more difficult, because commercial publishers are increasingly driven by short-term considerations. The corporate mentality seeks short-term returns for investment, sometimes at the expense of building up lists and reputations over time. Of the most commercial publishing houses are those that do not really publish academic books, but specialize in 'trade' books. There can be some degree of cross-over. Academics can and do sometimes write trade books, and some academic books become trade books, getting shelved and marketed with general books. But these are relatively rare. We shall return to the topic of trade publishing later in this chapter. For now we should say that for most academics and for most books trade publishing is unlikely – especially for a first or early book.

Not all commercial publishers are driven by high-volume sales. There is more than one way of making money out of selling a book. One means, which the large corporate houses like, is through volume sales to students. Those books are marketed relatively cheaply, and the profits (and the royalties) come from small amounts of money from large numbers of copies sold. If you sell, say, 10,000 copies of a book at £12.99, a small percentage of the cover price can mount up. But you can also sell, say, 1000 copies of a book at a higher unit price, say £49.99, and still turn over a decent amount of money. And there are plenty of commercial publishers who trade in that way. They produce smaller runs of books and sell them at a high cover price. They can still make a profit margin sufficient to justify publishing each title, and are just as commercially motivated as the 'trade' publishers or the publishers of textbooks and long print runs. They just operate with very different kinds of markets and economies.

Alongside these publishers are other kinds of academic publishers, including the university presses. University presses exist to publish scholarly work that is not primarily commercial. This is not a comment on the intrinsic value of what is published. On the contrary, university presses often produce academic works of high quality. One of our acquaintances – a very senior university manager – said to us once 'Oh, nobody bothers with university presses – they only publish what nobody else wants', as if the output of university presses was the residue after good publishers had had their pick. Of course, the crucial difference is partly the commercial interest. If the main commercial houses need marketable books, the university presses – like some niche publishers – can afford to take specialized monographs that will (they hope) attract critical approval but will never sell in large numbers. The major university presses in the United Kingdom – Oxford and Cambridge University Presses – stand out from and differ from the rest. They stand among the great publishing houses on an international scale (together with a small number of American university presses such as Chicago, Harvard and California). They are more like the large commercial houses in many ways. They produce very large lists, they have cheaper paperback editions of their more popular titles, and they publish textbooks as well as specialist monographs. In 2000 Oxford University Press decided to stop publishing its contemporary poetry list, and there was a furious correspondence in the serious press. They were acting like a commercial press, while their critics expected them to go on behaving as a major university press, setting intellectual standards rather than being driven by purely accounting concerns. The smaller university presses – Leicester or Aberdeen, for example – are not seen as arbiters of national 'standards' in the same way as OUP's stewardship of the poetry list was perceived. In the United Kingdom there are also old, well-established university presses that continue to fulfil their historic function of promoting specialist monographs and similar works that will not appeal to a commercial market-oriented press. These enjoy good reputations for the most part, and often produce well-made books of good quality. There are also some small – sometimes frankly obscure – university presses that carry little prestige, even though they have the limited function of getting work (usually by members of the same university) out into the public domain. University of Wales Press is a vital outlet for work on Wales, and on and in the Welsh language. Other regional university presses can perform equally useful functions of publishing social history of the region or other specialized materials. The presses of the universities will normally have specialist lists that reflect academic strengths of that university – but not restricted to that university for its authorship. Specialist lists may even reflect the enthusiasm of just one committed academic staff member, who carves out a niche with the local university press. The ability to publish specialized monographs in relatively short print runs, but reach the 'right' readership and library orders, is a valuable service performed by the university presses. They are certainly worth examining and getting to know: sometimes they can be virtually the only press able and willing to take on an esoteric topic.

Not all the commercial presses are large corporate undertakings. Every few years or so commercial houses merge or are taken over by corporate giants. The academic community laments the fact and expresses the fear that publishing is falling into fewer and fewer hands, while our collective and individual fates are governed by fewer and fewer gatekeepers such as commissioning editors. Then, from time to time, there emerge smaller publishers who occupy particular niches and meet the needs of readers and authors to put out specialist titles, and build up selective lists. Often these smaller houses reflect the interests and commitments of individual publishers – people who want to maintain relationships with their authors and who want to retain their personal commitment to 'quality' publishing.

There are three other types of publishing that need a brief mention. There are publishers who take camera-ready copy from the author or editor and reproduce it, so that their role is production and sales, rather than editing or proofreading. Current examples in the UK are Ashgate and Edwin Mellen. Their books are aimed at library sales, not bookshops, and they pay no royalties to authors. The status of a book produced in this way varies from subject to subject. Ashgate books in music and in medieval history can be high status, those in education are less so. We have edited an Ashgate series (The Cardiff Papers in Qualitative Research) which includes monographs of doctoral theses deemed 'not commercial' by more famous publishers, such as Pilcher (1996). Edwin Mellen operates in a similar way, but does not have stands at conferences or issue catalogues. Williams's (2002) biography of an American anthropology department, for example, has not been marketed to anthropologists in the UK at all.

Below these publishers in the hierarchy are the 'vanity' houses, where the author pays to have his book produced. These exploit sad people with bad poetry they want to see 'published'. Academics should avoid them completely. If there is no chance of getting published otherwise, self-publication is better than vanity production.

Now this is not an exhaustive listing of types of publisher – and a complete typology would not get this discussion very far anyway. Our point is to remind researchers and their colleagues of what they know already, that 'publishers', like 'books' are highly diverse. Consequently, when thinking about one's own publication strategy, or when thinking about the publishing career of one's junior colleagues, it is necessary to think about two things simultaneously: What kind of book are we going to write? What kind of publisher are we going to try to place it with?

Like everything else, successful publishing reflects some amount of 'research'. As we have suggested in relation to journal publishing, it is always surprising, although common enough, to find colleagues in the academy who will devote a great deal of effort and time to researching their *magnum opus* but are unwilling or unable to devote any serious time and effort to researching publishers and markets, or who do not think strategically about the publication of their work. So some sort of homework is required. Equally, careful thought needs to be given over to deciding what sort of book(s) one is aiming to produce.

One does not need to think in terms of just one book, after all. Many projects or groups of projects among a research group can potentially yield several books of different types. A major project on, say, the impact of tourism on the Lake District could potentially generate a specialist monograph with a university press or smaller monograph publisher, a more general textbook on tourism studies, or on the methods of tourism studies, and an introductory text for beginning students on the social aspects of tourism. These all imply different approaches.

Researching publishers

Whatever kind of book you and your colleagues decide to try to publish, however, there are certain recurrent things you need to bear in mind, and certain things you ought to do. As I have said, you need to research the publishers. An aspiring author is much more likely to succeed when approaching a publisher who has a track record and a list of titles in the relevant area. If you are trying to publish something on, say, housing as a social problem, it makes sense to seek out publishers who have already demonstrated some commitment and interest in social problems like housing and/or housing itself. This seems self-evident. A commissioning editor will feel secure in judging and commissioning books in a familiar area. Moreover, if the publisher has a successful list in a particular field, then the company knows that it can sell books of that sort, and it is able to reach the right sectors of the academic market. The publishers Multilingual Matters, for instance, specialize in books on language, especially on bilingualism and bilingual education. They would not want to see a proposal for a biography of the Hungarian composer Ferenc Erkel, or an exegesis of the theology of Dorothy L. Sayers. A perusal of the relevant catalogues is therefore a useful part of the research strategy, and helps inform the successful academic's current awareness of the field.

It also makes sense to know something of the way a publisher is thinking. It is useful to know about their future plans. Are they, for instance, thinking of moving into a different area of specialization? Are there particular niches they want to fill? Are there obvious gaps in their list that the commissioning editor(s) want to remedy? This kind of intelligence is not assembled from catalogues alone. It is therefore useful to meet and talk to members of the publishing houses. At one time in living memory, commissioning editors regularly did the rounds of the university departments, and talked to a considerable number of potential authors, teachers who knew what textbooks were needed and what were being used, or senior colleagues who could advise them about likely young authors, intellectual trends, and so on. Some still come on such visits, but they are less visible. But you can still meet publishers, of course. Luckily they and their representatives still go out and about. They are to be found at academic conferences. Big conferences have publishers' displays. These have a massively uniform character to them all over the world, whether they are held in large American convention centres and resort hotels or in tatty bits of UK campus universities. Rows of booths are stacked with the latest titles and promotional leaflets. Most people at the conference will visit the publishers' displays at least once during a conference. Apart from anything else, it gives you something to do if you find yourself at a loose end, on your own or otherwise idle. The publishers' exhibits are a good place to arrange to meet somebody. You can browse among the books on display almost indefinitely. Obviously you can find out what new books are appearing, with any luck find a title or two you did not know had come out. But this is not the only function of the publishers' exhibits. As well as the essential aimlessness of many of the conference delegates as they wander round the display, one can also observe that there are long periods in the conference when the representatives from the publishing houses are equally unoccupied. Apart from the rush hours between sessions, at lunch-time and so on, the publishers' hall is often fairly quiet. The people staffing the booths can be seen drooping rather listlessly by their wares; sometimes they are driven by boredom to look at their own or their competitors' books. Sometimes they are to be seen talking to each other. So why not give them somebody interesting to talk to? Talk to the publishers who are there. It is impossible to predict who they will be. At the large international conferences, the complement will often include one or more editorial staff, as well as people from marketing. And editorial staff will often be found at smaller conferences if they match the editor's specialist list. So getting to know publishers is not all that hard. They are an almost captive audience, sitting or standing by their display or in their 'booth'.

This is not the time to try a hard sell of your brilliant idea for a book. Button-holing a hapless publisher and fixing them with an obsessive look, like the Ancient Mariner, is not a recipe for success. But this may be the perfect opportunity to find out who the commissioning editor is, talking in general terms about your interests and finding out about theirs. If they have your business card, that's a handy way of having a record of who to approach later. (You have got a business card to give them, haven't you?) If you take their business card, then you have the name and address of someone to keep in touch with and approach in the future. This kind of informal networking is, after all, one of the most significant functions of academic conferences, and the useful relationships are not confined to those with fellow academics. Talking to publishers is a key aspect. Your discussions may come to nothing, but the time spent is usually more valuable than listening to yet another dull paper you sit through because there's nothing else to do or because you think you ought to.

One way or another, then, you need to build up a profile of the publishers in your field. What lists do they have? Do they publish research monographs, textbooks, a mixture of both? Are they specializing in relatively expensive hardback monographs only, or do they seem to be aiming at a wider market, with cheaper paperback books? Are there specific aspects of your discipline they seem to be interested in? Do they seem to be moving into new areas that include your own specialist field? Even if you do not get to meet the commissioning editor in your field, it is a good idea to find out who she or he is by name. After all, you are going to write to them.

Proposing a book

So if your research leads you to decide on a publisher, you need to reflect fairly carefully on how to approach them. First, some things to avoid at all costs. Do not send them your PhD thesis or the thesis of your prize student. The arrival of an unsolicited thesis – all 120,000 words of it, with all the characteristics of a thesis, such a boring review of the literature, or a discussion of methods and sources that seems interminably pedantic – is not going to seize many people's imagination. Even though many monographs in the social sciences and humanities start life as higher degree theses, they have usually been through a major transformation before they become publishable books. Publishers do not want raw theses, and they certainly do not want to have such manuscripts sent to them 'cold'.

Publishers also dread the regular trickle of letters they receive from the eccentrics. Handwritten on lined paper these letters try to persuade publishers – often quite the wrong publishers – to take this unique opportunity to publish a book of excruciating obscurity and oddness. The proud new PhD and the eccentric with a bee in his bonnet actually share many characteristics. They are both convinced that their obsessive interest in some out-of-the-way topic is actually shared by lots of other people, who are just dying to buy and read books about it. The reality is usually that they are not. In any event, you do not want to look like the more crazy of the would-be authors. You want to impress the publishers, not startle or amuse them. (Save that for when you know them better.)

By and large publishers do not want to receive unsolicited manuscripts of books. You want to approach a publisher in one of two ways. The first is by a letter in which you outline succinctly who you are and what sort of book proposal you would like to approach them with. The second – which may be a follow-up to the letter – is by means of a well-crafted proposal. The proposal is important. One of our friends who is a very experienced commissioning editor in the United States has said to us that a potential author probably has about thirty seconds to capture his attention. That may be an exaggeration, but it makes the point very well. Commissioning editors get a lot of approaches from would-be authors. If they work for or run a successful publishing house that receives a lot of approaches and proposals, then they can afford to be choosy. So the more you can do to make them feel good about your own proposal, or those of your colleagues, the better. Obviously an outline proposal is not necessarily the place where you are going to show off exactly how clever you are, but it is the place to demonstrate how professional you are.

Here is a hypothetical example, then, of how not to approach a publisher. It is one we invented for the purposes of staff development. You need to imagine that it is handwritten in green ink on lined notepaper. (Green ink is a special favourite of the odder and more hopeless of wannabe authors.)

Box 7.1
A bad book proposal

24 Railway Cuttings
East Cheam

The Social Sciences Person
Snipcock and Tweed
36 White Horse Lane
London WC1

To Whom it May Concern

I have been working for ten years on a book about the lives of train-spotters. It will be of enormous importance to scholars in transport studies, and might interest people working on 'men's studies' as the trainspotters are all men. My book uses a unique mix of Foucault and Balint – never before reconciled! – and relates the world of the trainspotters to the blood donors of Titmuss's famous work. The research methods were also unique.

   I am enclosing the typescript – my only copy so please don't lose it – which is a bit faint at places as my toner cartridge was running out. It is about 250,000 words long (I haven't actually counted them ha ha!), and I'm afraid the dog sat on the vital pages of the theory chapter after she'd had puppies so they are a bit bloodstained.

   I look forward to receiving a contract from you, and will telephone you next week to talk about your plans for my book.

Yours faithfully,

Ebenezer Scrooge (Dr)
Research Fellow in Leisure Studies

P.S. I hope Snipcock and Tweed publish academic monographs in leisure studies. I can't afford to buy books so I haven't seen any of yours.

Of course, this is a caricature. It would be very rare to find anything that combined quite so many disasters in one. But publishers do frequently report getting communications that are not much better than this, and responding accordingly. As you can see, this sort of approach offers absolutely no help to a potential publisher. Worse still, it inspires absolutely no confidence as to the competence and professionalism of the aspiring author. The unsolicited manuscript out of the blue, with no prior contact or acquaintance, is virtually doomed to failure.

   By contrast, a sensible and well-structured proposal will go a long way towards persuading a commissioning editor that you are at least worth treating seriously. A good proposal will by no means guarantee success. If your book does not fit their list, or capture an interesting new direction they want to pursue, then a commissioning editor will not publish your book however good the actual proposal is. On the other hand, any editor needs to be persuaded to take a book, even if it does fall squarely in their normal subject matter. That is where your initial approach and your book proposal come in.

There may not be a single model for all books and for all publishers, but there are certainly some things that every publisher is going to want to know about your proposed book and about you. Compiling your proposal around those key issues will go a long way towards getting a sympathetic reading. They will not guarantee that you will get a contract, but they will help the proposal to get serious attention. The main thing to get across is to display that you know what you are doing and you know what you are proposing. This may sound laughably obvious, but like most things we are advocating and urging here, it is astonishing how many people fail to do so.

So here are some of the basic things you need to demonstrate.

The readership

You really do need to know what readership you are aiming this book at. It is obvious that there is a world of difference, editorially and commercially, between a textbook aimed at first-year undergraduates and a research monograph or a book of advanced theory that will only be suitable for postgraduate students and your fellow academics. The advice here is to be realistic. Do not invoke that illusory category 'the general reader'. General readers (whoever they are) do not get to hear about and read academic books. There are exceptions, such as bestselling blockbusters by historians or cross-over books of popular science, but they are very unusual indeed when set against the vast numbers of academic books published each year. An editor will be more impressed if you have a clear sense of what you are aiming at, even if it is modest, than a vague promise to be a runaway bestseller.

The readership also implies *level*. You need to think and to be explicit about the kind of level at which the book will be pitched. This means thinking about the style. Is this a book that will be accessible to students or practitioners with little or no knowledge of the field? Will the reader be helped with worked examples, suggestions for further reading, annotated bibliographies and the like? Will the book build on other, more elementary works? Will the text explain carefully the technical terms, or will acquaintance with the specialist topic be assumed? This is not a case of publishers trying to have authors 'dumb down' and make everything as accessible as possible to as many readers as possible. It is a practical issue of where a book is going to sit in the market, and what it is setting out to achieve.

Competition

Your editor will want to know what other books exist in the same field, and how your book compares with and differs from them. However well informed a commissioning editor is, one cannot expect her or him to know the field as well as you do. While we might all like to think that our book is original and insightful, in reality we are often trying to compete with other books. This is especially the case if the appeal of a book is that it will be adopted for course use at some level or other within further and higher education. This is a crowded market, and editors and marketing managers (of whom more later) will need to be reassured that there is room for your book, that your book will be sufficiently different or better than the existing texts. Of course, this is not the same issue that you are facing if the book is an academic monograph. Here the issue is not persuading the publisher that you can 'beat' opposing texts. Rather, you may need to persuade her or him that there are other books out there that are like yours. Even monographs do not stand alone. They have to be placed in catalogues, lists, advertisements and so on. If there are no books out there, and no books with this publisher in your chosen topic, then you may have to work hard to persuade the publishers that anyone will be interested. More probably, you will find yourself pointing out not competitors but complementary books – showing how your new book fits into an established field, a developing trend in scholarship and so on.

Market

You might think that a commercial publisher would know much more about marketing than you do, and you would be asking them about it rather than them asking you. Of course, when it comes to actually publicizing and distributing your book they do know more about it than you do. But at the point of you trying to 'sell' your idea to the publishers, it helps if you have a clear sense of the market. For instance, if this is going to be a textbook, what courses is it likely to be adopted for? Are these large (for example introductory or compulsory) courses, or likely to be smaller advanced and optional courses? Would your book be the single required purchase, or is it likely to be a supplementary 'recommended' text? Will your book sell in an international market, or only in your own country? Some things are internationally marketable. In the social sciences, for instance, theory and methods are international. Other books are not. Obviously books about social processes and social problems in one country are not widely marketable elsewhere. If the book is a monograph, who is actually likely to buy it? University libraries only, or individuals?

It helps too to give the editor a sense of a more or less captive audience out there. If your monograph is in a specialized field, it helps if you can identify learned societies and conferences where like-minded people take an interest in what you do. Indeed, this is a general selling point. Are you a member of a learned society, or a research network, or a major conference at which your book can be marketed? Is there a membership list to whom publicity materials can be sent? These kinds of considerations will do three things. First, they will help the editor identify the intellectual market. Second, they will help the marketing department ascertain how they are going to publicize and sell your book. Third, they show that you have thought about the audience for your work carefully and will work with the publisher to sell it.

Contents

Again, this seems so obvious that it goes without saying. Clearly any book proposal will need to outline the envisaged contents. But you might be surprised to learn that some (unsuccessful) proposals do not. Or at least they do not do so in a helpful way. It is not going to cut much ice if the proposed contents consist merely of cryptic chapter titles with little or no indication of what each chapter will actually contain. Equally, a list of entirely predictable contents – such as the 'standard' contents of any textbook in the field – will not give the editor grounds to believe that you really can offer a fresh perspective or a style of treatment that will stand out from the rest. Too many inexperienced would-be authors give the editor far too little to go on, with no real evidence as to how the book will be constructed, how its arguments will be developed, how it will reflect a novel treatment, how it will relate to existing literature and so on. The chapter synopses do not have to be hugely elaborate. They do not have to be mini-essays. But they do need to provide enough information to persuade a reader (who does not necessarily share your passionate commitment to the subject-matter, or share your own faith in your abilities) that you have got a sensible, feasible and interesting approach.

Length

The length of a proposed book is a crucial piece of information. It has major implications for the marketability of the final product. A book that is too long and too expensive as a consequence will not reach the student market, if that's what you are aiming at. The issue here is not the absolute length of a book, but the appropriate length for the market. A comprehensive and authoritative textbook in law, say, can be long. Many of them are. The definitive reference work that all libraries have to buy, and that students will be required to buy too, will be an attractive proposition. This can be the sort of book that goes into successive editions. A first-year comprehensive textbook on sociology, or educational psychology, or media

studies can be long. Indeed, it will have to be long if it is to be comprehensive and provide the basis for a course that lasts a whole academic year
or a whole semester. But that does not apply to monographs and more
specialist books. Publishers often have price thresholds that they feel are
psychological barriers to purchasers. Obviously the money value of those
barriers creeps up with inflation, and historically the cost inflation of book
production and distribution have outstripped average headline inflation
levels.

Equally, publishers will not necessarily welcome proposals for books that
are too short. Short books are fine in particular market niches. There are
series of primers and introductory texts that are appropriately short, and
they are often very successful in intellectual and commercial terms. Self-
help books and books of practical advice fall into this category (just like this
one). But otherwise short books are not inherently more attractive than
long ones. The costs of warehousing, distributing and marketing short
books are no less than those of longer books, and so the unit price is likely
to be disproportionately higher. It works when you have a mass-sales series,
with a clear appeal to a particular student or professional readership. The
overall length of the proposed book will therefore be an important consideration for its marketing potential. The proposal should therefore
indicate the intended length of each chapter, and therefore of the entire
book.

You also need to indicate whether there are any special typesetting
requirements or other contents, such as illustrations, music examples,
maps, diagrams, tables and so on. They are all likely to increase the costs of
typesetting and printing. One certainly cannot assume that an editor will
get excited over a fully illustrated monograph if that is likely to price it out
of the market. Equally, an introductory book might well need some illustrative and diagrammatic material, depending on the subject matter. But
this needs to be specified and justified. Editors will need to be assured that
copyright for the reproduction of illustrative material will be obtained – and
that is normally the responsibility of the author. This latter point is more
important than it may sound: we know of colleagues who have prepared
manuscripts that have been very badly delayed because they intended to
include illustrations or other copyright material that is very expensive to
obtain, or where the ownership of the reproduction rights is difficult to
track down, or where the copyright owner takes a very long time to respond
to requests. It is, therefore, a good idea to establish what permissions you
need (if any) and the costs (if any) well before the manuscript itself is
finished and submitted. The kind of work we publish rarely calls for tricky
permission, but we have experience of publication being delayed (a little,
luckily) by the failure of a major publisher to respond to a request to
reproduce just four lines of verse.

Timetable

When do you intend to deliver your manuscript? Editors have annual planning schedules to organize. They need to have a good idea of how many titles they are going to produce in a year, and they need to have an estimate of the costings of commissioning and publishing. An estimate of the delivery date is therefore an essential part of the initial planning and of the proposal. An editor would rather have a realistic date than a hopeful one.

Now publishers will often help their authors in determining these kinds of things by supplying an author's questionnaire. Such questionnaires cover the kinds of things we have just outlined – sometimes in what feels like interminable detail. One might as well show one's professionalism by anticipating most of the critical issues by covering them in the outline proposal. It would be hubris on our part to suggest that we know how to craft the perfect book proposal. There is no such thing, anyway. But so that you can get a sense of what at least one successful book proposal looks like, we have incorporated as Appendix 3 the proposal we first sent the publishers of this book. It will also allow you to compare the proposal itself with the finished book. You will be able to see how we attempted to anticipate the main issues a publisher will want to know.

How publishers handle proposals

What then happens to your carefully crafted proposal? The commissioning editor will read it, giving it the thirty seconds or more that we referred to above. Some proposals will be weeded out at that stage. Despite good advice (like ours) authors often manage to send proposals for books that have little or no relevance for a particular firm. They will have a polite but firm rejection, saying that the book is not for them and wishing you better luck with your proposal elsewhere. Assuming you have passed that hurdle, it may well be sent to one or more readers. If your proposal is for a contribution to a series, then the academic who is the series editor will have a major voice. For stand-alone volumes, publishers often have a small set of academics they trust to give sensible advice on proposals. Whether the proposal goes to a series editor, a regular reader or an untried one, it will be sent out by the publisher to get advice from a reader. These are people in the field – academics for most of the books we are considering here. They are asked to comment on the proposal, often with a checklist of questions to consider. The questions will reflect the kinds of things we have just enumerated: Would you use or recommend such a book? Is this an original approach and treatment? What is distinctive about this proposed book? Like all peer reviewing, this is mostly a labour of duty rather than love, but it carries with it only a modest material reward, usually the offer of a small cash honorarium or books to a certain value.

Kieran Marcable opened his post. There is a letter from a publisher.

Dear Kieran,
Dr MacFadyearn of Mallingford has sent us a proposal for a book on
the dispute between Chagnon and Tierney about the ethics of research
on Amazonian indigenous people. I'm not sure if it is a book we could
sell in Britain, and I am not familiar with Dr MacFadyearn's work.
Could you look at the proposal and the specimen chapter for me? I can
offer our usual fee of £50 or £75 worth of books from our catalogue (a
copy of which is enclosed). Please reply by email, fax or letter.
See you at the York conference?

Best wishes,

Sophie Bedivere
Commissioning editor, Area Studies and Anthropology

If the book receives sufficiently favourable readers' comments, then that
does not guarantee acceptance for publication. If the editor want to publish
your book then she or he will often have to put it as a proposal to other
people in the company. She or he will have to make a case not just for the
intellectual merits of your book, but also for its commercial potential. This
is an especially crucial stage in primarily commercial publishing houses. If a
marketing director is not convinced, then the book will probably not get
published. These matters vary considerably from publishing house to
publishing house. Small publishers where the commissioning editor effectively controls the list may be able to make decisions very differently from
those where corporate finance and 'the bottom line' are important. This is
where the contrasts between Apple Press and Plum Press in Powell (1985)
are informative.

All of this takes time. Authors can be quite obsessive about their own
books. Indeed, they should be, otherwise they probably will not have the
commitment to undertake the laborious work of actually writing and
revising the manuscript. But they can often forget the work that has to go
on in the publisher's offices. So common-sense advice is not to start
phoning, emailing or otherwise pestering the editor for a response as soon
as you send the proposal. If you have not heard anything for several months,
then something may have gone astray, but do not expect an enthusiastic
acceptance of your proposal by return of post.

Sophie Bedivere is staffing the Polegate and Pettifer stand at the
annual conference of the British Society for Area Studies at the conference centre on the University of York campus. She is thoroughly
bored. Everybody who hasn't gone into town shopping for the morning
seems to have gone to a session. The publishers' display area is
deserted. She's already wandered round and looked at everybody else's
book display. She's done some routine paperwork and made some
phone calls back to the office. Her friend Kieran Marcable appears,

and they go for coffee. 'I sent you the MacFadyearn proposal last week. If you can turn it round quickly I'd be grateful. She has already phoned me twice, and she seems to email every day wanting a decision. It's driving me mad. I really need a clear steer from you as to whether enough people are going to carry on being interested in that controversy to make a book worth going with.'

Some would-be authors assume that they ought to have a literary agent. For the normal academic author it is not a requirement, and can be a disadvantage. An agent is important if you are trying to publish the kind of work that will really be a trade book. A book of popular science for a publisher like Penguin, or the kind of history book that will find its way onto bestseller lists might do well with an agent, who can negotiate the best deals for royalties, reproduction and serialization rights, and so on. But otherwise, an agent is not going to know any better than you do who the most suitable publishers are likely to be. You know who publishes in your field. You know which books are well regarded, and do well. You can do the homework to find out about the small number of publishers in your special field. Some commissioning editors would rather not deal with agents anyway – who (they feel) sometimes hawk manuscripts and proposals round rather than dealing carefully with a chosen publisher. In any case, literary editors are not usually very interested in taking on academic authors, and are also not interested in working with would-be authors with no track record. Once you have become famous, or when you have a trade book proposition, then you and an agent may find mutual benefit in working together.

It certainly is possible for academic work to become a 'cross-over' book and appear in the trade book lists, even the bestsellers. Among recent examples is Amanda Foreman's (1998) biography of Georgiana, Duchess of Devonshire, which has become a popular book for the general reader. It helped that Foreman is beautiful and was prepared to pose nearly naked for publicity shots, and that Georgiana's life paralleled Diana, Princess of Wales's. In the United States work by the late socio-linguist Deborah Tannen (for example, 1990, 1995) on the communicative differences between men and women has also resulted in several books that have been marketed very successfully as trade books. Books such as these are often promoted in the same way as overtly commercial books. An agent may be invaluable in managing the publicity, such as getting spots on national radio or television chat shows.

You might think that an agent will get a better financial deal for you. As we have said, that might be the case if you are going to produce a book like *A Brief History of Time, Fermat's Last Theorem,* or *Longitude.* Otherwise, publishers have more or less standard contractual terms and conditions. These differ from publishing house to publishing house, and from type of book to type of book. Some do not pay any royalty: they publish the book, and you benefit on that score. They produce a short print run with relatively little profit for them from each title. The deal is mutually advantageous if it means that a monograph appears in the public domain, but this is not in itself a money-making deal for the author. (It can convert into material rewards indirectly, and we say more about that elsewhere.) Note that this is not necessarily 'vanity publishing' – although in a sense all authors are vain, and so all publication feeds their vanity! Small monograph presses and some of the university presses pay no royalty. Sometimes there may be a deal whereby no royalties are paid on the first print run, and royalties only result if copies are sold beyond that, after the book has covered initial costs ('washed its face').

More commercial deals, including the publication of textbooks, do generate royalties. These are normally at standard rates and are not normally matters of negotiation. Most of us would be lucky indeed if we had such a hot property that we could find ourselves talking up the royalty by a percentage point or two. Unless you have reason to think that there is something really odd about a contract, then having your lawyer inspect it is probably pretty pointless. In any case, for many books you will have paid more for the legal advice than you will get back in royalties.

Hitherto you will note that we have assumed that you are trying to get a contract for your book, or you are helping your colleagues get a contract, without having written the book first. On the whole, writing books speculatively and then trying to find a publisher is dangerous. You may find that you have written a book entirely to your own satisfaction, but that does not fit any publisher's current interests. If you have completed the manuscript, then you will not have had the chance to shape it in accordance with a publisher's own advice and interests. You may find yourself having to re-write the entire thing to accommodate a publisher, or – even worse – you may find that you have a completely unpublishable manuscript. This is clearly a terrible waste of time and effort. It is also a long and harrowing business trying successive publishers.

Equally, if you or your colleagues are first-time authors, with a modest track record, a publisher may well want you to prepare a specimen chapter before committing herself or himself to issuing a contract. This is usually a reasonable way to go. Editors would not normally ask an established author to do so, as they should be able to assure themselves that the author can write and can deliver. But if you have a colleague who wants to write a first book, then it is no bad thing to have a specimen chapter already prepared, or at least to be prepared to write such a chapter if asked by a commissioning editor.

We have mentioned at several points in the chapter differences between textbooks, general academic books and specialist monographs. Before leaving the single-authored text for a discussion of joint projects, we will just rehearse a few points about different types of book. Publishers usually want textbooks, especially textbooks they can sell outwith the UK. In sociology that means texts on issues that are universal, especially methods or theories. By textbook here, we mean university textbooks, not those for school children: those are very specific to one particular nation. In the UK if you can write a successful school textbook it will make you money, and it can boost recruitment to your department, but it will damage your academic reputation, unless you have previously and subsequently published very serious scholarly works. Textbooks for Year One undergraduates, or for groups like trainee nurses, social workers, teachers or dentists, are potentially lucrative, but do nothing for their authors' reputations as scholars. Books that could be used for second- and third-year undergraduates, as long as they contain material useful to lecturers, can escape the stigma of being textbooks, and earn both royalties and academic credit for you. Hammersley and Atkinson's (1983, 1995) *Ethnography: Principles in Practice*, for example, is used for undergraduate and graduate classes, but is also read by other academics. Publishers prefer such books. It is only a slightly caricatured picture to envisage an author offering a detailed exegesis of the manorial rolls of the Wallace-Gromit family between 1503 and 1543, and the publisher asking for an undergraduate text on 'Tudor England' or 'The Wars of the Roses and the Rise of the Tudors' or some such broad topic. The young scholar offering the detailed book on the views of the British cabinet or the Berlin airlift is likely to be asked to write generally on the Cold War in Europe, or the impact of Yalta. In each of these cases, the scholarly reputation of the author will be enhanced by the exegesis, as will their income and that of the publisher. Sometimes the solution is to write both: to negotiate a contract for the precious work of scholarship and the text the publishers think they can sell.

So far we have been discussing book publication as if a single-authored book was the sole possibility. Obviously that is not so. First, there is the option of joint authorship. Second, there is the possibility of editing collections of papers.

Joint authorship between two or more colleagues is one of the ways in which collaborative work between members of a research group can be manifested. While many people will reckon that a research-active career in the humanities and social sciences really needs solely authored monographs – and that is right on the whole – joint authorship among a research group is an important way of promoting and capitalizing on collaborative research. There are different methods of joint writing. There is no right way to do it, of course, but like most practical tasks it is worth thinking about what works for you and your colleagues. Collaborative writing can be extraordinarily productive and enjoyable. But it can also place an enormous strain on personal and professional relationships. If things go wrong, or if partners turn out to be incompatible, then the experience can be a stressful one. So it is in everybody's interests to avoid stress by thinking sensibly about how to approach and how to organize joint authorship.

A jointly written book is just like any other in terms of writing the synopsis and the proposal, and planning out the timetable. From there, one way of proceeding is to have each author take prime responsibility for different chapters. If two authors do about half the chapters each, they can then swap first drafts and re-work from there. This is fine so long as you agree fundamentally about what you are arguing. It can go awfully sour if each takes apart the other's draft and changes things radically. That can happen. Instead of working productively on the book, authors find themselves locked into a destructive cycle of drafting. This is avoided if they make sure they agree a common approach and stick to it. It is also avoidable if each author suppresses some of his or her cherished ideas, at least until there is a complete first draft that is broadly satisfactory to both of them.

Another way of working is for one partner to undertake the planning or the first draft, and the other to take the next stage and so on. Again, this is fine. It can go wrong if such an arrangement is not explicit. Otherwise, the author who takes responsibility for doing the first drafts can feel exploited, especially if the partner does not seem to do much re-drafting. Even worse, of course, is when the second author is negatively critical of the first drafts. Again, it is possible for even close colleagues to fall out, each thinking (and sometimes saying) 'Well, why don't you do it yourself then, if you know so much better.' This is best avoided.

Many joint authorships have the added complication of a status difference between the partners. There are many advantages to authorship between a more senior and a more junior author. It can be an excellent opportunity for the younger or more junior colleague to benefit from the experience of a more experienced and more senior collaborator. The older partner can benefit from new ideas, energy and motivation from a younger colleague. Sometimes that can lead to a fruitful partnership that is avowedly unequal – so long as it is not exploitative. The more senior partner can help map out the general direction and the main ideas, while the junior partner does more of the donkey work and the detailed drafting. Such an unequal division of labour is all right, provided it is explicitly recognized and negotiated to the authors' mutual benefit.

However you decide to divide up the work, and however joint responsibility is allocated, the most important thing is to make sure that all parties are comfortable with the arrangements. Fruitful writing partnerships are not best founded on misunderstandings and mutual resentment. It is also important to have a reasonable sense of how one's co-author prefers to work. As we have already discussed, each person's writing style can differ, as can the ways in which she or he organizes personal work. Some people like to work steadily and to a plan. Others are less organized, and some of them write things in a great rush at the last minute. If your work timetables and rhythms are not compatible at that level, then you will have to find ways of accommodating to otherwise uncomfortable work styles and patterns. Joint authorship is not necessarily an easy solution. In many ways the graft of drafting chapters is shared among the co-authors, and so reduced for any one of them. On the other hand, co-authorship creates its own stresses and strains. We have just alluded to some of them. If you are going to embark on writing jointly with one or more colleagues, therefore, you need to have some practical understanding of the following issues.

The division of labour

How are you going to divide up the tasks? Will one person be responsible for doing the first drafts, and then the other will re-draft, and so on? Will each do the first draft of a different chapter or section and then swap? Is one of you better at one aspect, and will have a first shot at that?

Intellectual style

Do you both actually agree sufficiently to write together? You may both be interested in and committed to 'the same' topic, but that does not actually guarantee that you will agree as to the argument of a paper, a chapter or a book. You need to be able to find sufficient common ground to be able to create a joint product. Moreover, you need to be able to pool your ideas and expertise in such a way that the sum is greater than the parts – so that the writing collaboration is more than or better than what each one of you could have done separately: this involves a certain suppression of individual pride.

Who's taking the lead?

However much you approach co-authorship on an egalitarian footing, you will probably find that one of you needs to be the prime mover in order to keep the project moving. It can help to decide who is going to have that role from the outset. In practice, it can change over the course of the project, and it can certainly change if the writing partnership becomes a long-term one. If there is a status difference between you, you need to make sure that it is not unduly influencing the intellectual work. It is important to make sure that the more junior author is not suppressing her or his ideas, and being unduly deferential towards the more senior partner. Equally, it is important to guard against intellectual exploitation or even bullying on the part of the senior author.

We say these things not in order to put our readers off working together, but to help them make co-authorship productive. There is, however, one further word of caution. Writing with one or more partners is a good thing in principle. In many disciplines it is the norm and is good in cementing research groups and other collaborations. But in some disciplines – especially in the humanities and social sciences – it carries some dangers. It is important in those kinds of disciplines to establish one's own presence in the field and one's own reputation as a sole author alongside any joint publications. The world of appointing panels and promotions committees can get uneasy if a candidate appears to have no separate and individual intellectual identity. We ourselves have published a number of things together and have worked together for a long time. We have academic interests in common. But we made a very clear and conscious decision to avoid publishing too much together in the earlier years of our careers. Academic couples who publish together a lot can run the risk of always being thought of as a matching pair. Vice-chancellors, referees and others need to know that you have an academic reputation in your own right. So collaborative authorship is something to be pursued, if at all, alongside other commitments that establish one's own credentials separately.

We have not, so far, said anything about producing books that compose the writings of others: editing collections, translations, or the texts of others. These, in moderation, do not harm a career, but they are very time consuming. Translating the work of non-English-speaking scholars is invaluable for colleagues, but will not advance your career. Collecting the papers of a dead colleague, or an eminent person, will also be welcomed by others, but does little for your career. Robert Burgess (1995), for example, did not advance his career by collecting the papers Howard Becker had published on education, although it is useful for educational researchers to have them all in one volume. We have not discussed such compilations any further here.

Editing collections of papers

Editing a collection of papers, either individually or in collaboration, is another publishing activity that has benefits and some potential dangers. In this day and age of Research Assessment concerns, it must be recognized that editing volumes in and of itself is not always highly valued. Being the editor of a book does not carry anything like the same weight as writing a book, or even writing a good journal article, so it should not be thought of as a substitute for original authorship. Does this mean that it is not worth doing at all? Certainly not. One just has to know what one is doing and why.

An edited collection of papers can arise from a number of sources. It may be the result of a conference you have organized or helped organize. It is fairly common to at least try to publish selected papers from a conference or symposium: the potential for publication is an incentive for your conference participants. Moreover – and this is the real point – it can help to stake an intellectual claim to a particular academic field. If you are bringing together experts, possibly on an international basis, in your field, and opening up new avenues of scholarship, then the proceedings of the conference can be a valuable research contribution in their own right. (See our remarks on conferences as mechanisms of dissemination and networking in Chapter 8.)

In the same way, an edited collection of original papers that maps out a major set of contributions to the field – reporting on new approaches, new theories, new scholarship or whatever – can in itself be an important contribution. This is especially so if the editorial work that is performed is in itself 'value added'. In other words, as the editor, you need to ensure a number of things. First, the edited collection needs to be coherent, addressing a substantial topic or theme that is intrinsically significant.

Second, the contributions need to be of uniformly high quality. This means that editorial work should be quite demanding. People who have not done this kind of work sometimes think that there is nothing more to it than slinging together a series of papers written by other people, and then claiming the result as a 'publication'. But putting together a random collection of papers of patchy quality will not enhance your reputation, and will do nothing for the reputation of your research group or department. Success calls for proper editorial effort. That means: making sure your contributors have something worth writing about; working hard on their draft chapters to ensure that the final versions are all of high quality; working on the volume overall to ensure even quality; putting effort into the editorial matter. This last means ensuring that there is an editorial essay or introduction that is a substantial contribution in its own right, that does more than simply introduce and list the contributions, and lays out the intellectual rationale for the volume as a whole, staking the claim for its originality and its importance for the academic community.

If you look at the disastrous proposal for an edited collection in Box 7.2, you will be able to find plenty of reasons why no publisher would be interested in it.

Box 7.2
Proposal for the edited collection

School of Social Sciences
Cardiff University
King Edward VII Avenue
Cardiff CF10 3WT
Wales, UK

Ms Lettuce Wyn-Jones
Social Science Editor
Snodgrass and Pettigrew
36 White Horse Lane
London WCQ 4RX

Dear Ms Wyn-Jones

I am writing on behalf of a small group of young scholars at Cardiff University. We ran a conference on 'masculinities and the new nationalism' here last month. We would like to publish the best papers in an edited volume, and enclose the proposed contents. Would you be at all interested in it?

Yours sincerely,

Jacob Marley MA, PhD
Lecturer in Sociology
e-mail *MarleyJ@cardiff.ac.uk*

Masculinity and Nationalism

Introduction	J Marley *et al.*	10,000 words
Scotland	J Marley	10,000 words
Latvia	X Wilderbeest	3000 words
Peru	Z Trueba	5000 words
Manchuria	P Williams	5000 words
Macedonians in Melbourne	L Danforth	not known
Conclusions	J Marley *et al.*	10,000 words

N.B. Danforth did not come to our conference, but we think he might be interesting.

You will have spotted several problems with this proposal, including the plan to include a paper by a big name (Loring Danforth) who was not at the conference and clearly has not been asked for a contribution yet. Danforth (1995) produced an important book on Macedonians in Melbourne, and if he were interested in being in a book it would increase its attraction for a publisher: but the wannabe editors would need to show that he was committed to sending them a chapter. Other problems with this proposal, apart from the total lack of details on market, delivery date and so on, are the preponderance of contributions by Marley (in number and length) and the wide geographical range it covers. Potential readers interested in both Scotland and Manchuria are probably rather rare and unusual people. Such a proposal is likely to get sent back with a cursory 'we are not commissioning any edited collections at present' letter. Good conferences do not make good books without considerable editorial work.

Books and esteem

We know that not everybody needs to publish books, and not everybody therefore needs to be unduly concerned about the processes and decisions we have outlind in this chapter. That does not absolve them from having some understanding of the issues, however. Laboratory scientists who restrict their publications to journals may find themselves on promotions committees, looking at the curricula vitae of specialists in humanities and the social sciences. There is, therefore, a need for a wider understanding of publishing. (Equally, our humanities colleagues need to have an informed understanding about the cultures of scientific publishing, for the same reasons.)

In the current climate of competitive evaluation of personal and institutional performance in research and publishing, one finds some unhelpful beliefs about publishing and book publishers. First, one should be careful of evaluating the quality of published work solely on the basis of the reputation of the publishing house. Some outstanding work does not get published by the big houses on commercial grounds. There are always smaller and less well known publishers who occupy niche markets, who can break even on a smaller volume of sales, and who often publish good books. Equally, therefore, while aspiring academics will often want to have their work published by one of the prestige publishers, they should not despair or think that their reputation will not be enhanced if they cannot do so.

Second, the current emphasis on the publication of *research* does not mean that books also aimed at more 'textbook' markets are beyond the pale. In the humanities and social sciences, we do not gain kudos from writing basic school- or college-level introductory textbooks. But if one looks at a lot of books that are published – including those by big names in the field – then a lot of them are what are becoming known as 'hybrid' books. They are books that are somewhere between original works of scholarship and textbooks. They often mingle the author's research with broader and more didactic content, which can include introductory discussions of general theory, methodological perspectives, or *tours d'horizon* of the field – espcially emergent new specialisms. One should not necessarily avoid such publications, simply because they are not 'research' in the pure sense. Research monographs just will not get published in many cases, or will only get published by smaller publishers. The more general books will get published, will reach a much wider readership, and have the chance of reconfiguring the field. They may bring new ideas or new syntheses of ideas into the mainstream of the discipline. They are often the vehicle whereby their author establishes her or his position in the field, and builds a reputation nationally and internationally. Be wary, therefore, of collegial advice that is so fixated on the most narrow of evaluative criteria that they cannot see the bigger picture of how one actually moves forward the discipline and one's own position within it.

8

Other dissemination: 'expeditious diffusions'

'Their function was not merely to make knowledge but to diffuse it as expeditiously as possible' (Stewart 1976: 162). Pattullo is here describing two successful scholars, but it should apply to all academics. In the previous three chapters we have discussed writing, publishing in the academic journals, and publishing books. In this one we turn to other forms of dissemination: reports to funding bodies and feedback to those studied, doing conference posters, giving conference papers, running a conference, the pros and cons of departmental working papers, websites and other electronic disseminations, editing journals and starting a new journal, influencing policy making and dealing with the media. These are all part of being a successful academic in the twenty-first century.

> It is September in Perth, and the annual conference of the British Association for Narrative and Life History Studies is in full swing. A multidisciplinary society, across humanities and social sciences, Roger and Dermot are both members. They are having breakfast together and discussing their publication and dissemination plans. Dermot has had a small grant from the British Academy, and is preparing his final report. Roger has been asked by a friend to appear on a radio programme to talk about his research, and wonders if he should accept.

These are the sorts of opportunities for dissemination that shrewd scholars seize upon.

Reports to funding bodies

There are two kinds of document here: reports on standardized forms and those you have to structure yourself. The big funders, such as the Research Councils and the big charitable foundations, have official forms for the final report, and prescribe the format. Other, smaller funders, such as local government bodies, small charities and bodies who only give grants occasionally, do not usually have a set format for their reports, but will expect a coherent account of the results in a usable style. We deal with each type in turn.

The precise structure and content of a final report will be dependent on the requirements of the funding body and the structure of their final report form (if they have one) and their instructions to award-holders. Clearly, the sensible thing is to think about the nature of the final report well before your sponsor's deadline. Just because it is called 'final', that does not mean that it has to be the last thing you do as part of the project, nor that it is done at the last minute. The end-of-award report need not be burdensome. We all encourage our students and younger colleagues, after all, to 'write early and write often', when preparing doctoral theses, book drafts and papers for publication. We should apply that maxim to topics like reports too. Most of the key contents will be self-evident, and one can certainly draft many of the key components well before the actual termination of the award.

The practical advice, therefore, is to find out what is expected of an end-of-award report and start preparing draft materials well before the end. One can certainly expect to include all or most of the following things:

- The original aims and objectives of the project;
- The conduct of the research (for example, data collection, analysis);
- Any problems you encountered or departures from the original research design;
- Research highlights and key findings;
- Implications for policy;
- Publications and other outputs from the research – actual and planned.

You may be required to accompany the report itself with selected papers. Sponsors will very likely want to have an executive summary. They may also want an even shorter summary, as the basis for press releases, or their own annual reporting. Your institution's finance office or research office will also need to provide a final summary report of the financial side of the research award.

As well as being a part of your dissemination strategy, and a contractual obligation anyway, these reports are also part of the general patter of peer review. Most bodies have end-of-award reports read by peer reviewers, and they may award a grade on the basis of such reviews. Hence the project will have received two grades – once when it was awarded an alpha grade to get funded, and once after the research has been completed. Just as with the research proposal, good evaluations of final reports rest very much on the clarity with which the research is reported. The original aims need to match up with the outcomes. The research needs to have been conducted in accordance with the original research design, or departures from the original plans need to be explained and justified very explicitly. The outcomes, highlights and implications need to be expressed clearly and explicitly. Executive or non-technical summaries also need to be what they say they are: comprehensible to a non-specialist. Since you know roughly what you will be expected to produce, you can certainly draft most of the report as the research progresses.

Intellectual property

One impediment to dissemination can be disputes over who owns the ideas and results: the ownership of intellectual property rights (IPR). There can be problems when a funding body believes that it owns the results, and problems when the funders feel they need to keep the results confidential, either because commercial rivals can benefit from them or because they do not agree with the research results. Often funding bodies are ignorant about the needs of academics for publications, and this too can lead to disputes.

It is important to get the IPR issues clear when the grant is being awarded, and to set out the procedures for any vetting of potential conference papers, journal articles and books. If you are seeking funding from any body which is not a mainstream funder such as a Research Council, it is sensible to consult the experts in your institution about any restrictive or potentially restrictive clauses in the contract. If the funder has not mentioned IPR or publication at all, then it is wise to find a standard 'freedom' clause and get it inserted.

In the 1960s and 1970s there was a body in England called the Schools Council which funded evaluations of curricula innovations. When reports came in, they could not be published until a committee, dominated by representatives from the teaching unions, had approved them. These union stalwarts had no knowledge of the demands on university researchers to publish. Many potential publications were stopped, were delayed for many months, were effectively censored. We therefore know much less about curriculum change in England than we should do. In Cardiff we did some research for the Welsh Office in the 1980s that the civil servants and the advisory committee hated: they flatly refused to believe the findings, they objected to the lack of positive case studies, they quibbled about the pseudonyms (not Welsh enough). We changed the pseudonyms – a school we had called Artinswell became Aberelwy – because that was trivial. We went back and found half a dozen exemplary teachers in our data whose successes could be written up as positive role models: we had no desire to suggest that there were no teachers managing the innovation. However, we could not change the main findings: in most schools, most of the time, the innovation had not happened, the schools were ignoring it, implementing it by breaking the Sex Discrimination Act, or subverting it in clever ways. The Welsh Office never published the bulk of the report: they disseminated the exemplary case studies to 'prove' that the innovation was a great success. They did not, however, censor the academic publications that we wrote.

When commercially sensitive material is collected for a PhD thesis, it is normal to put an embargo on access to that thesis for several years. Such embargoes can also be imposed if there are data in the thesis that could be dangerous to the informants: if, for example, the data were collected in a country with a dictator who might send secret police to read the thesis and trace the respondents, to damage them or the researcher.

When the research is not for a thesis, the possibilities of embargoing the report, and the consequences for the investigator's career of non-publication, are much more problematic. Sometimes it is helpful to find a senior person – a professor, a pro vice-chancellor, a dean, even a vice-chancellor – to talk to the funding body: especially if they do not understand how vital publications are for the individual career and the RAE. A compromise may be possible.

Feedback to informants

In social sciences there is frequently a commitment, or a desire, to provide feedback to the people who were studied: so, for example, if the project was an evaluation of an after-school club, there might be feedback to the children, the parents and the playleaders, as well as the formal report to the government department that funded the evaluation. These reports might need to be done rather differently: for example, the children might get their feedback in a comic strip, the parents in a parents' meeting and a newsletter, the playleaders might get a copy of the report to the funding body with a covering letter.

Departmental working papers

In social science the coming of the web has revitalized the old idea of working papers. In the 1960s and 1970s many groups or departments 'published' working papers: usually pamphlets, which were sold, or circulated free, to disseminate work. The RAE largely killed them off, because they were not a peer-reviewed form of output yet could be expensive to produce and distribute. Hard copies of departmental working papers can have an ISBN, which places them in the public domain, and therefore gives them a 'proper' standing. Production of such working papers in hard copy entailed a legal requirement to deposit copies with the copyright libraries (the British Library, Oxford, Cambridge, the National Library of Scotland, the National Library of Wales, and Trinity Dublin). However, with the arrival of the web, many social scientists have launched new series of working papers to disseminate their research. Issues of cost are now relatively unimportant because nowadays they are being placed on websites or circulated electronically. Currently there is no legal requirement for electronic documents to be deposited in copyright libraries, so that 'cost' is also avoided. Nor is there an agreed system of ISBNs for electronic working papers if no hard copies are produced.

Pre-prints

In the sciences, the circulation of pre-prints served the same function as the working paper in the arts and social sciences: ideas were disseminated quickly by pre-print. Again electronic circulation has replaced the old roneo-ed or xeroxed text sent by post or faxed. In the sciences the circulation of new ideas among core sets who are advancing the research in specific areas is a precursor to peer-reviewed publication which allows the people at the cutting edge to restrict current awareness of brand new research to the core members of international networks. The consequence is that marginal groups or individuals remain outside the loop. It is, therefore, important to try to break into networks of circulation, including the circulation of preliminary findings.

Conferences

Academic life is permeated with conferences of all shapes and sizes. Arts and social science conferences are described in novels: most famously in David Lodge's (1984) novel *Small World*. Science and engineering meetings are less prominent in novels but just as important in the real world – in many ways more so. In the latter, the abstracts, or proceedings, of conferences are recognized as a form of peer-reviewed publication, and entries in such conference proceedings are routine on the curriculum vitae of scientists and engineers. In arts and social sciences there are some conferences with little peer review, the peer-review status of many conference papers is obscure, and there is no tradition of the abstracts being published, or recognized as publications. The work done on preparing conference papers is rewarded in science and engineering because the conference proceedings are a recognized 'publication'. This is less common in humanities and social sciences, and so it is vital that you and your team colleagues and doctoral students submit conference papers to journals, and make good efforts to turn them into 'real' publications as soon as possible.

When building a research career it is vital to strut your stuff at relevant conferences, and when you are building a research group you need to ensure that the group's work is profiled successfully. There are five main ways to perform at conferences: the poster, the round table presentation, the paper, or being the chair or the discussant in a session or symposium. Additionally, there can be scope to organize sessions, or symposia, or short training courses, or even to give one of the invited addresses, and, most demandingly, to run the whole meeting. We have discussed each in turn.

In the UK, conferences are frequently held in universities, while in the

USA they are usually in hotels. David Lodge (1984) describes a typical British conference, held in the University of Rummidge, in the industrial English Midlands, where the delegates sleep in rundown student rooms without private lavatories or showers, and eat dull institutional food. Fifty-seven people attend the Rummidge English literature conference which opens Lodge's novel, but readers are told that there would have been 150 if it had been in Oxford or Cambridge because these are attractive cities with great bookshops and are the alma mater of most UK lecturers. At such a small meeting, there would only be one session at a time, or perhaps two parallel sessions, and probably only one publisher would attend. UK-wide organizations can have annual meetings with 1000–5000 people at them, but 300–500 is normal for an arts or social science meeting. At the other end of the scale are the big American conferences, such as the Modern Language Association (MLA), the American Education Research Association (AERA), and the American Psychological Society (APS) or the American Medical Association (AMA). The MLA has 10,000 delegates, AERA 11,000, the APS about 30,000.

The AERA has 66 parallel sessions in two-hour blocks from 8.15 a.m. to 6.00 p.m.: each of which has four or five papers in it: a total of about 2000 conventional papers, plus the same again in posters and round table pre sentations. In the UK the timings of conferences vary a little because they are usually planned for the vacations. A learned society which always meets in the week before Easter will find its conference scheduled for any time between 12 March and 20 April, depending on the date of Easter. In the USA many of the big meetings occur in term time: the anthropologists and the criminologists meet in November, for example. The big meetings move around the conference cities: those with big hotels and conference centres. The MLA, which occurs between Christmas and New Year, is usually in New York. The AERA moves around those few cities with enough hotels, and takes place from Easter Monday to the following Saturday. In 2001 it was in Seattle, in 2002 in New Orleans, in 2003 in Chicago. Chicago is one of America's big convention cities, and there are two novels about big academic conferences set there. Emma Lathen (1982) features a massive American plant science conference in Chicago, but there is a detective story set at the MLA (Jones 1993) when it is taking place in Chicago. The Lodge novel is the most famous fictional account of the full range of academic conferences and includes the MLA. Lodge calls the MLA 'a market as well as a circus' (pp. 313–4) and that does very well as a description for the AMA, or any other whopper. Big conferences are markets for people, for books and journals, as well as for food, souvenirs and sex. The American higher education institutions do a good deal of recruiting at the big conferences, so a dean or departmental chair may spend all five days interviewing prospective lecturers in a hotel suite, and never attend any papers at all. Between the small national conference and the enormous American and international jamborees, there are, in many disciplines, intermediate events either pulling together specialists in a small field (for example, just catalysis specialists not all chemists) or researchers from neighbouring countries. In educational research, there is a Nordic/Scandinavian conference, one for the Australian association, one in the South Pacific, and one for Europe. For most disciplines in Britain, the British conference and the American conference are particularly important because the language is English. European conferences can be important, but British scholars rarely have good enough language skills to present papers or understand them in anything but English. (Some European conferences have adopted English as their language, of course.) Few British scholars go to Latin American conferences, although they will go to international meetings when they are held in Latin America. Australasian conferences are very expensive to get to for many would-be delegates from North America and Europe, and that can be a deterrent to them. In general a good career is built on regular attendance and presentations at the British conferences with occasional performances at an American one.

These conferences are a vital part of the American academic year, but also serve as international conferences because scholars from all the other countries attend. It is easier to meet two Australians, a Japanese and a Chilean collaborator at the American conference than to assemble them anywhere else. Confusingly, the American meetings sometimes take place outside the USA: in Canada, or Mexico. The Society for Applied Anthropology (SfAA) is a largely American society, but in 1981 it met in Edinburgh.

In many disciplines there are also enormous international meetings which move round the world, and take place once every two, four or five years. In sociology there is the ISA, which meets once every four years, and has been in, among other places, Varna, Aix-en-Provence, Mexico City (polluted, and dangerous), Gothenburg (expensive), Delhi (upset stomachs and visa problems), Madrid (too hot), Bielefeld (no hotels, long bus rides) and Brisbane. These meetings are useful on the CV, but are rarely academically stimulating.

Generally, there are only funds to go to conferences for those giving papers: so planning needs to start up to a year ahead. Usually the 'call for papers' goes out 12 months before the meeting, with a deadline for abstracts about 9 to 10 months before the event. Such calls are usually in the newsletter of the learned society and on its website. If you are not a member, find a colleague who is, and borrow the 'call'. Some learned societies only accept papers from members, others are open, others will take papers from non-members if a member sponsors them. It is often easier to get a symposium, or a session, into a programme, rather than an isolated paper, especially if you can persuade a big name to be the notional organizer, or to act as chair, and/or to act as discussant of the session or symposium. Whether you are submitting a proposal for a poster, a round table paper, a full paper, a whole session, or a symposium it is vital to help the referees and the conference organizers to handle your application quickly. Like work on journals, most people refereeing conference submissions are doing it on top of a full-time job as an altruistic task, and so the easier their task is, the better your chance of getting accepted. The submission may be by email, but it can be a matter of completing forms and enclosing stamped addressed envelopes and postcards, or international reply coupons. Be careful to supply all the information required in the correct format – if it is going overseas be careful to ensure it all goes airmail, or if necessary is couriered.

Small, regional and local conferences are usually glad to have papers offered, unless they are elite and/or by invitation only. With large, national or international conferences it may be harder to get a full paper onto the programme, so junior people may need to settle for a poster or a round table session. If you are building a research group, it is a good idea to check that the team all know about poster sessions, round tables, papers, panel sessions, plenary lectures and other sessions called things like fireside chats, 'meet the author', business meetings, short courses and social events. They will also need guidance on how to make the most of their time at the conference – you need to ensure that they know why they are going, and what the aims of attendance are, for them and for the group. It is too easy for the novice to treat the conference as a holiday, a party, or to be overwhelmed and baffled. If you are the senior person, you need to help them choose the sessions to attend, the people to meet, and how to use the publishers' exhibits. You may need to help colleagues grasp conference politics and impression management. If you or a colleague is presenting, then ensure that your paper is rehearsed, runs to time, and that you can cope if the pre-ordered audiovisual equipment fails. Ensure that there is an opening slide with name, address and affiliations clearly displayed. Acknowledge the funding body, and absent colleagues. A coherent paper that is audibly presented and finishes promptly is quite rare: one that is crisp and makes a couple of memorable points even rarer. You and your team can shine quite easily. Check that the slides or Powerpoint presentation are legible from the back of the room, and do not assume people can assimilate large amounts of data in small typefaces at high speed. Tell them the data are available if they email, or are visible on a website. Dress in a bright colour, one that does not immediately show sweat marks if you are nervous. Do not read the paper: speak up and out at the audience.

Audience behaviour is also important, and different conferences have different conventions about criticism and tough questions that you and your team need to learn. In the social sciences, American conferences are more polite than British ones: opponents tend to boycott sessions by scholars they disagree with, not attend and confront. Asking a question is a good way to publicize yourself and your group, but a constructive, even sycophantic question is more productive for network building. Criticisms of the work of others can be done better in print. Standing up and saying 'I'm Dermot Garroby from Wedmarsh in the UK. I really enjoyed the paper, and we have some parallel results', or 'I'd like to ask for more details about ...', or 'for some clarification of ...' or 'some further expansion about ...' gets your group good exposure. Saying 'Why have you left out Bahktin?', or 'You should have used multiple regression on Table 13', or 'I don't believe your detector will ever find any gravity waves' is only sensible when you are such a big name that you can say anything.

At American social science conferences there is often a discussant, who has prepared an overview of all the papers in the session. If your session has such a person, it is vital to get a copy of the paper, or at least the main points of its argument, to the discussant so they can assimilate it. This ensures your paper gets discussed, gets discussed sensibly, and may even get you useful feedback. Once at the AERA Philip Jackson opened his presentation as discussant by saying he had not been given one paper at all, and a second had been pushed under the door of his hotel room at 9.00 p.m. the previous evening, so he was not going to refer to them at all. He focused his praise and analytic skills on the two he had had by the deadline.

Everyone should come home with a set of business cards, a set of emails to use for further contact, some new friends, and an enhanced sense of self-worth. It is also important to turn all the conference presentations into publications as soon as possible. Based on the poster, the round table or the paper, there should be a journal article.

There are several different strategies for choosing which papers to attend. Many Americans choose only sessions with high-status people from top institutions and/or sessions featuring themes and ideas they agree with. When one of us is at an American conference, we try to hear papers about topics that do not get into the UK literature or the journals taken in UK libraries. Some younger colleagues like to go to sessions where they can see 'big names', so they have a face and a performance to go with their reading of that person's work. (It is often a salutary experience to discover that big names do not necessarily make good speakers.) As the editors of a journal, we are frequently hoping to hear papers we can solicit as submissions for it. There is also a strategy of going to a session because you expect a friend to be at it, so you can see them; or going hoping to introduce yourself to the panel at the end to widen your circle of acquaintance.

Running a conference

Organizing a conference is a thankless task, but it has to be done. It is possible to stage a conference for a specific purpose, or to organize one of the regular meetings of an existing body. The former can be risky – because it is possible that no one will come. The latter is bound to draw core members of the existing body. Many meetings are very dependent on the energy of a particular group of people: there were two very well-attended day conferences in 1997 and 1999 at the Crewe Campus of the Manchester Metropolitan University on controversies in educational research, but when the prime movers changed jobs the series died. In 2002 a planned meeting of an American-based group, which was to be held unusually outside the

USA in Manchester, had to be cancelled because so few people had registered for it that it would have been uneconomic, although a previous UK-
based meeting of that group in 1996 had been attended by about 80 to 100
people. Generally, organizing the regular conference of an existing body is
less risky, because the members will be expecting a conference at that time
of year, and have budgeted and planned for it. Usually, learned societies
advertise for bids to host or organize the conference several years ahead:
that is, in 2004 they will ask groups who want to run or host it in 2006 or
2008 or 2010 to prepare a bid. Organizing the bids, the meeting rooms, the
audiovisual, the breakfasts, the vegan banquet and the transport from the
station is all pretty miserable. If the event is to be on a campus, there may be
a good conference office who will deal with that. There are also professional
firms who run the practicalities, although they push up the costs. Until you
have seen how unable most academics are to fill in a simple form stating if
they need Powerpoint for their paper, or a double room, or a kosher diet,
you have not really become a battle-hardened scholar.

Organizing the academic programme is more intellectually interesting,
especially deciding which papers to accept and reject and which papers to
put together in sessions. Finding chairs for sessions is important, briefing
them to be tough enforcers of the timetable even more vital. Running a
successful conference can be a very good way of showcasing your university,
your department or your research group. You can invite influential people
to be plenary or keynote speakers, and you can encourage key research
groups to give papers or present posters. This in itself is an excellent way of
networking and building reputations. Regular conference series on a particular theme can help to make your department or group well known as a
centre of influence or excellence.

Of course, if you are going to follow that strategy, then it follows that what
you provide must be reasonably impressive. If you are going to encourage
people to come – and certainly if you ever expect them to come again –
then you need to make sure that things run well, and that the facilities are
appropriate. Not all hotels are equally well geared up to run a conference
(whatever their publicity materials say) and not all universities are equally
good at looking after delegates. There is one major UK university – which
had better remain nameless here – whose halls of residence have given Paul
food poisoning on two occasions: the last time he presented at a conference
there he stayed elsewhere, touched no food, and had as little to do with the
physical setting as possible. Other delegates who had not been forewarned,
many from overseas, complained bitterly about the squalid accommodation,
barely edible food, and poor facilities.

Other possible benefits and spin-offs from conferences can include the
publication of edited papers, or even series of papers. If people have gone
to the trouble of preparing a paper or a plenary address, then they may well
be willing to have it included in an edited volume. A conference with a clear
theme, or with clearly themed strands, can often yield a series of papers
that make a genuine contribution to the intellectual field. Many of the

interesting edited collections that one encounters have started life as a conference, or a symposium.

Editing a journal

It may not be obvious why we have included editing a journal as part of our discussion of dissemination. In a narrow sense, of course, it is not. If you are editing a journal, then you cannot publish any of your own papers in it, and you have to be very scrupulous about publishing anything by close colleagues. However, there are several ways in which taking a spell at the helm of a journal can enhance the reputation of a scholar, her research group, her ideas and her intellectual priorities. If Dr MacFadyearn of Mallingford University becomes the editor of *Latin American Anthropology*, then scholars from all over the world will know that Mallingford has a reputable anthropology department and that Dr MacFadyearn exists. The publishers ought to provide some money, so that there will be some clerical support and some funds for editorial expenses. There may be travel money to go to conferences. Being the editor of a journal can lead to appearances on panels, at pre-conference workshops, at summer schools and so on. The ongoing editorial work can provide postgraduates and postdoctoral staff with valuable experience of peer-reviewing and the exercise of academic judgement. While they cannot do the decision-making (that is the prerogative of the editor(s)), they can be party to it and contribute to it.

The amount of freedom editors have to make a difference to a journal varies a good deal. But while *Latin American Anthropology* is at Mallingford it might be possible for Dr MacFadyearn to make her mark in Latin American studies in several ways. It is possible to have a special issue that becomes well known in its own right, showcasing a new trend, helping some younger scholars into print, or establishing a network. It may be possible to re-shape the journal somewhat, so that it covers areas that reflect aspects of the field that she and her colleagues at Mallingford value. The editorial board sometimes needs to be restructured or renewed, refereeing practices altered, the pool of potential reviewers widened, and so on, in ways that reflect MacFadyearn's own sense of what is important in the field. (This is not a recipe for unbridled self-interest; we are describing how one can contribute to shaping a field, not recasting it completely in one's own image.) Editing a journal gives some scope for patronage and for helping to redefine intellectual agendas. Of course, such (limited) power should not be used to undermine the reputation of the journal, or to display favouritism and publish only the work of a clique. But it is legitimate to encourage the publication of good papers by reputable people, in new areas of intellectual interest, to promote debate in the discipline, and so enhance the reputation of the editor and the host department. Like everything else, this means doing it well. Editorial work takes a certain amount of time and effort. It needs regular attention if one is to keep on top of the flow of submissions and the production schedule, and to ensure that editorial decisions are made as promptly as possible.

The term of office of an editor varies from discipline to discipline and from journal to journal. Three or four years is quite a common term of office in those social science journals that circulate, although five or six is not unusual. As a rough generalization, journals that are owned by a learned society usually have an editorial team chosen by a committee or elected by the membership. Those journals such as *The British Journal of Psychology*, core journal of the British Psychological Society, or *Sociology*, from the British Sociological Association, usually have a fixed term for an editorial team. When our colleague Derek Blackman edited the *BJP* the term was six years. Such editorships are of high prestige. They normally come with an editorial board chosen by the learned society, a committee to oversee the work, possibly with a chair different from the editor and answerable to the learned society itself. While owned by learned societies, many of these journals are published by commercial publishers, and the business side of the journal is their responsibility. The commercial rights in the journal title itself will be shared by the two parties (arrangements differ widely).

Many journals are not controlled by a specific learned society but are owned by the commercial publisher itself. Here there may be less democracy or corporate control. Editorships do not have to circulate. Publishers may be happy to leave a successful editor in post indefinitely. *The British Journal of the Sociology of Education* is 25 years old in 2004. It has had the same editor, Len Barton, for all that time.

As well as being 'the' editor, it can be sensible to edit a special issue of a journal, or to be book reviews editor. The latter is a good way to build up a large network of contacts in the discipline, for future reference as well as for the task in hand. A reviews editor learns who is and who is not reliable about hitting deadlines and following guidelines, and that is always potentially useful information.

So journal editing is a potential part of a dissemination strategy in that it can help individuals and local groups to participate in setting the agenda for their specialism. It can be a marker of esteem both for the editor and for the department or group she or he is associated with, and so help to establish one's presence and the currency of one's own research engagements in the wider world.

Starting a new journal

Starting a new journal is exciting and is one way to open up new specialist areas. If the journal 'takes off' then the founding editor(s) can consolidate their academic reputation or build one up. Our own colleague at Cardiff, Barbara Adam, was the founding editor of *Time and Society*, which helped establish the significance of that specialist area of social science scholarship, which was her own, and so helped to consolidate her career in the process. Part of the lasting legacy of Nate Gage (Stanford University) to educational research is the journal *Teaching and Teacher Education*, which reflects and has developed out of his particular intellectual and professional commitments.

The opportunities to be a founding editor are various. If a society wants to start a journal, then being chosen as founding editor is an honour and a major opportunity to shape the future of the journal itself and of the academic constituency it serves. Sometimes a commerical publisher thinks that there is a gap in the market and invites an academic to be the founding editor, put together an editorial board and so on. Sometimes some academic group – a special interest group or network, or members of one department – decide to propose launching a journal, sometimes on the back of an existing newsletter or regular conference series. Such a foundation can be an excellent way of establishing one's position in the field and helping to set the intellectual agenda.

We have been involved with several new journals. The medical sociology group of the British Sociological Association started *Sociology of Health and Illness* just over 25 years ago, with a commercial publisher. It had an uncertain editorial start, as the original editor had to give it up almost immediately, and when Paul took over the editorship it was far from established. But working on the journal in its earliest days, and nurturing it to safety – indeed towards considerable success – provided some opportunity to establish a distinctive ethos, to encourage particular types of publication, and to help promote a distinctive approach to the field. In this way the journal established a distinctive niche in the intellectual and commercial marketplace. In contrast Sara was involved from the earliest days with *Teaching and Teacher Education*, which had the financial support of Robert Maxwell's Pergamon Press behind it, and was expected to make money within a specified timeframe. Much more recently, we were asked by Sage Publications if we would like to start a journal focused on qualitative research methods, and so we became founding editors of *Qualitative Research* in 2001. As we write this book we cannot yet know whether it will be a commercial success and viable in the long term. But we see it as a space in which good work can be published, and where work from a very diverse range of social science disciplines can be published in the same covers. By helping to provide intellectual spaces – for medical sociology, for research on teaching, and for qualitative research methodology, we have helped to enhance our own careers, promoted our interests in the social sciences, and helped to profile social science at Cardiff University. The work is time consuming. In the immediate term, it can feel like a series of thankless tasks. Like a lot of things in academic life, it seems to be a matter of more headaches than rewards. In the longer term, it is a way of disseminating work and perspectives we care about, and promoting good research publications.

Influencing policy

By no means all research in all the disciplines has actual or potential impact on policy. There are, however, many topics that are potentially policy-relevant. Such research is by no means confined to research on social problems and public policy. A great deal of pure and applied scientific research has implications for policy, and is of potential relevance to public debate. Indeed, there are many domains of contemporary scientific development that are especially high profile: genomics, nanotechnology, sustainable energy, climate change, information technology are among them. These are not just popular in the mass media and in the more popular ends of science publishing or broadcasting. They are also of considerable interest to statutory and voluntary agencies, interest groups, politicians and others involved in the policy process. A lot of economic and social research is of equal relevance to a wider variety of policy advisers, government departments, local agencies, charities and pressure groups.

One important aspect of one's dissemination strategy is, therefore, to devise ways of engaging with the relevant groups and individuals. The growing emphasis on evidence-based policy means that there are many contexts in which research findings may become incorporated into policy and practice. (Cynics sometimes suggest that just as often we get policy-based evidence: that research findings are selectively reported or endorsed in order to support policies that have already been decided upon on the grounds of political expediency, resource allocations and the like. But that does not mean that one should never engage with the overall policy process.)

It is important to have a clear strategy in this context. One cannot hope to gain the ear of the relevant influentials or public bodies just by happenstance. One also has to be prepared to *work* at the process. There are some basic precepts that can inform such a strategy. Like everything else we have been commenting on, it normally requires only the application of common sense and the sorts of intellectual capacities that academics should have anyway.

First, one needs to identify the right channels and bodies. These may be included in the array of users and beneficiaries you have assembled in the course of the research itself. There is no generic 'policy-maker' and no generic 'politician'. One should acquaint oneself with how the relevant bodies and procedures work. In the United Kingdom, for example, that could certainly include a general understanding of how the parliamentary system works – how debates, parliamentary questions, and select committees operate. It would also involve a recognition of different levels of government. Post-devolution there are important policy-making and political contexts in Scotland, Wales and Northern Ireland. Regional and local agencies also have considerable significance. On a wider scale, UK academics also need to be aware of the European dimension. A great deal of public policy is regulated or influenced by European legislation. Again,

Europe calls for an appreciation of how its bodies work, how the various Directorates work, how European networks of researchers and experts can be put together and how their work can feed into policy formation. One's attention does not need to be confined to governmental bodies or political parties. So-called think-tanks can have disproportionate influence. They regularly produce reports and media briefings that receive close attention by public influentials of all persuasions. Informing their reports can be an important, indirect way of getting the implications of research into a broader domain.

Second, we need to understand the appropriate forms and rhetorics that will reach the right people. Influentials do not commit themselves to reading journal papers or lengthy research reports. They expect executive summaries, with clear bullet points, equally clear conclusions, and explicit steers on the practical and policy implications of research. (This applies to dissemination via mass media: see below.) Members of government departments and senior people in major charities regularly complain that academics are singularly poor at presenting their work in the right ways. We are all too often given to providing equivocal conclusions, with lame recommendations that 'more research is needed' and insufficient precision, and we are not always alert to the timetables and deadlines that government needs. Of course, academics can often retort that central and local government are too eager to get 'quick fix' recommendations, are too impatient to await the results of in-depth research, cannot be bothered to master the relevant arguments or understand the evidence, and are generally unsympathetic to real research, as opposed to opinion. Both sides of the argument are true up to a point. Here our advice is not to damage one's research and one's reputation by trading in over-simplified reports or recommendations. It is, however, important to acquaint oneself with the methods and needs of one's potential audiences. The Economic and Social Research Council has published a booklet on *Influencing the UK Policymaking Process* (McGrath n.d.), which is a very useful brief source of advice. Although written for social scientists, its advice is relevant to scientists and humanities people as well. As in all things, it pays to extend one's 'research' to include these aspects of dissemination. They can and should also form the basis of staff development within the department or the research group.

Dealing with the media

One does not have to aspire to becoming a 'telly don' – with one's own prime-time series of popular science or history – in order to think about the media. Both broadcast and print media may take an interest in your research. Your research sponsors may have an interest in seeing 'their' research widely reported, and your institution may well want to see its members' achievements in the local, national and international media. Some larger research grants and programmes may *require* you to have a communication strategy that includes dissemination via the mass media as well as through academic conferences, reports, briefings and so on.

It can, therefore, pay dividends to have some sort of communication plan for your research. Moreover, it may be useful to have some level of media training available for members of your research group, or for principal investigators across the institution. These paragraphs do not substitute for such training or for a proper plan. We offer some very general precepts that form the basis of such a plan.

The fundamental principle that all academics and researchers need to keep in the forefront of their minds and their preparations is that they need to try to stay in control of the media representation of their work. Being reported in print, or appearing on TV and radio, is just one of the many contexts in which you can be a 'victim' again. It is easy to have one's work misrepresented. This is not because journalists are malign. But it reflects the kinds of pressures that they work under – with very pressing deadlines and severe limits of time and space. Consequently they need to try to encapsulate sometimes complex ideas into simple formats. As a consequence, over-simplification and distortion can creep into the process.

Consequently, it is important to try to exercise control over what is put out. Whether you are writing a press release or preparing for a broadcast interview, you need to keep asking yourself: 'What am I trying to get across?' In other words, be clear what your 'story' is (and the media do like to think in terms of stories). Then stick to that story. Do not let an interviewer sidetrack you into departing from your own agenda. Answer the questions you want to answer (not necessarily the questions the interviewer puts) and give the answers you want to (not what the interviewer may try to put into your mouth). Obviously you will need to think about your potential audience. A science programme on public service radio will imply a different audience from a morning magazine show: the time available for the interview also will be different, and the style of presentation will be different too. It is important to be able to hit the right level.

While high-profile or controversial research may result in your being cold-called by journalists, the great majority of research gets reported because people put out press releases and other information. This often goes to specialist publications or specialist journalists. Consequently, if you want to reach the right audience, you probably need to do some research on outlets and journalists. If necessary, you probably ought to get to know the right writers or broadcasters. They are often very knowledgeable and very helpful. Working *with* a journalist who is knowledgeable in her or his own right can be very rewarding for both parties.

The ESRC publish three short guides to dissemination: *Heroes of Dissemination* (Walker n.d.), *Developing a Media Strategy* (Vaitilingam n.d.) and *Television and Radio: A Best Practice Guide* (Gaber n.d.). *Heroes* docs include one woman, Ruth Lister, who is an expert on poverty, but she is outnumbered by nine men. Each talks about how they have chosen to use the media, and the consequences their exposure has had for them. Vaitilingam explains why all social scientists should have a media strategy, and explains how to write press releases, set up websites, organize public meetings and how to run media training for the whole team. The pamphlet on broadcasting explains how the TV and radio systems work in Britain, differentiating between current affairs, chat-shows, documentaries, the commissioning process, and the production processes. There are then some guidelines for appearing on radio and on TV. Again these would be equally useful for academics outwith social science.

The Rhind Commission (2003) argued that British social scientists were spectacularly poor at communicating their work to policy makers or the media. But social scientists are not alone in that. All funding bodies express concerns from time to time about the relative failure of academics to exploit the possibilities of mass media to disseminate the processes and the results of research as widely as possible. Intellectually speaking, an ability to engage with wider publics should be part of researchers' crafts skills and competence. Morally speaking, publicly-funded research deserves to be in a genuinely public domain; and if we believe in democracies of well-informed citizens, then it is our job to contribute to the flow of information.

9

Research assessment exercises: 'the susceptibilities of scholars'

Not for the first time that year Roger Clatworthy at Beauminster looked glumly at a memo in his hand. It came – as usual – from the department administrator, whose job seemed to involve the periodic distribution of requests for information from all academic staff, accompanied by cryptic references to various agencies and information-gathering exercises. All sorts of people seemed to want more or less the same information, though usually in subtly different formats, relating to different timeframes and expressed in different categories. Roger had spent ages trying to work out what proportion of his working time was devoted to various kinds of activities, pouring over the list of categories that was itself incoherent and barely comprehensible, all in aid of a 'transparency' review. Nobody had explained to him what was meant by 'transparency', who was conducting the review, and why. In any event, it was abundantly clear that 'transparent' was the last adjective any sane person would have attached to the exercise, which was patently an exercise in 'garbage in, garbage out' management statistics. Likewise, he had painstakingly classified his meagre list of annual publications into the 'CVCP categories', although it remained completely baffling as to why such august and distant personages as the heads of all the UK universities wanted to know how many book reviews he'd published last year. It was especially mystifying, as nobody ever seemed to publish the data using those categories. But he had gamely yielded up his tiny quanta of information, along with similar exercises for various internal reviews conducted by the department, the faculty and the university as a whole. They had all been swallowed up into the giant maw of the university's management information system. Some of it had appeared – several years out of date – in published statistics produced by HESA, another agency that produced statistics nobody much had great faith in, and fewer people ever read.

Now this request for information had a sharper edge to it. This one couldn't be fudged, or guessed at, and it seemed to matter to everybody. The memo was headed 'Research Assessment Exercise' and it asked all members of the academic staff to list all their publications for the past five years, and to put an asterisk next to the four 'strongest or most significant' publications. Unlike the other information-gathering exercises, this was not a shadowy or insubstantial one. It was more than just a paper exercise, more than just troublesome bureaucracy. Roger knew that much. He knew because there had been anxious discussions about 'The RAE' at successive staff meetings, and various more senior colleagues had muttered about it. Roger had confessed to himself that he didn't really understand what it was all about or what he was sup-posed to contribute to it all. He'd rather avoid it all if he could – but it seemed to be pressing down on so many people in the university that it was really too hard to avoid it. So it had arrived, here he stood, holding the memo. Another memo. He really must find out more about it. But how to do so without displaying his ignorance, and – worse still – his craven fear?

Poor Roger. Roger is clearly in need of some staff development, but his annual publication return is a small matter compared to the impact the Research Assessment Exercises have had and will have on Beauminster. The rest of the chapter focuses on the RAE. For readers not in Britain we hope that it has some interest, if only because of what it reveals about British academia. The obvious problem for people like Roger is that they are vic-tims of research assessment. He seems powerless and ignorant. The fact that he does not know how to categorize his publications is symptomatic of his more general ignorance. (We have explained the system in Appendix 2.) We do not advocate the view that one's research plans and research strategy should be driven entirely by the exigencies of research assessment pro-cesses. On the contrary, the development of a research culture and the promotion of research-led careers depend primarily on the intrinsic value of the research. Moreover, the rewards of successful research – research funding, high-quality publications and so on – should be sufficient if fur-ther extrinsic rewards are sought. If successful research is being pursued, then any form of internal or external assessment should be a matter of reporting it. Research assessment and its outcomes are driven primarily by the quality of research and outputs that have been achieved, and not by the dark arts of 'spin'.

Background

The Research Assessment in the United Kingdom has grown enormously in scale and significance since its earliest days. It began in the 1980s, applying originally only to the 'old' universities, with the collection of detailed information on science and technology – where research is expensive – and relatively little data collected in arts and social sciences. Then in 1989 more information was collected and the resulting grades were used to distribute the 'R' money more differentially. In 1992, when all the former poly-technics became universities, a third RAE took place, to which over 100 institutions could submit data on their performance. The 1996 RAE led to a still more steeply graded allocation of R monies, so that lowly graded units received nothing. Again, after the 2001 RAE the rewards were even more unequal, as we explain later in this chapter. So over a 15-year period there have been five RAEs which have progressively led to the concentration of R money in a small number of universities. That cluster of leading research-led and well-funded universities constitute the Russell Group (named after the hotel in which the group first met).

The Research Assessment Exercise is a remarkable invention. It creates fairly stable rankings among all UK universities, from which are derived the formulae for distributing a substantial amount of those universities' core funding. It impinges directly or indirectly on virtually all academic staff, and a great many administrative and support staff too, in all higher education institutions in the United Kingdom. Unlike Roger Clatworthy, therefore, one should really understand how it works, what it does, what to expect, and how to succeed. Moreover, the creation of successful research groups, cultures and careers is fundamental to success in the RAE itself. Successive RAEs are not really exercises in self-presentation and drafting: they reflect the kind of planning and development we have been discussing in the previous chapters. While UK universities have for a long time resisted the direct imposition of differential tiers of institutions (teaching only, mixed and research-led), in many ways they have diligently competed in the assessment exercises, vigorously trying to outdo one another, and in the course of it transforming the higher education sector into a strongly dif-ferentiated and stratified one.

The pressures of successive RAEs have been felt by individuals, by research groups, by departments, and by universities. The consequences of universities' local decisions, taken in the light of RAE outcomes, have ripple effects across the entire sector – not least when under-performing depart-ments are closed or merged.

The individual and the department

One cannot succeed in the RAE as an individual academic, of course. Individuals are not graded: departments, or parts of departments, are. But the grading of those 'units of assessment' is ultimately predicated on the performance of individual academics in those departments. As in all things, the individual research career and the collective research culture are inextricably linked. The fate of the individual depends on the fate of his or her department and his or her university. The fate of the department depends on more than just the efforts of individuals, however. The eva-luation of a department depends on all sorts of objective performance indicators and on subjective judgements made about its research and research culture. The ethos of a department is important, therefore, as is its external reputation and the impression it creates among the key networks of academics.

It is a recurrent theme throughout this book that one should try to avoid being a victim. We all need to decide whether we are going to let external demands and pressures overwhelm us, or whether we are going to stay in control. People who are in control can take reviews and assessments in their stride. They create a good deal of work for somebody, that is true, and they can often prove intrusive and disruptive. But they do not have to be a great worry. The successful research-active academic should be able to anticipate activities like the RAE the way a particularly good student can contemplate degree examinations – a chance to shine and display one's achievements. We tell our students not to panic about exams, we should tell ourselves the same sort of message.

The origins of the RAE are to be found in the culture of accountability that has afflicted higher education, along with just about everything else in the public sector, over the past decades (Atkinson and Coffey 1997, 2004). Roger Clatworthy is by no means alone in groaning with weary resignation every time his administrator or head of department asks for the same information yet again, or seems to have invented yet another form of scrutiny and enumeration. The demands for information and evaluations grow cumulatively more burdensome, and are in danger of becoming a significant waste of time and money. Moreover, they become a form of displacement activity: if academics are not careful, they put more effort into making the performance indicators look good rather than performing well.

The RAE also fits a rather different aspect of UK academic culture that pre-dates contemporary fashions for accountability and surveillance. It captures the kind of snobbery and competitiveness that inform British cultural and intellectual life, and have done so for generations. For those individuals and institutions that can do so, the exercise permits 'top' people to have their elite status confirmed. It also holds out the possibility of upward mobility for the hard-working and the enterprising. It thus satisfies the two pervasive value-systems of the academy – elitism and meritocracy. To that extent, therefore, it satisfies that streak of Protestantism that so many academics endorse – the belief in self-improvement through hard work. While it has promoted a certain amount of short-run mobility, and a small number of more dramatic improvements, the RAE has tended to reflect the Matthew principle: to those that have shall be given. The exercise has tended to confirm the overall hierarchy between UK institutions, validating them through 'objective' measures. Unlike most exercises of this sort, however, we have all been constrained to participate in the competition between 1992 and 2001. Even though there is a high degree of stability in the system overall, any given institution and any given unit of assessment still has to try to optimize its own position, in the attempt to attract better levels of resourcing from the Funding Councils.

The RAE is a comprehensive exercise through which all 'units of assessment' are graded on a common scale. The scale is: 1, 2, 3b, 3a, 4, 5 and 5*. (There is something uniquely British in the way a historical five-point scale has been turned into a seven-point scale while retaining and elaborating on the original numerical categories.) Each grade attracts a different level of 'R' funding for the institution. The precise level of funding depends on: the academic discipline, the RAE grade and the volume measure. The latter reflects the actual number of academic staff returned for a given unit of assessment which is a discipline or subdiscipline. Units of assessment in laboratory science, such as physics or veterinary medicine, are given more 'R' money than library-based disciplines such as philosophy or law. So a grade 5* for 50 staff in molecular genetics brings Wedmarsh far more money than a 5* for 50 staff in politics: but, as the management of Wedmarsh would point out, the genetics department is much more expensive to run and costs Wedmarsh far more to operate. The units of assessment are based on a standard classification of academic subject areas. They vary from very general to very specific ones, apparently reflecting historical developments rather than systematic planning. They do not necessarily correspond to academic departments. Departments may find themselves submitting returns, or being part of returns, to several different panels. A department of urban studies might find that some of its staff are returned with geography, some with politics and some with social policy, for example, because the management has decided that there is no suitable panel to which to send the whole department together, or because the grades and income are likely to be higher if urban studies staff are added to three other groups. Equally, several departments may form one 'unit of assessment' for the purposes of the RAE. Indeed, the preparation and planning for RAEs can involve a good deal of strategic thought about how disciplines and departments can most advantageously be returned.

The RAE is important because it drives one important component of universities' funding. In very broad terms each university is funded via two main income streams, teaching (T) and research (R). Teaching resources follow the students that are enrolled. The unit of resource is determined by categories of course. The T element of resourcing comprises the larger slice of all institutions' income from Funding Council sources, and it is relatively inelastic. The R stream, on the other hand, is the competitive element, driven by Research Assessment gradings. Note that this R income is quite different from the research income derived from grants and contracts from Research Councils, charities, UK government, industry and so on. The R money we are referring to here is core recurrent funding. It reflects the fact that, overall, the 'dual support' system means that the higher education sector is funded to carry out teaching and research. In other words, for an individual academic staff member, funded by the Funding Council, one can think of a proportion of her time being funded for her to do research and a proportion of her time being funded for her to teach.

The distribution of T and R money to universities is governed by formulae. Although it is not really of relevance to this discussion, you should be aware that the different territories of the UK have different agencies. There are separate Funding Councils for England, Scotland and Wales, while Northern Ireland has its own funding arrangements. (There were different Funding Councils from 1992 before parliamentary devolution and the establishment of the Scottish Parliament and the Welsh Assembly.) The different Funding Councils can and do allocate R money on different principles. It is, for instance, open to the Councils to decide on different step-functions in funding as between the different RAE grades. Consequently, one must be careful not to refer to 'the' Higher Education Funding Council, and one must realize that the funding of higher education is one area in which there are territorial differences within the UK. Once the relevant Funding Council has made its allocations to each individual university, the institution has discretion over how its allocations are made internally. A university is not bound to 'pipeline' the resources to each department precisely in line with the formula that determined the funding overall. For heads of department and for individual academic staff members, it is important to understand two broad sets of issues: i) the generic mechanisms that determine the institution's overall income; and ii) the mechanisms whereby the resources are allocated internally. It is possible and entirely legal, because universities are autonomous decision-makers, for a university that gets a 5* social policy department to take the money from the Funding Council and spend it on the dental school. This is an entirely fictitious example. Whatever mechanisms and practices exist in any particular university, it is vital that the staff of that institution understand them.

Luckily for the present discussion, the fact of different Funding Councils is not a major problem, as they all subscribe to the same RAE so there is a common exercise, with a common method, even though the funding outcomes can differ. It is important that every member of staff, from the most senior member of the department to the most junior lecturer or researcher, has an understanding of the Research Assessment. It is important, as far as is possible, for all members of the department to 'own' the process. Why? Because their collective fate will be largely determined by its outcomes. The reputation of their department and of their institution will be coloured by RAE results.

Although the volume measure has an impact on the funding, the increasing selectivity of funding increasingly drives institutions towards the highest possible gradings, and hence to the more selective approaches. The funding attached to RAE outcomes has got progressively more differentiated. In future it is clear that only units assessed as 4, 5 or 5* (or the equivalent in some future gradings) will be funded for research. Consequently, it is vital to try to achieve the highest possible grade. In the longer term, a higher grade will help to recruit the best staff and attract the best postgraduate students. It will help in the national and international competition for research grants and contracts. In terms of reputation, it is the grade that people remember and that carries worth, rather than the volume of staff returned.

Individual researchers can do relatively little to affect research assessment. The essence of the RAE return is that it reflects the collective strength of a department or a division. But collective strength is impossible without individual strength, and any academic who has ambitions to build a research-based career needs to have more than half an eye on the RAE and its consequences. The relative novice who is embarking on a research-led career, then, needs to know and do a small number of things. They all reflect the kinds of things that we have been discussing throughout this book.

The research literature on the impact of the successive RAEs in British academic life is gently expanding. Lisa Lucas (2001) has compared the strategies used to maximize RAE scores in biology and sociology in two English universities. David Pearson (2002) has interviewed academics in physics, chemistry, music and philosophy in two UK universities, to discover what impact the successive RAEs have had on their working lives. In the next six pages, we have drawn on Pearson's data and his commentary upon them at some length. They show the impact of the RAE, and different disciplinary responses to it. Pearson's informants were ambivalent as individuals, and divided within and across disciplines about the merits and disadvantages of the RAE. A physicist, Professor Wigmore, articulately captured some of the common tensions:

> The problem is, it just grew. Once you put a system in, you begin to believe the system for its own virtues rather than why you put it there, and the original reasons get lost and you're lumbered with something that may not be what you want. Remember that the Research Assessment Exercise was something which was designed to work out how to spend money in research ... You can, it is true, presumably, make some sort of judgement about the worthwhileness of research for research's sake, which is what they were doing in that exercise, and then you can make your judgements accordingly and what has been useful so far is to give unto those that have you give even more those that hath not you take away even that which they hath got.

These last phrases are a rare example of an almost direct biblical quotation. The so-called 'Matthew effect' is a concept widely applied to scientific practice by sociologists of the Columbia School of Science Studies, following Merton (1968/1973).

Among Pearson's articulate and thoughtful respondents, Prof. Redfern, a physical scientist, is enthusiastic, while Prof. Adey, a philosopher, is more ambivalent. Here, Prof. Redfern repeats his point that the RAE measures what 'you ought to be doing anyway'.

> The RAE influences what you do because it makes you think about what you publish, the way you publish, and it makes you think about interactions with people outside your own department, which are going to not only enhance your work but enhance the perception of

your work. So I think it influences lots of things that you do to not only try and improve the quality of your work but also make that demonstrable. . . . I think a lot of the things that the RAE leads you to put stress on are things you should put stress on anyway if you're a good researcher and doing good research. . . . the things that you need to do to perform well in the RAE are things that you ought to be doing anyway. . .

And I think anyway, as a scientist, there's no point in obtaining new information, new knowledge, gaining new insights, unless you share them with other people. And so I would argue that you're not really doing science effectively if you're not publishing your work. . . . But I think you can't claim to be doing science if you're having great thoughts and keeping them to yourself. . . . So all our work goes into highly regarded journals, so I suppose that's the biggest impact of the RAE: making you think hard about that, but again I think, you know, you ought to be doing that anyway. . . . But I think it's emphasised what we all ought be to doing anyway is trying to do good science. And I think it's made that very visible and has put that right at the top of the agenda.

He explained to David Pearson how even during the previous two RAE periods (1989–96) research had moved up the agenda, out of the private and into the public domain. Here he contrasts the early 1990s with the present (1999):

(Research) was a very personal activity which in some ways people didn't share with other people. . . . I'd been here a little while and I put a notice up to say I was giving an invited talk at a conference and I was going to rehearse it. Anyone was welcome to come along to the rehearsal. People heard comments – you know – were chatting in the post room. 'Don't think much of this new professor we've got if he has to rehearse his talks.' Of course the rehearsal was to make sure we got the timings right; make sure that the things were right and the whole presentational thing was right; so I think that really surprised me – that people would sit away working in their own room doing something; send it off for publication without thinking to discuss it with anyone else . . . I think things have changed.

Redfern is a scientist. Pearson's interviews with academics in philosophy and music produced a less enthusiastic picture. Humanities academics talk of restriction, as if their intellectual freedom to explore has somehow been confined to the structures of research favoured by the RAE panels. Although Prof. Adey, a philosopher, struggles to capture precisely what he thinks he has lost, his words express very well the feeling of restriction:

I think as I experience the RAE personally, it made me feel much more under pressure to work with very definite publishing outcomes in view. I felt much less able to read around; to keep discussion papers; to indeed think of – you know – putting one – you know – new lecture courses on – if you like – a speculative basis in a sort of free and unstructured way, because – you know – as I've just said – of the sense of the need to focus on publishing outcomes of the work I did and I have to say that personally I didn't find this altogether welcome. I could see that in some ways it meant that I – and I think others – worked in a more focused and in a more productive way if – you know – productive means – you know – actually delivering written work on paper. But at the same time I felt it – to a degree – that it forced on me a narrowing of activity of a kind that I didn't actually welcome personally and I'm not convinced was academically all that beneficial, because I think this – you know – what I call this more speculative and unstructured reading and writing actually had a lot of not so easily quantifiable benefits in terms of – you know – coming across things that you wouldn't otherwise have come across and so on and just widening your interests and things of that sort.

This feeling that there is a new sense of pressure and the need to achieve is especially characteristic of academics in the arts disciplines, particularly music. Take two music professors for example:

Prof. Rendle: . . . it's woken us all up to the competitive world outside: that we can't sit down and meander through life doing some teaching and doing some research, and if it's published, all well and good. So I think it's bucked up a lot of people. I could use a different initial to the word 'bucked' up a lot of people as well
Prof. Eyers: . . . one has to be far more organised about research and far more up-front about it and far more up-front about making grant applications. It's actually much more exciting than it used to be, I have to say.

These professors were speaking before the 2001 RAE. Since then a review of the system and proposals for its future development have been published.

In 2002 the four higher education Funding Councils in the UK set up a review of the Research Assessment Exercise. Chaired by the master of an Oxford College (Sir Gareth Roberts, President of Wolfson) who had previously been the vice-chancellor of a red brick university (Sheffield) the steering committee began its inquiry in the autumn of 2002. The invitation to submit evidence and opinions was issued in October 2002. A submission period effectively of about six weeks was provided in the autumn of 2002. An initial report, based on that consultation and the deliberations of the working party, was published in late May 2003 (Roberts 2003). There was a 12-week formal consultation period from May 2003. The main impetus for the Roberts committee to be set up was a perceived 'crisis' in the RAE system which followed the fifth exercise. There was an RAE in 2001 that the government, and therefore the HEFCE, could not or would not fund. In late 2002 the HEFCE decided that a new category, in effect a '6', should get generous funding. At first there was a plan to re-convene the 2001 panels, but instead, UOAs in England that had got a 5* in both 1996 and 2001 were treated as a 6. The extra funds were channelled to the 6s by removing R funds from the 4s in England. Had anyone in academic life known in 2002 that this was even a possibility, different decisions about the 2001 submissions would have been made all over the UK. A philosophy professor, Daniel Hutto, wrote to the *The Higher*, pointing out that only Oxford met the 5* twice criterion in his discipline (18 April 2003 p. 15).

It follows that cutting funding from ten 4-rated philosophy units to better fund one 6* unit threatens support for 20 to 30 international researchers. Some universities are clearly preparing to take a strategic view of research. They will focus funding only on units that have clear potential to achieve a 5 rating. What will become of the internationally excellent research in the 4-rated units? In philosophy, 73 per cent of units rated 4 in the 1996 RAE were rated 5 in 2001. This suggests that previous funding levels were effective in raising the amount of international research. It could be argued that funding a few select units at the expense of many others creates 'critical mass'. But this assumes, falsely, that all research is primarily collaborative or team-based, requiring researchers to be located in a single institution. What does that leave for disciplines such as philosophy in which research is often conducted by individuals working alone?

Daniel Hutto. Head of Philosophy, University of Hertfordshire

The Roberts Report proposed several changes to the RAE, but many features were left as they had evolved since the 1980s. The RAE is to remain a UK-wide exercise based on peer review conducted by subject panels. Higher education institutions (HEIs) will be able to choose whether to apply for a full Research Quality Assessment (RQA) or a less competitive Research Capacity Assessment (RCA). If this is introduced, it will have major implications for individuals and departments. The Roberts committee envisage a closer scrutiny of institutional research strategy, staff development, equal opportunity policy and research dissemination to decide whether any particular HEI can be funded for its research. Part of the new system is to have fewer units of assessment (about 20 to 25) with about 60 subpanels, and allowing the panels to develop a range of criteria. Another change proposed is that any department going for a full RQA will have to submit a minimum of 80 per cent of its eligible staff: thus preventing the strategy of a tiny fragment of an otherwise mediocre department getting a high grade. Finally the grading system will be changed.

The most significant change from the previous RAEs will be in the grading system. Rather than the present rating scale for departments of 1 to 5*, each submission would be given a composite rating indicating the proportion of:

- 3* research (broadly equivalent to the top half of the research considered international in RAE 2001)
- 2* research (the bottom half of international research), and
- 1* research (the top half of national research)

Consequently the output from the RQA will be a Quality Profile for each submission indicating the quanta of one star, two star and three star research.

If the changes are introduced then many institutions will adapt their strategies. However, for the individual, or the head of department such as Lalage, many of the lessons from the previous system will still be relevant, and it is to these we now turn. We are not obsessively concerned with the minutiae of the UK's assessment exercise, or speculating about its precise future shape. In many ways, the general principles of research culture, esteem, and research performance hold true, irrespective of the specific details that are applied in the UK or elsewhere.

Research development and institutional culture

In this section we explore briefly some of the issues that confront academics at all levels in thinking about the assessment of research and the promotion of a collective research culture. This applies at the most senior levels of university management. It applies – perhaps most crucially at the level of the school, department or division – and hence at the level of deans, heads of department or their equivalent. It also has implications for individual scholars, although we and they have to recognize that their individual efforts are very largely dependent on collective, institutional strategic development. For some elite research-led institutions, the problems are not about developing a research culture, but ensuring that world-class research is sustained, recognized and adequately rewarded. For others – the majority – there is still work to be done in enhancing research performance, and that implies changes in the organization and culture of the university. Our remarks are aimed primarily at colleagues in such academic contexts.

> Theo Beatock, a Senior Lecturer at Wedmarsh is having lunch with Tom Kentallen, who was his PhD supervisor at Mallingford. To his surprise, Tom announces he is moving to Penbury as Deputy Vice-Chancellor (Research). 'I'm stale – I'm not going any higher at Mallingford – the kids are gone, and they're offering a lot of money – it'll be a challenge. The new V-C really wants to build up research and says he will give me all the support I need.' Back with his wife Theo wonders if Tom is wise: building up research across all the disciplines at Penbury seems to him to be a hard, and possibly thankless task. His wife speculates that Tom plans to be a V-C himself, and sees this move as a

stepping stone to get status and experience outside Mallingford where he has been for most of his career. Theo is on the research committee at Wedmarsh, and is director of research in his department, and he cannot imagine what Tom's new job will be like. Wedmarsh has a reasonable research culture, and the tasks are hard enough there. Penbury has no track record to speak of, and little infrastructure to support the development of a research culture.

In this case study we explore the ways in which institutional officers, such as Tom Kentallen have to do at Penbury if it is to have a serious chance of being a research-led institution. Penbury, being a former polytechnic, had no government infrastructure money to underpin research from its origins in 1918 to 1992, and the majority of the staff were appointed to teach, and to liaise with local businesses, unions and government agencies. Their academic work was not interpreted primarily in terms of attracting research grants, conducting major research projects, or publishing prolifically. Only staff appointed since 1992 have had the requirement of research in their contracts. So Tom Kentallen has a much harder job than Lalage, the head of department.

Tom Kentallen has accepted the post of Pro Vice-Chancellor (Research) at Penbury. This is a new post, because the new Vice-Chancellor, an energetic 48-year-old whiz-kid, is determined to change Penbury into a research and teaching university. Tom believes that they can work together to change Penbury. He is now planning a research infrastructure for his new university, based on long conversations with friends in a dozen other places. Penbury needs radical change at every level from the individual to the institutional. Tom would probably not have time to run a research project himself, although if he could that would be an excellent example. But even if he cannot run his own research projects or group in this new context, he needs to find ways of continuing to have a credible presence in his own discipline, as a leading scholar, still publishing and – most importantly – contributing to the university's research planning as an actively research-oriented academic.

Tom Kentallen sketches out how Penbury will need to change. Things the university needs to do include:

1. A Research Support Office, to service the whole university, needs to be established or strengthened. This office would gather information about funding opportunities, disseminate them inside Penbury, encourage applicants and work with them to write the bids, do the costings, and ensure compliance with the funders. Tom would be based in this office, and finding an energetic and skilled staff for it will be vital.
2. At university level, there needs to be a Research Committee with funds to disperse to start promising projects off, or to help collaborations inside or outside the institution.
3. In each faculty, there will have to be a sub-dean of research, who would

run staff development on research and publication in their area, help the academics form teams, advise on the intellectual content of applications, on publishing, and on raising the profile of the research in other ways too.

4. In each department there will need to be a director of research, and a research committee, appointed with a clear mission and targets for that department.

5. Tom knows that there needs to be a culture shift in all the academic and administrative departments, so that the new V-C's mission is known, *and supported.* There has to be commitment to it, for example, in the conference office, because research-led conferences will have to be lured to Penbury with good deals. Then every new post, and every promotion, will have to be decided by research-led criteria, so every member of every appointment and promotion panel has to understand the new mission, and work to implement it.

6. Every department and every faculty will have to produce an action plan, with one-year, three-year, five-year and seven-year targets about
   (a) applying for grants;
   (b) getting grants;
   (c) submitting publications;
   (d) persisting until research actually gets published;
   (e) attracting academic conferences in their discipline to Penbury;
   (f) getting the editorships of learned journals in their discipline to Penbury;
   (g) getting Penbury people into office-holding posts in relevant learned societies.

7. Every individual will have to have a research-oriented appraisal with a research active colleague (or a research active subject specialist brought in as a consultant from elsewhere), so they can draw up an action plan, which should include what staff development they need. That will have to be provided quickly while the impetus is there.

8. There is a need for money to be released centrally or earmarked in departments, to underwrite the costs of new investments, and to ensure competent Penbury staff can go to all the important conferences at which they can display Penbury research. Of course only research active staff should be going to conferences.

9. There will have to be a public relations effort to demonstrate the new culture to funding bodies. The key players from the Research Councils, the charities, the government departments and so on will have to be invited to Penbury, and shown the changing institution.

10. Some of the big multi-disciplinary high-profile meetings – such as the British Association for the Advancement of Science – need to be hosted at Penbury. Such events bring influential people, and the media, to the host institution.

11. There will have to be some strategic head-hunting of research active figures – 'stars' – who have a track record of building up research

groups. Their contracts will have to build in the culture changes they are required to lead.

Research stars need to be attracted to spend sabbaticals at Penbury to act as role models: overseas research-leaders, for instance, can be attracted as visiting scholars, provided that the right facilities and support can be provided. Not only can they contribute directly to renewed research initiatives, they can also help to build international research links and collaborations.

Some of the facilities – such as the library and the computing – will need upgrading to support research, and a culture change will be required to make them accessible 360 days a year. Some staff will have to change their working patterns. Penbury, like many other post-1992 universities, has longer teaching terms than top research universities. Oxford and Cambridge only teach for 24 weeks per year, Russell Group universities for 30: Penbury currently teaches for 33 and staff are then examining for a further 3 weeks. The 33-week teaching loads are heavy, so many staff are currently on holiday in the student vacations. These have to be lengthened from 19 weeks to 22 weeks, but staff have to learn to be in work for research. The teaching hours and office hours will have to be reduced for the research active. The current system reduces teaching loads for administrative duties but not for research, instead it is administration that has to be removed from academics so research can be done, this may mean funding administrative and clerical staff or slicing away tiers of administration, or both.

The scientists and engineers will need access to good research labs. This probably means arranging a partnership with Castleton University in the old county town six miles away, because there is no way Penbury could ever build up its own research labs. Penbury was not funded to do research in science and engineering from 1892 to 1992, and the government funding of research laboratories has been heavily concentrated in a few elite universities since 1985. Sharing research facilities on a regional basis can, if imaginatively managed, mitigate this. This is the Manchester solution and is explained below.

The staff in humanities and social sciences are in some ways better placed to develop new research – because they do not need laboratory and similar facilities. They can be helped into productivity. These departments can launch working paper series in electronic format, and it might be possible to think about book series – if as rumour has it Castleton University Press is struggling financially, perhaps they could inject some money and make it the Castleton and Penbury University Press. They do, however, need good library facilities: not just book and journals, but a renewed library and information service that sees the support of research as one of its core activities.

Not everything can be provided at once and on a single site. There may, therefore, be a place for strategic research alliances and collaborative arrangements. The Manchester solution has been energetically promoted by the Vice-Chancellors of the four universities in the city of Manchester for a decade. The four universities, Manchester, Salford, UMIST and Manchester Metropolitan, have different histories, but are within a five square mile radius of each other. It is not possible, with UK funding for HE, to envisage four HEIs all strong in research in all disciplines. Instead, there is a solution. The expensive research areas, such as chemistry, electrical engineering, biophysics – where a rich funding stream from the government and from grant-giving bodies needs laboratories with expensive, up-to-date equipment and skilled technicians – are concentrated in the old universities which have a long tradition of such funding. Staff in the newer institutions join research groups in these universities, and do their research there: as a quid pro quo undergraduates use the teaching-centred libraries in the new institutions, or have their undergraduate teaching in the labs there.

Attracting some research stars to come as visiting fellows will not initially be easy, which is the reason for the incentives: help with schools for children, housing, work or other occupations for a spouse are all other incentives a good personnel department could help with. If Penbury is not in itself an attractive city, potential sabbatical fellows might be encouraged to live in historic Castleton instead, and provided with attractive information on the region. The research visitor could be offered a postdoctoral research assistant and conference expenses – perhaps on the explicit agreement that he or she provides some staff development of a 'masterclass' kind.

Head-hunting research stars to permanent jobs as research professors or even research deans is a high-risk strategy. It is possible that the people who will come are actually past their best, and will coast to retirement on past glories. Regis (1988) argues this about many of the distinguished scientists who reached the Institute of Advanced Study at Princeton and were then very unproductive. Some others will be entirely selfish, and will not share their expertise and do institutional or staff development unless they are required to. Some others will be so unhappy in a lower status institution they will not settle at Penbury: they can damage the new mission by moaning about the place. This means that if Tom Kentallen is going to head hunt, he needs a budget for infrastructure for his stars: if, for example he is going to recruit someone in English literature, they will need texts, critical apparatus, journals. Some of this can be provided on CD ROM and electronically, some could be systematically bought. However, if our notional 'star' in English literature has been at Perth, with a library stocked regularly since 1583, and the National Library of Scotland an hour away by train, she or he is going to find Penbury's library a poor thing. Travel funds, a research assistant, and some PhD students, plus a budget for research materials are needed to keep the Perth star productive, happy and pro-Penbury. There is also a need to keep promises about no teaching, no administration and none of whatever they hated where they were. If a person has been lured to a new university by promises of no teaching and no administration, as long as they are highly productive, that promise has to be kept.

However, parachuting such stars into departments can cause enormous resentment, so it is vital that their expected contribution is explicit and to explain to overworked colleagues why such promises are made, and what benefits will accrue to them if the 'star' performs. Of course, if a 'star' comes to Penbury and fails to get grants, write for publication, provide leadership, or be a catalyst, then the managers will have to insist that the person takes up a normal role. Tom Kentallen would probably use it to get the new research mission of Penbury clear to and shared by all the deans, or the heads of departments.

Such institutional change has to take place if Penbury is to become a research-led university. Some of those changes would be very visible to all staff, some less so, some not at all. For academic staff who are at an early stage in their career, it may not be clear what they should do to be ready for future research assessments, whether or not they take the form of the RAE, whether or not the Roberts vision of the exercise comes to pass. Our basic message is that the things we have referred to throughout this book – the kinds of activities that help to build a successful career, and help to create successful research groups – will help to create a good RAE return. The pervasive culture of research assessment should not bear down oppressively on more junior staff. But they need to understand how their individual efforts, and how their various successes, can contribute to the overall departmental and institutional strategy. Their successes need to be supported and celebrated. They therefore need to be helped to feel that they are valued as part of the larger collective effort. For such colleagues, the general advice includes the following.

Have a secure publications strategy

One cannot expect someone who is just embarking on their career to have the kind of publications profile that one would expect of an established academic. It is, however, important that one should be 'returnable'. In other words, you want to be among the academic staff listed as research active in the department, and to be part of a strong research group. Assessment panels repeatedly stress that they want to see evidence of younger scholars' work and their participation in the research culture of the department. The Roberts Report (2003) specifically focuses upon the institution's career development structures and the insistence that 80 per cent of staff employed on Funding Council money being returned so that those with emerging careers will not be excluded by the fearful or ageist institution in future. It is, therefore, important that rising stars have a strategy, follow it, and are helped to get enough 'returnable' items.

Become known

It is important to go to conferences, to make yourself known to the leading figures, and to get good publicity for the work you have published in the quality press and learned society newsletters. At conferences, colleagues can often make introductions, and even famous people are pleased when they are asked a positive, sensible question. Most people like to be asked for advice, so a network can be increased by seeking help from some new links every few months.

Build alliances

One way to increase a person's 'returnability' is to carry through some joint publication projects. Doing something with a more senior person can increase your visibility, and if the collaborator already has enough items for themselves their unneeded item can be one of your star listings. Working with someone at the same level so you both get two joint publications although each of you has only written one of them is sensible.

Collect intelligence

Find out which journals are short of papers, which new ones are starting up, and target them. Leave the ones with long waiting lists until you have banked enough items to get by. Colleagues in the network will have lots of news, have heard rumours, will be able to ask editors for you: use them.

Contribute to the research group

Research groupings provide the opportunity to collaborate and to develop. The group – whether it is a formal centre, or a less formal grouping – provides a collegial and supportive environment in which to grow research ideas, draft collaborative research bids, and publish together. If it is not such a supportive environment, work at making it so.

Do not whinge

Never, ever tell anyone in academia that you cannot publish because of teaching, administration, illness, pregnancy or emotional turmoil. Always present yourself as someone who is working on some publication project. That means always having a project to burble about, but, of course, it need not be any of the actual projects you really have in mind, so it cannot be held against you later. Mutter about a paper based on a talk at a conference, or jointly authored with an absent colleague, or being planned for a possible special issue of a journal. If you are drowning in teaching or administration, take a long cold look at it: are you being too conscientious? Or are you using them as a displacement activity or an alibi? If you are ill, pregnant or in emotional turmoil, find a trusted colleague and strike a bargain: if they write something with both your names on *now*, you will repay the favour later. Dust off some unpublished conference papers and submit them to journals. Find a promising postgraduate or research assistant, and get them writing something for the two of you, with their name first. (If it gets published you will look magnanimous.)

In the final chapter we turn to the career-crowning rewards that the successful strive for and which are among the markers of success for top institutions and the top people within them.

10

Conclusions: 'stoking a modest imagination'

It would not be appropriate to have a long or elaborate conclusion. Our intention was to provide some strategies that would encourage academics to take charge of their careers, rather than feeling like clueless or defenceless victims. We meet a good many Roger Clatworthys every year: our intention is to help more people become like Althea Sclander or Dermot Garrowby. Our friend Andy Hiken works with the motto 'Action Overcomes Fear'. That is a good motto for academic career-building.

For much of the book we have been offering strategies for coping and succeeding at things that every academic can and should be doing, such as publishing papers and raising research grants. We do not regard teaching as an alternative to such activities. After all, research is to teaching as sin is to confession: if you have not done the former, there is nothing to talk about during the latter.

However, we do recognize that it is very easy to become absorbed in everyday academic life, and not to see or understand the contests in which the senior people in higher education are involved. So in this final chapter we have sketched in a few of the issues that can preoccupy those in the upper echelons of UK higher education. The details may be unfamiliar, but the underlying structural concerns of networks, of peer review, and of reward, are quite similar to those we have emphasized throughout. If we return to Althea Sclander's university, Arlinghurst:

> It is June at 8.30 in the morning, and the Vice-Chancellor of Arling-
> hurst (Professor Sir Marcus Burgoyne, FRS) opens his emails. The head
> of Physics, Prof. Inglestone FRS has written: 'Good news: Barharrow's
> got appointed to the Council of PPARC.' Sir Marcus replies immedi-
> ately 'Splendid!' and emails Prof. Barharrow to congratulate him, and
> the chair of the Research committee to tell her. His secretary buzzes
> him on the phone 'Dean of Engineering for you about the Materials
> Research Society award': he takes the call.

For many people, even *inside* universities, it is not clear what has actually happened here, or why it matters. One of the aims of this book has been to dispel such ignorance.

Elite distinctions: peer review at the top

Some of the most senior people in higher education are still subject to peer review, and many of them are busy providing peer reviews of their contemporaries and immediate successors. In the scenario of the Vice-Chancellor of Arlinghurst we can see several aspects of elite peer review. To demystify that scene, we have spelled out some of the cryptic clues about each person and institution mentioned.

First, the Vice-Chancellor. He has been knighted, 'given his K', for services to higher education and science. That shows he is acceptable to the establishment; an equivalently successful woman Vice-Chancellor is made a Dame. Sir Marcus's success as a scientist is shown by his FRS: the letters that mean he has been elected a Fellow of the Royal Society, or as he probably calls it 'The Royal'. Being elected an FRS is the highest scientific honour a scientist can get inside the UK: above it are some international honours such as the Lasker Prize in bioscience and the Nobel Prizes in sciences and economics (Zuckerman 1977). Sir Marcus would have been elected an FRS by his peers: every year panels in each discipline decide who should be elected to join them. There is a fixed size for the total number of Fellows: people retire, and some die, so the number elected each year can vary slightly. Election to the Royal Society is an elite form of peer review.

In the UK the distribution of fellowships of the Royal Society is very uneven across the universities: they are much commoner in the golden triangle (Oxford, Cambridge and the 'old' constituents of London University such as Imperial and Kings) than outwith it. Our imaginary Arlinghurst might have three to five, including Sir Marcus and Prof. Inglestone. Professor Barharrow's appointment to the Council of PPARC, the Particle Physics and Astronomy Research Council which disperses government research funds to those subjects might be a sign that he too is on his way to honours in British science such as election as an FRS. Serving on one of the Research Councils is a heavy task, involving reading a great many grant applications and other bids before every meeting. However, it is an honour to be chosen, and the insights gained, as well as the expansion of one's networks that results, mean that the work is undertaken willingly.

The Dean of Engineering is likely to be, or hope to be, a Fellow of the Royal Academy of Engineering, and have FREng after his name. The chair of the Arlinghurst University Research Committee, a very distinguished medieval historian, Professor Freda Kinsey-Hewitt, is the institution's only FBA: a Fellow of the British Academy, which is the equivalent of the Royal Society for arts disciplines. Election as an FBA also draws upon an elite peer review process.

The final peer review issue in the first scenario is the Materials Research

Society Prize. This is awarded by the society, which is based in Philadelphia, to a young (under 36) scholar who has 'contributed in an innovative way to the progress of materials research' and 'show promise as a developing leader'. It only pays 3000 dollars, but the status of 'outstanding young investigator' is worth more. Once again, candidates have to be nominated, and the candidates are peer reviewed. If someone at Arlinghurst has been shortlisted, or even won, then that young scholar, the Faculty of Engineering and the Vice-Chancellor will all be thrilled. So things are going well in the Vice-Chancellor's office – even though it is only breakfast time.

Success and failure: the badges of esteem

Probably because academic life is not well paid, markers of success and prestige are rarely monetary: indeed producing a bestseller, doing a successful TV series, writing a column in a tabloid, or winning a car or cash on a game show are all despised. It is necessary to learn what the indicators of prestige and success are, and how to recognize some of the 'badges' worn. You may despise many of the issues we raise in this section, but you should know the enemy: despise from a position of knowledge.

The highest degrees

Above the PhD/DPhil are two kinds of higher doctorate: Honorary ones, given to prime ministers, ageing rock stars, football managers and so on, and the ones *earned* for scholarly distinction. In Science and Engineering the DSc and the DEng are relatively common – in that successful researchers planning on promotion to professorships apply for them. The usual format is a portfolio of publications with a covering application explaining the contribution made. There are equivalents in non-science areas DLitt, DMus, DTheol, LlD, but they are much more rarely sought after. If you look at the poshest list of staff in your university, and count the number of scientists with DScs and the number of Humanities Scholars with DLitt's the ratio is usually 60:1. In Cardiff in 2001, for example, of 35 Readers and Professors in Biosciences 19 had higher doctorates, in the Business School of 35 Readers and Professors none had a DScEcon, in Social Sciences of 25 Readers and Professors two had DScEcons. There are certainly scholars in the Cardiff Business School who could reasonably apply for a DScEcon, and would probably be awarded one by their examiners. In Cardiff, the DLitt is also rare: in English and Philosophy, of 19 Readers and Professors none had a DLitt although there are certainly distinguished scholars who could submit an application. The University of Wales offers a DScEcon: at the time of writing there is only one holder on the staff of all six universities. One deterrent is the cost to submit for the higher doctorates. In 2003, to submit for a DSc in the University of Wales costs £328 plus the cost of providing the examiners with copies of all publications. But the big issue is disciplinary culture. In Science and Engineering the culture is more geared to stepwise merit ladders. Investing in a DSc or DEng is more career-enhancing than a getting DScEcon or a DLitt would be. In medicine, the MD is, in the UK system, also a higher doctorate, based on the submission of *research*, in contrast to those systems – like that in the USA – where initial medical training is at postgraduate level, so that the MD is the primary medical degree.

Prizes and awards

Scientists and Engineers have many more awards and prizes than other disciplines, and a clearer hierarchy. There are some landmarks that everyone needs to know about. Top of the lot is a Nobel Prize: these are awarded annually in three science areas, physics, chemistry, and physiology or medicine and in economics. There is nothing for maths, and much of biology is not eligible. Earth Sciences is also excluded. Each prize can be shared by up to three people and there are no posthumous prizes. The jury in Sweden decides but nominations are sought from top scientists in that discipline across the world. In the USA and the UK universities boast about how many Nobelists, or Laureates they have produced, have, and have had on their staff. The prize is a substantial sum of money, but the prestige is far more important. There is a book about the American scientists who have won the prize (Zuckerman 1977) which is a fascinating read.

Berkeley is also the setting for an amusing story. Andy Hiken is a sociologist, but also a locksmith. He was doing a PhD as a mature student at UC, Davis, when Paul was there as a visiting professor. One weekend he and Paul travelled down to Berkeley together. They called in to see Billy-Bob, a locksmith friend of Andy's, who was overworked. Berkeley has drugs and crime problems: locks are always needed. Billy-Bob said that some professor had been complaining because Billy-Bob had not yet fitted his garage security system: Billy-Bob had replied: 'I got six laurettes (*sic*) waiting for me to fix their locks. You ain't published nothin'. You'll wait!'

Below the Nobels there are high-status international prizes in each area of science. In biomedicine the Lasker is significant (Pert 1997). The Lasker Awards were established in 1946, and 59 winners since 1946 have gone on to win the Nobel. There is also the Crafoord Prize, awarded by the Royal Swedish Academy of Sciences since 1980, for research in maths, astronomy, biosciences especially ecology, geosciences and polyarthritis. At national level most countries have big prizes, such as the US Medal of Science Winners, the Leibniz in Germany, and the French Physical Society Prizes.

As well as academic prizes, which can be large sums of money, but can also be a medal and a scroll of no extrinsic worth, there are many exclusive academic clubs. Membership of these confers prestige. These are, again, particularly important in the natural sciences, such as Fellowship in the

National Academy of Sciences in the USA, or the Royal Society in the UK. There are equivalents in many other countries, from Austria to the Ukraine: there is for example a Croatian Academy of Sciences and Arts. Historically, these bodies were created by men, and they still have a minority of women members. The American Academy of Sciences was founded in 1863, had 1904 active members in 1999 of whom 118 were women. The Royal Society of London was founded 1660 and in 1999 had 1185 fellows, of whom 43 were women. The 'of London' is rarely mentioned although there is also a Royal Society of Edinburgh. Here we refer to the London one as The Royal Society.

In Britain election as a Fellow of the Royal Society (FRS) is a great distinction: but unlike a prize it costs you money. There is an annual subscription to pay to stay a member. British universities can be ranked as centres of scientific research excellence by the number of FRSs they have. The elections to the ranks of the FRS are done by committees in each discipline, and the results are then published. The most famous C.P. Snow novel *The Masters* (1951), has as one of its core themes the desperation of an unsuccessful research chemist to get an FRS, which everyone else knows is totally out the question. Indeed, all C.P. Snow's academic and scientific novels, *The Search* (1934), *The Masters* (1951), *The New Men* (1954), and *The Affair* (1960), have the Royal Society looming over the characters: the successful treat its existence and their membership/fellowships as a part of the landscape of science and its normal rewards, while those whose scientific careers are failing see it as an impenetrable citadel forever excluding them. The importance of the Royal Society in British science, and in many universities is considerable. The equivalent bodies for other disciplines are less well known, less often appear in fiction, and do not occupy so much discussion within higher education. However, ambitious young academics such as Althea Sclander and Dermot Garrowby need to know of their existence.

In the UK there is the British Academy for those in some Humanities and some Social Sciences disciplines, the newer Royal Academy of Engineering, and the newcomer, The Academy for the Learned Societies in the Social Sciences. The British Academy was founded in 1902, now has 729 fellows (84 women), in 18 sections of which six are for social science. The sections are unbalanced, compared to the distribution of disciplines in universities. More than one third of the humanities sections are for history, including history of art, but there is no English section. The role of the British Academy is more contentious in academic life than that of The Royal Society: many scholars do not believe that the award of the FBA is an objective measure of scholarly achievement – they see the elections as dominated by Oxford, Cambridge and London (the golden triangle) and by traditional disciplines such as classics and Hebrew with a total exclusion of exciting new fields such as cultural studies, and new approaches such as poststructuralism. One past president, quoted in the *THES* (28 January 2002), reinforced this view by saying:

> There is no point in pretending that intellectual distinction is evenly
> spread over universities or over the country. As soon as anyone in Hull,
> say, writes an important book and is elected to the British Academy, it is
> as likely as not that they will move to Oxford or Cambridge.

These top awards and elite bodies may seem very far removed from the
everyday lives of ordinary university staff with essays to mark and grant
applications to write. However, the networks and insights gained by those
on the decision-making bodies can and should be harnessed to help more
junior colleagues.

Let us return to Arlinghurst:

> Rick Dyne is having lunch with Prof. Barharrow. He is depressed
> because his latest grant application to the EPSRC, his third, has once
> again been rated Alpha but not funded. Prof. Barharrow tells him
> several stories about other young scientists, including himself, who
> experienced this. After lunch Prof. Barharrow wanders into the office
> of the Head of Department, Prof. Inglestone, and mentions Rick 'not
> my area, Bill – but can we do something for him?'

During the next two years the two professors invite six members of the
relevant EPSRC panel down to Arlinghurst, to give papers, to examine PhD
theses, to advise on rebuilding one of the labs, to a university 'feast', to the
regional conference, to meet a visiting Australian. In each case Rick is
included in the event: he chairs that departmental seminar, he is the
internal examiner, he shows the visitor the lab, he meets the dinner guest
from the train, he sits next to the visitor at the conference dinner. He had
not met all these top figures as a colleague before. To his surprise, but not,
of course, the surprise of either professor, his next application to EPSRC
not only gets an alpha, it also gets funding. Neither professor tells Rick what
they did. They only did it because of the alpha ratings. Their behaviour does
not demonstrate any lack of 'faith' in peer review. They both believe Rick's
work is good, and that the problem with funding was that he was not
'known': all they did was ensure he got 'known'. Because they moved in
elite circles, they knew that good work must not only be done, but it must be
seen to be done. They used their insights to hypothesize that Dr Dyne's
academic potential was not yet widely known, and their networks to ensure
that key figures in UK physics met Dr Dyne, and had a chance to decide for
themselves if his work was potentially valuable. Junior people who do not
talk to their more senior colleagues, and do not listen to the stories about
Nobel ceremonial waistcoats, locksmiths, or what the funding bodies'
priorities are, are likely to miss out on career opportunities. The lessons in
Cornford's (1908) book are still valid: young scholars in a hurry can damage
their prospects without ever knowing how and why. Knowledge is an
excellent protection against being a victim.

Appendix 1: Further reading on writing and publication

These are books that could usefully be held not only in the library of your university, but as a staff development collection in a department, signed out from a reliable secretary. There are five sections:

1. Books on grammar, punctuation and style;
2. Books on writing (practical help);
3. Books on publishing and dissemination;
4. Books on all stages of research projects;
5. Reflexive works on how texts are produced.

We have annotated the entries when their content is not immediately obvious from the title.

1. Books on grammar, punctuation and style

Oxford University Press have a useful series: *One Step Ahead*. These are small, cheap books, all of which would be helpful to any author.

Allen, R. (2002) *Punctuation*, Oxford: Oxford University Press.

Allen, R. (2002) *Spelling*, Oxford: Oxford University Press. The other titles in this series appear in the section on dissemination.

Collinson, D. *et al.* (1992) *Plain English*, Buckingham: Open University Press.

Cutts, M. (1990) *The Plain English Guide*, Oxford: Oxford University Press.

Dummett, M. (1992) *Grammar and Style*, London: Duckworth.

Kirkman, J. (1993) *Full Marks*, Marlborough: Ransbury Books.

Kirkman, J. (1996) *Good Style*, London: Spon.

Manser, M.H. (1990) *Bloomsbury Good Word Guide*, London: Bloomsbury.

Ritter, R.M. (2002) *The Oxford Guide to Style*, Oxford: Oxford University Press. This is too big and daunting for students to buy, but it is sensible to ensure it is held in the library reference collection so you can consult it.

Whale, J. (1984) *Put it in Writing*, London: Dent.

The Bloomsbury *Encarta Concise Dictionary* was created for students, is based on research into current mistakes in usage, and its usage notes do not assume an unrealistic level of grammatical and syntactical expertise.

Turabian, K. (1996) *The Manual for Writers of Term Papers, Theses and Dissertations* (6th edn), Chicago and London: University of Chicago Press. Turabian died in 1987 at the age of 94, but her invaluable book lives on, as useful in 2007 as it was in its original 1937 version. Over six million purchasers cannot be wrong. There have been British editions, the first in 1982 by J.E. Spink.

It is also helpful to have available at least one guide to writing without racism and sexism, such as:

Frank, F.W. and Treichler, P.A. (1989) *Language, Gender and Professional Writing*, New York: The MLA of America.

Schwartz, Maria (1995) *Guidelines for Bias-Free Writing*, Bloomington, IN: Indiana University Press. This is the official guide produced by the Association of American University Presses.

2. Practical help with writing

There are books for social scientists about how to settle down and actually produce something.

Becker, H.S. (1986) *Writing for Social Scientists*, Chicago: University of Chicago Press. This is marvellous – helpful *and* funny.

Becker, H.S. (1998) *Tricks of the Trade*, Chicago: University of Chicago Press. This is a companion to his book on writing, this time about thinking – excellent.

Booth, W.C. *et al.* (1995) *The Craft of Research*, Chicago: University of Chicago Press. Part 4 is all about presenting your material and is excellent.

Fox, M.F. (ed.) (1985) *Scholarly Writing and Publishing*, Boulder, Co: Westview Press. Chapters 7–10 present accounts of people solving their writing problems.

Richardson, L. (1990) *Writing Strategies: Reaching Diverse Audiences*, Thousand Oaks, CA: Sage. Tells you how to redraft the same material for different types of audience, such as an academic journal and a trade book.

Wolcott, H.F. (1990) *Writing Up Qualitative Research*, London: Sage. This is similar to Becker, but less funny.

Zerubavel, E. (1999) *The Clockwork Muse*, Cambridge, MA: Harvard University Press.

If you have to oversee undergraduates, or graduates, who seem to lack basic skills in constructing a coherent argument, they would benefit from:

Bailey, E.P. and Powell, P.A. (1987) *Writing Research Papers*, New York: Holt, Rinehart and Winston. This is an American book, mostly about 'term papers' – but British students can use it with advantage.

Cuba, L. and Cocking, J. (1994) *How to Write about the Social Sciences*, London: HarperCollins. The British equivalent.

For all graduate students, the chapters on writing in the books for PhD students can be useful.

Cryer, P. (2001) *The Research Student's Guide to Success*, Buckingham: Open University Press.

Phillips, E.M. and Pugh, D.S. (2000) *How to Get a PhD* (3rd edn), Buckingham: Open University Press.

The American equivalent is:

Rudestam, K.E. and Newton, R.R. (2001) *Surviving your Dissertation*, London: Sage.

The advice book for supervisors also has a chapter on writing (Chapter 8).

Delamont, S., Atkinson P. and Parry, O. (1997) *Supervising the PhD*, Buckingham: Open University Press. This could be helpful if you have to supervise people who are having writing problems.

There are some books for doctoral students specifically about writing, which can be helpful for research assistants, associates and fellows also – indeed for experienced authors too:

Bolker, Joan (1998) *Writing your Dissertation in Fifteen Minutes a Day*, New York: Henry Holt. Written by an experienced writing coach, this is empowering and encouraging.

Murray, Rowena (2002) *How to Write a Thesis*, Buckingham: Open University Press. Murray, who is an experienced 'coach' of graduate students and of supervisors, provides lots of guidance and ideas on how a thesis can be written, set in a wider context.

Brause, Rita S.(2000) *Writing Your Doctoral Dissertation*, London: Falmer. This is an American version of Murray. Because of the structure of the American PhD, this book would be particularly useful to candidates doing Professional Doctorates. Brause has two very useful lists of further reading, on doctoral dissertations and on academic life.

Dunleavy, Patrick (2003) *Authoring a PhD*, London: Palgrave. Too dull and 'worthy' for our own tastes, compared to Murray or Becker. However, some students and colleagues might well find it reassuringly professional and dispassionate.

Glatthorn, Allan A. (1998) *Writing the Winning Dissertation*, Thousand Oaks, CA: Corwin Press. Allan Glatthorn has chaired about 100 dissertation committees in the USA. His book distills his best advice. We can all learn from it, not just American colleagues.

Woods, Peter (1999) *Successful Writing for Qualitative Researchers*, London: Routledge. In this volume Woods mixes autobiographical and didactic material to cover all aspects of writing and publication for qualitative researchers. This would help anyone in arts and social sciences.

3. Books on dissemination and publishing

A. Dissemination

In the Oxford University Press series *One Step Ahead* the following are self-explanatory:

Baverstock, A. (2002) *Publicity, Newsletters and Press Releases*.

Dorner, J. (2002) *Writing for the Internet*.

Seely, J. (2002) *Writing Reports*.

B. Conventional publication: books and journals

Barzun, J. (1986) *On Writing, Editing and Publishing*, Chicago: University of Chicago Press. This is helpful for people in humanities, where Barzun is a guru.

Day, R.A. (1995) *How to Write and Publish a Scientific Paper*, Cambridge: Cambridge University Press. This is clearly written and would help any scientist prepare work for publication.

Derricourt, R. (1996) *An Author's Guide to Scholarly Publishing*, Princeton: Princeton University Press. Derricourt uses the format of letters to authors to demystify all aspects of publishing books (and starting a new journal). If you imagine that you had a friendly publisher prepared to explain everything you ever needed to know, this is what they would tell you over a couple of years.

Fox, M.F. (1985) *Scholarly Writing and Publishing*, Boulder, Co: Westview Press. This is a useful collection on getting published *and* on working effectively. Chapters 1–6 are about publishing articles and books.

Germano, W. (2001) *Getting it Published*, Chicago: University of Chicago Press. This is a thorough guide to getting academic work published, which is not an entertaining read but covers all angles in a helpful way.

Pechenick, J.A. and Lamb, B.C. (1995) *How to Write about Biology*, London: HarperCollins. Does exactly what it says on the cover. It guides young scholars in the biosciences towards professional production of scientific prose.

Peters, A.D. (1996) *How to Get Research Published in Journals*, Aldershot: Gower. The author is an editor and publisher, not an academic. We found some of the ideas to be rather strange (Peters seems to think quadruple blind referencing means using four referees) but there are many helpful insights in the book.

Powell, W.W. (1985) *Getting into Print*, Chicago: University of Chicago Press. This reports an academic study of two publishing houses, Apple and Plum. Only a keen person should read it through so it will not work as a quick fix, but would be wonderful background reading for a team.

Richardson, L. (1990) *Writing Strategies: Reaching Diverse Audiences*, London: Sage. This is a useful book, because the author shows how she wrote up the same material for an academic book, a journal, and for a mass media piece.

4. Research projects through all stages

Booth, W.C., Colomb, G.G. and Williams, J.M. (1995) *The Craft of Research*, Chicago: University of Chicago Press. Leads the reader through all the stages of an arts or social science research project. Experienced researchers would learn from it, and for novices it is invaluable.

5. Reflexive works

There are books designed to make us reflexive and self-conscious about the texts we read and those we write. Such books can be intimidating and paralysing for some people, while others find them stimulating and even liberating.

Nigel Gilbert's essay 'Writing about social research' in his edited collection *Researching Social Life*, London: Sage (1983, 2001), is a good introduction to the genre: if that seems pointless and annoying, the reflexive works are not for you.

Laurel Richardson (1994) has a famous essay 'Writing: A Method of Inquiry' in N. Denzin and Y. Lincoln (1994) *Handbook of Qualitative Research*, London: Sage, which is reprinted/revised in the 2000 second edition. It is deeply ethnocentric, but worth reading. She develops her ideas in Laurel

Richardson (2002) 'Poetic Representation of Interviews' in J.F. Gubrium and J.A. Holstein (eds) *Handbook of Interview Research*, London: Sage. Richardson is famous, or infamous, in social sciences for using unconventional ways to present her results, such as poems and plays. Reading her papers from 1994, 2000 and 2002 shows the development of her ideas.

Jonathan Spencer (2001) provides a useful overview of the issues, in his paper 'Ethnography after postmodernism' in P. Atkinson, A. Coffey, S. Delamont, J. Lofland and L. Lofland (eds) (2001) *Handbook of Ethnography*, London: Sage.

Some other relevant works in this vein are:

Atkinson, P. (1990) *The Ethnographic Imagination*, London: Routledge.

Atkinson, P. (1992) *Understanding Ethnographic Texts*, Thousand Oaks, CA: Sage.

Coffey, A. (2000) *The Ethnographic Self*, London: Sage.

Coffey, A. and Atkinson, P. (1996) *Making Sense of Qualitative Data*, Thousand Oaks, CA: Sage.

Wolf, M. (1992) *The Thrice Told Tale*, Stanford, CA: Stanford University Press. In this book Wolf reflects on her research in Taiwan, using a short story, her original notes and her academic publications.

Appendix 2: CVCP publication categories

The CVCP categories are a relatively straightforward way of classifying publications and other outputs which has been used since the mid-1980s. All the universities in Britain collect a list of all the output of all the staff each year, and the categories are also used in the Research Assessment Exercises.

1   Authored Books
2   Edited Books
3   Short Works
4   Conference Contributions, Refereed
5   Conference Contributions, Other
6   Departmental Working Papers
7   Edited Works, Contributions
8   Editorships, Journals
9   Editorships, Newsletters
10 Journal Letters, Notes, Short Papers or Abstracts
11 Academic Journal Papers
12 Professional Journal Papers
13 Popular Journal Papers
14 Official Reports
15 Review Articles
16 Reviews of Single Academic Books
17 Other Publications, Research
18 Other Publications, Research Equivalent
19 Other Media, Research
20 Other Media, Research Equivalent

Most of the categories are self-explanatory, but it is worth quoting the explanations of the three types of journal article.

Journal papers (categories 11–13)

The three categories provided, academic (category 11), popular (category 13) and professional (category 12) are meant to cover all possibilities. For the purpose of this survey, academic and professional journals should be defined as follows. An academic journal (category 11) normally contains research papers aimed primarily at the academic and research community. The papers will normally be refereed, but may not be. A professional journal (category 12) is normally aimed at practising members of a profession and mainly contains papers informing members of current developments in the profession rather than communicating research results. Such papers will not normally be refereed by the academic and research community, although they may be. Clearly, Category 11 is the high status one in academia, but it can be useful to publish things in Category 12 because that is a form of dissemination to users and beneficiaries, or Category 13, because popular journals pay fees. Categories 17 or 18 are designed to include music scores or scripts. Categories 19 or 20 can include performances of music or plays and works of art such as sculpture or paintings. Other possible entries here are architectural or engineering designs, or maps or software.

So each year institutions collect data on publications and other output, classified by the RAE Unit of Assessment, the CVCP category and the fraction attributable to that institution. Sara's return for 2001 is given below, listed as Unit of Assessment 42. You will see that each entry starts with a code. The first number is the 1992–2001 Unit of Assessment 42, which is Sociology and Social Policy. The second number is the CVCP classification code. The third is the fraction of the publication attributable to Cardiff: you will notice that the last item is only 75 per cent attributable to Cardiff because one of the authors is from another institution.

[# 42/1/1.0] Delamont, S., *Changing Women, Unchanged Men: Sociological Perspectives on Gender in a Post-Industrial Society*, Buckingham, Open University Press (2001), pp. *ix* + 128, ISBN 0 335 20037 0

[# 42/7/1.0] Delamont, S., Las ovejas negras: los gamberros y la sociologia de la education, *La Sociologia de la Education: Balance y Perspectivas* [Editor: J. Varela], Madrid: Ministry of Education (2001) 61–78 (Special Issue of *Revista de Education* No. 324, April), ISSN 0034–8082

[# 42/7/1.0] Delamont, S., Bernstein, Basil, *A Tribute to Basil Bernstein 1924–2000* (Editors: Sally Power, P. Aggleton, J. Brannen, A. Brown, L. Chisholm and J. Mace), London: Institute of Education (2001) 104–5, ISBN 0 85473 6514

[# 42/10/1.0] Delamont, S., Sociological Research on the PhD, *Network*, 79 p. 15 (2001), No ISSN

[# 42/11/1.0] Delamont, S., Reflections on Social Exclusion, *International Studies in Sociology of Education*, 11, 1, (2001) 25–40, ISSN 0962–0214

[# 42/11/1.0] Delamont, S. and Atkinson, P., Doctoring Uncertainty:

Mastering craft knowledge, *Social Studies of Science*, 31, 1, (2001) 87–108, ISSN 0306–3127

[♯ 42/16/1] Delamont, S., Review of 'Constructing Female Identities', Amira Proweller, New York: State University of New York Press (1998) pp. 198, ISBN 0 9719 3771 X. *Qualitative Studies in Education* 14, 3 (2001), 453–5, ISSN 9951 8398

[♯ 42/16/1] Delamont, S., Review of 'Taking sides in Social Research' Martyn Hammersley, London: Routledge (2000), pp. 196, ISBN 0 415 20287 6, *British Journal of Sociology of Education*, 22, 1, (2001) 157–160, ISSN 0142–5692

[♯ 42/6/0.75] Delamont, S. Atkinson, P.A., Coffey, A. and Burgess, R.G., *An Open Exploratory Spirit? Ethnography at Cardiff 1974–2001*, Cardiff: School of Social Sciences [2001] Working Paper No. 20, 56 pp., ISBN 1 872 33058 4, http://www.cardiff.ac.uk/socsi/publications/workingpapers.html

You will also see that the ISBN of all books and the ISSN of all periodicals is given. (All books have a unique International Standard Book Number, all journals an International Standard Serial Number.)

Appendix 3: Book proposal

We presented our book proposal with the following letter to the publisher:

> Cardiff School of Social Sciences
> Cardiff University
> Glamorgan Building
> King Edward VII Avenue
> Cardiff CF10 3WT

John Skelton
Open University Press
Celtic Court
22 Ballmoor
Buckingham MK18 1XW

Dear John,

We enclose a proposal for a new book. It incorporates material and ideas that we have been using for some time in staff development programmes, as well as drawing on our research in higher education and our own professional experience.

W have three chapters in preliminary draft, and – as you will see – a fairly clear idea of the contents in outline. We would expect to complete a MS for delivery in April 2002. We think it would make a rather good addition to your list, and would complement out book on supervising the PhD.

We look forward to hearing from you in due course. In the meantime, our very best wishes.

Yours sincerely

Sara Delamont   Paul Atkinson

Building research careers and research groups

Sara Delamont & Paul Atkinson

Address for Correspondence

Cardiff School of Social Sciences
Cardiff University
Glamorgan Building
King Edward VII Avenue
Cardiff CF10 3WT

Email AtkinsonPA@Cardiff.ac.uk

Background and rationale

The development of research is a major preoccupation for contemporary academics in the United Kingdom and elsewhere. Research is decreasingly a matter of 'private' scholarship, and increasingly a topic for collective and strategic commitment. Successful academics need to develop careers that are shaped primarily by the trajectory of their research. While the collective planning and management of research is well established in the natural sciences, it is a less familiar process in the humanities and the social sciences.

This book is aimed primarily at academics in the latter categories. It is intended to provide practical advice on the development of research-led careers and research groups. It will be used on an individual basis by academics, and will also provide a resource for the ever-increasing number of staff development seminars and training programmes in higher education.

It is hardly possible to do justice to the entire range of disciplines in the academy. This is aimed primarily at the humanities (including the arts and performing arts) and social sciences (including business and law).

The competition and the market

The market is primarily researchers and academics in higher education, mainly in the United Kingdom. Although some general issues will be of relevance beyond that readership, it is not possible to make such books of equal relevance beyond national boundaries.

There is virtually no direct competitor. There are specific topics covered elsewhere – such as how to get research grants – but they are predominantly American and do not travel well. They include the Sage series of survival guides for academics, such as *Proposal Writing* by Coley and Scheinberg, or *Proposals that Work* by Locke, Spirduso and Silverman. Among similar books in the UK, the Open University Press has a very successful series of guides for students and academics. One covers similar ground – *The Academic Career Handbook* by Blaxter, Hughes and Tight – but the two are complementary rather than direct competitors. Inevitably, there is some degree of overlap in subject matter. But our proposed book covers a more restricted range of topics, such as publishing and research funding, than the Blaxter *et al.* (which itself includes teaching and other professional activities), and covers them in greater depth. Moreover, it includes issues that neither the Blaxter nor any other book covers – such as the Research Assessment Exercise and the development of research groups.

Style

In keeping with the envisaged market, the book will be written in a direct, accessible style. We shall write as if addressing the readers – our professional peers – directly, rather than writing in a very impersonal way. We shall draw on our own research, our own professional experience and – where available – published research. We shall illustrate the chapters with 'boxes' giving specific examples, potted cases and so on. Where possible, guidance will be given for further reading and references to other sources of information, such as websites. The reader who works her or his way through this book will be well placed to understand key issues and processes within the contemporary university, and will understand how to promote not only her or his own research career, but also the research success and career development of research students and junior colleagues.

The authors

We can build upon extensive knowledge and experience in these matters. **Sara Delamont** has, amongst other things, been Dean of two different Faculties at Cardiff University, and Head of the School of Social and Administrative Studies. She is the national convenor of the Standing Conference of Arts and Social Sciences. She is a Past President of the British Educational Research Association. She has written extensively on education at all levels, gender, and research methods. Her books include: *Knowledgeable Women, Fieldwork in Educational Settings, Feminism and the Classroom Teacher, Fighting Familiarity, Sex Roles and the School, Interaction in the Classroom*. **Paul Atkinson** has been a Pro Vice-Chancellor and a Head of Department at Cardiff University. He is a member of the Economic and Social Research Council's Research Resources Board. His books include: *The Clinical Experience, Ethnography: Principles in Practice, The Ethnographic Imagination, Understanding Ethnographic Texts, Making Sense of Qualitative Data*.

Together (with Odette Parry) we have conducted ESRC-funded research on the processes of higher degree supervision and research training in the natural and social sciences. That research has resulted in a monograph (*The Doctoral Experience*) and a book of practical advice for academics (*Supervising the PhD: A Guide to Success*) which has proved successful, has been well received, and is used for staff development purposes in higher education.

We are also the co-editors of the new journal *Qualitative Research* and of the new *Handbook of Ethnograph* for Sage.

We are well placed to write this book. We have experience of running a successful department in a research-led university. In successive exercises we took our own department from lowly Research Assessment grades to a 4 for over 30 research-active academics. We have a track record of funded research that includes grants from ESRC, the Wellcome Trust, the Leverhulme Trust, the Welsh Office, the DHSS and the European Union. We have supervised a steady stream of PhD students in the sociology of education, medicine, qualitative methodology, and work and professions, as well as about 100 Masters dissertations. We have built a research group and a research tradition at Cardiff that is widely recognized as one of the best of its kind.

We have conducted staff development seminars on these issues at Cardiff University and at other institutions for some years.

Synopsis

1. Introduction: research imperatives

In this introductory chapter we outline the significant themes of the book by discussing the imperative for research success in the contemporary university. This will include a brief discussion of the significance of research success for the prestige of academic institutions, their international standing and their funding. It will outline how research development and career development are interlinked in the contemporary academy. It will also emphasize the intrinsic rewards of research success as well as the extrinsic rewards and pressures facing today's academy. It will stress the positive virtue of being in control of one's own career trajectory and one's research, rather than being a victim of the pressures. Career building and the contingencies of promotion in academic life require advice and explicit management, on the part of the academic him- or herself, and by advisers and mentors. We shall consider the kind of research-related criteria that are invoked by committees in considering individual candidates for appointment to posts or internal promotion.

4000 words

2. Peers and peer reviewing

A great deal of the activities and judgements we discuss are predicated on various processes of 'peer review'. Research careers and research groups are predicated on the peer review of research bids, research publications, curricula vitae (for promotion) and exercises like the Research Assessment Exercise. Here we introduce those issues through an exploration of what peer review means and how it is conducted. We explain what is meant by 'peer review' and why it plays such a central role in academic life. There have been reviews of the peer-review process, and although it is recognized to be imperfect, it is also regarded as the best available system. It is intended to ensure high standards of scholarship, and equitable treatment of submissions. It enshrines the principle that academic work is judged by fellow academics and other experts and, to that extent, a certain principle of democracy in academic work. It is not, however, egalitarian: it produces hierarchies of esteem. In addition to explaining the processes and principles of peer review we also discuss the processes of becoming part of the peer-review system, building networks and becoming part of the 'core sets' of one's academic field. We thus explore how to build networks, how to make contacts, how to establish and position oneself, how to develop patterns of research collaboration. This chapter introduces themes that are discussed in more detail in subsequent chapters.

6000 words

3. Building a research culture and a research group

Research success in today's academy can be promoted through a collective commitment. In the most general sense, this depends on the university itself promoting a research-led culture throughout the institution. It requires research-oriented academic leadership at the top. That needs to be repeated and reinforced at the level of the school or department, where the management of people and resources needs to promote research. This is not just a matter of exhortation. It requires the development of a pervasive culture in which research and publishing are treated as core activities, as part of the collective commitment, as having visible benefits, and as part of the departmental ethos. Although not traditionally part of the disciplinary culture, there is increasing need in the humanities and social sciences for the development of 'research groups'. They may not be quite the same as the research groups as found in the laboratories of the natural sciences, but there are good arguments for the promotion of groupings of academics with a shared research focus, some collaborative projects, a collective strategy. The research grouping also provides the environment within which junior staff can be mentored and helped by more experienced senior colleagues, and within which research students can be socialized into a departmental and disciplinary culture. Research groupings and collective strength have benefits for the profiling of research, and in the external perception of research, including the Research Assessment Exercise.

8000 words

4. Supervising and mentoring

The development of the research group depends on successful processes of mentoring and supervision. Research students need to be supervised. This involves more than just the intellectual oversight of their individual research projects. Increasingly, it also involves the creation of a research environment. The movement is towards systematic research training for all research students. This includes not only the provision of specific research skills and intellectual direction. It also implies socializing research students into the craft skills of academic life; introducing the apprentices to the 'mysteries' of the craft; promoting self-confidence and self-management. Likewise, the development of a research group involves mentoring and developing one's research workers. Contract researchers are not just 'hired hands' who are casualized labour. They represent a major investment, and need to be brought on. Whether their career develops within the same research group, or whether they are mobile, in the longer term everybody benefits if research workers are made part of the research team, are granted proper recognition within the research group, the department and the university at large.

8000 words

5. *Research funding*

Research funding is of central importance in the promotion of research, as well as its external assessment. It is not vital to have research funding to do good research of many sorts – but there are few research activities that cannot benefit from external funding. We shall consider how to plan funded research for oneself and/or one's research group, and the role of external funding in creating and maintaining one's research group. We shall discuss the main steps in constructing a fundable research proposal, with particular reference to the Research Councils (including the AHRB), Europe, and the major charities. We shall discuss the function of the small personal research grant, the project grant, and the programme-level grant. We shall provide basic advice on how to construct grant proposals that capture the attention of reviewers and funding committees. We shall outline the basic elements of research planning and costing that go into proposals. We shall discuss the vexed questions of indirect costs or 'overheads'. We shall provide practical advice on how to avoid the commonest mistakes in preparing and submitting research grant bids. UK funding agencies are all over-subscribed, and the purely numerical odds are always against success. One must, therefore, do all one can to reduce the unnecessary mistakes and hostages to fortune that can mar the proposals from inexperienced (sometimes experienced!) would-be researchers. We shall discuss the merits of collaboration and inter-departmental, inter-disciplinary and inter-institutional collaboration. We shall also discuss the management of funded research once the grant-getting has been successful. Planning needs to be carried forward from preparing a bid to preparing for the research itself.

8000 words

6. *Writing*

Research is about writing. If research is not published, then it is pointless. If an academic does not publish successfully, then her or his career will suffer in consequence. Surprisingly large numbers of academics find difficulty in writing – or at least in getting things written. There seems to be a gulf between the capacity to write as a student, a research student or research associate, and the ability to turn research into writing for publication. This is not just a matter of personal 'gifts', and all academics can face writing problems at some stage or another in the course of their career. In this chapter we explore how to turn writing into a non-threatening kind of activity, how to promote it as a craft skill to be taught and talked about, rather than a mysterious and private thing. We discuss how to develop writing circles, how to share written work among the research group. We also discuss the personal and professional issues concerning collaboration and co-authorship. Writing and its management form a key aspect of the work of the research group, and the encouragement of writing is a key function of the research group leader or the individual mentor. There are strategies for writing that can be developed and shared.

8000 words

7. *Publishing in journals*

Publication in decent academic journals is one of the key outcomes of research and writing. We outline for the reader the basic mechanics of journal publishing, and provide insight into the editorial process. We help the reader to think about how to choose a journal to send their work to, and what to do when they get an editorial response. We offer advice on how to avoid the commonest problems and pitfalls in submitting work to academic journals, and therefore how to minimize one's own rejection rate. We discuss how to conduct one's own 'market research' on journals, and how to recognize that journals need their authors just as much as authors need the journals. We use the chapter to provide practical advice on how to be a good reviewer for academic journals. Being a good reviewer helps one become a better author, by developing the right critical faculties. We also discuss how to have one's own journal, for one's own department or research group.

8000 words

8. *Publishing books*

We discuss how to prepare a proposal for an academic monograph, and a textbook. This includes the preparation of a synopsis of the book, with the kind of information that publishers require: how to think about the market, the level and readership, the international appeal (if any), the courses it may be adopted for, competitor books, the book's distinctive features and selling points. We discuss the importance of realism in making claims about such features, and also being realistic about the proposed length of the book and the deadline for the delivery of the manuscript. We also provide advice on how to approach publishers' commissioning editors, and how to get to meet them. In addition to the single-authored book, we also comment on collaborative authoring, and the production of edited collections. We discuss how co-authoring can fit into the more general pattern of research groupings and their development. We also discuss the tensions and synergies between commercial publication, personal advancement, research assessment, and the external promotion of one's reputation.

8000 words

9. Research assessment

Academic judgements and peer reviewing find their most dramatic and pressing manifestation in the periodic review of research performance. Academics in today's universities and other institutions are subject to constant assessment and inspection. The academy is the site of 'audit' and 'transparency' of all sorts. None is more pressing that the Research Assessment Exercise, which is the highest-profile assessment exercise in higher education. Not everyone understands the process and its outcomes. In particular, the mix of 'objective' performance indicators and the more 'subjective' evaluation of research culture is not always understood. All academics need to understand the basic principles and procedures involved in these exercises. Although the details of successive RAEs change, the underlying logic remains the same. We therefore explain clearly and succinctly what it means in general, what it means for a department, what it means for a research group and what it means for an individual. We also discuss how it works in principle. We then go on to offer general advice about how to prepare for the research assessment process – irrespective of the precise mechanics of any given exercise after the 2001 RAE itself. We go back over the issues we have already discussed in the book in order to show how each of the issues we have covered enters into the research assessment.

8000 words

10. Conclusion: taking control

In a brief conclusion of this book we assert once more what we take to be the main message: that academics should try to exercise control over their careers, and over their intellectual destiny. This involves exercising control over their research careers. This also has implications for the rest of their professional activities. While this book is focused exclusively on research and its outputs, taking control of research has direct implications for other key functions: teaching and learning within a research culture; administration within a research environment; the development of the research-led university. Success also brings extrinsic rewards as well as the intrinsic intellectual rewards of the research process itself.

4000 words

Total length 70,000 words

References

Abbott, Andrew (1999) *Department and Discipline*, Chicago: University of Chicago Press.

Aisenberg, N. and Harrington, M. (1988) *Women of Academe: Outsiders in the Sacred Grove*, Amherst: University of Massachusetts Press.

Atkinson, P.A., Bachelor, C. and Parsons, E. (1996) The career of a medical discovery, *Qualitative Health Research*, 6(2): 224–55.

Atkinson, P.A., Bachelor, C. and Parsons, E. (1997) The rhetoric of prediction, skill and chance in the research to clone a disease gene, in M.A. Elston (ed.) *The Sociology of Medical Science and Technology*, Oxford: Blackwell, pp. 101–25.

Atkinson, P. and Coffey, A. (1997) Analysing documentary realities, in D. Silverman (ed.) *Qualitative Research*, London: Sage, pp. 45–62.

Atkinson, P. and Coffey, A. (2004) Analysing documentary realities again, in D. Silverman (ed.) *Qualitative Research* (2nd edn), London: Sage.

Barzun, J. (1986) *On Writing, Editing and Publishing*, Chicago: University of Chicago Press.

Becker, H.S. (1986) *Writing for Social Scientists*, Chicago: University of Chicago Press.

Bell, Colin (1977) Reflections on the Banbury research, in C. Bell and H. Newby, (eds) *Doing Sociological Research*, London: Allen and Unwin.

Blaxter, L., Hughes, C. and Tight, M. (1998) *The Academic Career Handbook*, Buckingham: Open University Press.

Booth, W.C., Colomb, G.G. and Williams, J.M. (1995) *The Craft of Research*, Chicago: University of Chicago Press.

Broad, W. and Wade, N. (1982) *Betrayers of the Truth*, New York: Simon and Schuster.

Brouns, M. (2001) Male bias in assessment and decisions for scientific grants, in A. Colosimo *et al.* (eds) *Women and Science*, Brussels: European Commission.

Brown, G. and Atkins, M. (1988) *Effective Teaching in Higher Education*, London: Methuen.

Burgess, R.G. (ed.) (1995) *Howard Becker on Education*, Buckingham: Open University Press.

Caplan, P.J. (1993) *Lifting a Ton of Feathers*, Toronto: Toronto University Press.

Clark, B.R. (ed.) (1994) *The Research Foundations of Graduate Education*, Berkeley: California University Press.

Coffey, A. and Atkinson, P.A. (1996) *Making Sense of Qualitative Research*, Thousand Oaks: Sage.

Collins, H.F. and Pinch, T. (1993) *The Golem*, Cambridge: Cambridge University Press.

Collins, H.F. and Pinch, T. (1998) *The Golem at Large*, Cambridge: Cambridge University Press.

Cooper, J.E. and Stevens, D.D. (eds) (2002) *Tenure in the Sacred Grove*, Albany: SUNY University Press.

Cornford, J. (1908) *Microcosmographia Academica*, Cambridge: Bowes and Bowes.

CUDAH (2002) *Doctoral Futures: Career Destinations of Arts and Humanities Research Students*, Leicester: De Montfort University, for the Council of University Deans of Arts and Humanities.

CVCP (1987) *Academic Staff Training: Code of Practice*, London: Committee of Vice-Chancellors and Principals.

Danforth, L. (1995) *The Macedonian Crisis*, Princeton: Princeton University Press.

Deem, R. and Brehony, K. (2000) Doctoral students' access to research cultures, *Studies in Higher Education*, 25(2): 149–65.

Delamont, S. (ed.) (2002) *Academia 2010*, Cardiff: SCASS.

Delamont, S. (2003) The marriage analogy?, in C. Pritchard and P. Trowler (eds) *Realizing Qualitative Research into Higher Education*, Aldershot: Ashgate.

Delamont, S. and Atkinson, P.A. (2001) Doctoring uncertainty, *Social Studies of Science*, 31(1): 87–108.

Delamont, S., Atkinson, P.A. and Parry, O. (1997a) Critical mass and pedagogic continuity, *British Journal of the Sociology of Education*, 18(4): 533–50.

Delamont, S., Atkinson, P.A. and Parry, O. (1997b) Critical mass and doctoral research, *Studies in Higher Education*, 22(3): 319–32.

Delamont, S., Atkinson, P.A. and Parry, O. (1997c) *Supervising the PhD*, Buckingham: Open University Press.

Delamont, S., Atkinson, P.A. and Parry, O. (1998) Creating a delicate balance? *Teaching in Higher Education*, 3(2): 157–72.

Delamont, S., Atkinson, P.A. and Parry, O. (2000) *The Doctoral Experience*, London: Falmer.

Delamont, S. and Galton, M. (1986) *Inside the Secondary Classroom*, London: Routledge and Kegan Paul.

Derricourt, R. (1996) *An Author's Guide to Scholarly Publishing*, Princeton: Princeton University Press.

Devos, A. and Casson, C. (2002) *Researching Women. An Evaluation of the Second Year of the Women Research 21 Program*, Kensington, Au: University of New South Wales.

Dooley, P., Graham, N. and Whitfield, R. (1981) *Survey of Educational Researchers in Britain*, Birmingham: University of Aston, Department of Educational Enquiry.

Eggleston, J.F. and Delamont, S. (1982) *Supervision of Students for Research Degrees*, Kendall: Dixon and Co. for Bera.

Etzkowitz, H., Kemelgor, C. and Uzzi, B. (2000) *Athena Unbound*, Cambridge: Cambridge University Press.

Floud, R. (2002) Reflections, in S. Delamont (ed.) *Academia 2010*, Cardiff: SCASS.

Foreman, A. (1998) *Georgiana, Duchess of Devonshire*, London: HarperCollins.

Fox, M.F. (ed.) (1985) *Scholarly Writing and Publishing*, Boulder, Co: Westview Press.

Fox, M.F. (1995) Women and scientific careers, in S. Jasanoff, G.E. Markle, J.C. Petersen and T. Pinch (eds) *Handbook of Science and Technology Studies*, Thousand Oaks: Sage.

Freedman, E.S., Patrick, H., Somekh, B., McIntyre, D. and Wikeley, F. (2000) *Quality Conditions for Quality Research*, Nottingham: British Educational Research Association.

Gaber, I. (n.d.) *Television and Radio: A Best Practice Guide*, Swindon: ESRC.

Galton, M. and Simon, B. (1980) *Progress and Performance in the Primary Classroom*, London: Routledge and Kegan Paul.

Galton, M., Simon, B. and Croll, P. (1980) *Inside the Primary Classroom*, London: Routledge and Kegan Paul.

Galton, M. and Willcocks, J. (1983) *Moving from the Primary Classroom*, London: Routledge and Kegan Paul.

Germano, W. (2001) *Getting it Published*, Chicago: University of Chicago Press.

Glover, J. (1999) *Women and Scientific Employment*, London: Macmillan.

Gornick, V. (1983) *Women in Science*, New York: Simon and Schuster.

Grant, J., Burden, S. and Breen G. (1997) No evidence of sexism in peer review, *Nature*, 390: 438.

Hammersley, M. and Atkinson, P. (1983) *Ethnography*, London: Tavistock.

Hammersley, M. and Atkinson, P. (1995) *Ethnography*, 2nd edn, London: Routledge.

Harris, M. (1996) *Review of Postgraduate Education*, 2 vols, Bristol: The Higher Education Funding Council for England.

Harris, M. (2002) Reflections, in S. Delamont (ed.) *Academia 2010*, Cardiff: SCASS.

Hess, D.J. (1991) *Spirits and Scientists*, University Park, Pennsylvania: Pennsylvania State University Press.

Hood, J.C. (1985) The lone scholar myth, in M.F. Fox (ed.) *Scholarly Writing and Publishing*, Boulder, Co: Westview Press.

Jones, D. (1993) *Murder at the MLA*, Athens, Georgia: Georgia University Press.

Kevles, D.J. (1998) *The Baltimore Case*, New York: W.W. Norton.

Koch, J. (2002) Coping with feelings of fraudulence, in J.E. Cooper and D.D. Stevens (eds) *Tenure in the Sacred Grove*, Albany: SUNY Press.

Labinger, J.A. and Collins, H.F. (eds) (2001) *The One Culture?*, Chicago: University of Chicago Press.

Lathen, E. (1982) *Green Grow the Dollars*, London: Gollancz.

Locke, L.F., Spirduso, W.W. and Silverman, S.J. (2000) *Proposals that Work*, 4th edn, London: Sage.

Lodge, D. (1984) *Small World*, London: Secker and Warburg.

Lodge, D. (1988) *Nice Work*, London: Secker and Warburg.

Lucas, L. (2001) *The Research Game*, unpublished PhD thesis, University of Warwick.

Lurie, A. (1967) *Imaginary Friends*, New York: Penguin.

McGrath, C. (n.d.) *Influencing the UK Policy-making Process*, Swindon: ESRC.

Merton, R.K. (1968) The Matthew effect in Science, reprinted in R.K. Merton (1973b) *The Sociology of Science*, Chicago: University of Chicago Press.

Morley, L., Leonard, D. and David, M. (2002) Variations in Vivas, *Studies in Higher Education*, 27(3): 263–74.

Mosley, W. (2000) Holiday is not an option, *The Guardian*, 26 July, 12–13.

Mullins, G. and Kiley, M. (2002) It's a PhD, not a Nobel Prize, *Studies in Higher Education*, 27(4): 369–86.

Newby, H. (1977) Editorial note, in C. Bell and H. Newby (eds) *Doing Sociological Research*, London: Allen and Unwin.

Parry, O., Atkinson, P.A. and Delamont, S. (1994) Disciplinary identities and doctoral work, in R.G. Burgess (ed.) *Postgraduate Education and Training in Social Sciences*, London: Jessica Kingsley.

Parry, O., Atkinson, P.A. and Delamont, S. (1997) The structure of PhD research, *Sociology*, 31(2): 121–9.

Parry, O., Atkinson, P.A., Delamont, S. and Hiken, A. (1994) Suspended between two stools?, in A. Coffey, and P.A. Atkinson, (eds) *Occupational Socialization and Working Lives*, Aldershot: Avebury.

Pearson, D. (2002) *Pressure Points in Academic Life*, unpublished PhD thesis, University of Wales, Cardiff.

Pert, Candace (1997) *Molecules of Emotion*, New York: Simon and Schuster.

Peters, A.D. (2003) *Winning Research Funding*, Aldershot: Gower.

Pilcher, J. (1996) *Women of Their Time*, Aldershot: Ashgate.

Platt, J. (1976) *The Realities of Research*, Brighton: Sussex University Press.

Porter, M. (1984) The modification of method in researching postgraduate education, in R.G. Burgess (ed.) *The Research Process in Educational Settings*, London: Falmer.

Powell, W.W. (1985) *Getting into Print: The Decision-Making Process in Scholarly Publishing*, Chicago: University of Chicago Press.

Punch, K. (2000) *Developing Effective Research Proposals*, London: Sage.

QAA (2001) *The Framework for Higher Education Qualifications in England, Wales and Northern Ireland*, Gloucester: QAA.

Rees, T.L. (2001) Mainstreaming gender equality in Science in the European Union: The ETAN Report, *Gender and Education*, 13(3): 243–60.

Regis, E. (1988) *Who got Einstein's Office?*, London: Simon and Schuster.

Reskin, B. (1978) Sex differentiation and the social organisation of science, *Sociological Inquiry*, 41(1): 6–37.

Rhind, D. (2003) *Great Expectations: The Social Sciences in Britain*, London: Commission on the Social Sciences.

Richardson, L. (1990) *Writing Strategies: Reaching Diverse Audiences*, Newbury Park, CA: Sage.

Roberts, G. (2002) *SET for Success: The Supply of People with Science, Technology, Engineering and Mathematics Skills*, Bristol: Higher Education Funding Council for England.

Roberts, G. (2003) *Review of Research Assessment*, Bristol: Higher Education Funding Council for England.

Rossiter, M. (1982) *Women Scientists in America: Struggles and Strategies to 1940*, Baltimore: Johns Hopkins University Press.

Roth, J. (1966) Hired hand research, *The American Sociologist*, 1 (August): 190–6.

Scott, S. (1985) Working through the contradictions in researching postgraduate education, in R.G. Burgess (ed.) *The Research Process in Educational Settings*, London: Falmer.

Simon, B. and Willcocks, J. (eds) (1981) *Research and Practice in the Primary Classroom*, London: Routledge and Kegan Paul.

Snow, C.P. (1934) *The Search*, London: Gollancz.

Snow, C.P. (1951) *The Masters*, London: Macmillan.

Snow, C.P. (1954) *The New Men*, London: Macmillan.

Snow, C.P. (1960) *The Affair*, London: Macmillan.

Sokal, A. (1996) Transgressing the boundaries, *Social Text*, 46/47: 217–52.

Sonnert, G. and Holton, G. (1995) *Who Succeeds in Science?*, New Brunswick, NJ: Rutgers University Press.

Stewart, J.I.M. (1976) *A Memorial Service*, London: Gollancz.

Swinnerton-Dyer, P. (1982) *Working Party Report on Postgraduate Education*, London: HMSO.

Tannen, D. (1990) *You Just Don't Understand*, New York: Morrow.

Tannen, D. (1995) *Talking from 9 to 5*, London: Virago.

Tescione, S.M. (1998) A woman's name: implications for publication, citation and tenure, *Educational Researcher*, 27(8): 38–42.

Tierney, W.G. (2002) Tenure and academic freedom in the academy, in J.E. Cooper and D.D. Stevens (eds) *Tenure in the Sacred Grove*, Albany: SUNY University Press.

Tinkler, P. and Jackson, C. (2000) Examining the doctorate, *Studies in Higher Education*, 25(2): 167–80.

Tooley, J. (1998) *Educational Research: An OFSTED Critique*, London: OFSTED.

Topkis, G.S. (1985) Book publishing: an editor's eye view, in M.F. Fox (ed.) *Scholarly Writing and Publishing*, Boulder, Co: Westview Press.

Torrance, M.S. and Thomas, G.V. (1994) The development of writing skills in doctoral research students, in R.G. Burgess (ed.) *Postgraduate Education and Training in the Social Sciences*, London: Jessica Kingsley.

Toth, E. (1997) *Ms Mentor's Impeccable Advice for Women in Academia*, Philadelphia: University of Pennsylvania Press.

Vaitilingam, R. (n.d.) *Developing a Media Strategy*, Swindon: ESRC.

Walker, D. (n.d.) *Heroes of Dissemination*, Swindon: ESRC.

Wakeford, J. (1985) A director's dilemmas, in R.G. Burgess (ed.) *The Research Process in Educational Settings*, London: Falmer.

Wenneras, C. and Wold, A. (1997) Nepotism and sexism in peer review, *Nature*, 347: 341–3.

Williams, M. (2002) *The Ethnography of an Anthropology Department*, Lampeter: Edwin Mellen Press.

Winfield, G. (1987) *The Social Science PhD*, 2 vols, London: ESRC.

Woods, P. (1986) *Inside Schools*, London: Routledge.

Woods, P. (1996) *Researching the Art of Teaching*, London: Routledge.

Zerubavel, E. (1999) *The Clockwork Muse*, Cambridge, MA: Harvard University Press.

Zuckerman, H. (1977) *Scientific Elite*, New York: The Free Press.

Zuckerman, H. (1996) Introduction to the Transaction edition, *Scientific Elite*, 2nd edn, New Brunswick, NJ: Transactions *xiii–xli.*

Index

Page numbers in **bold** refer to main discussion, *a* indicates appendix.